The Fondas

The Fondas

The Films and Careers of
Henry, Jane and Peter Fonda

by JOHN SPRINGER

The Citadel Press   New York

First Edition
Copyright ©1970 by John Springer
All rights reserved
Published by Citadel Press, Inc.
222 Park Avenue South, New York, N. Y. 10003
In Canada: George J. McLeod Limited
73 Bathurst St., Toronto 2B, Ontario
Composition by Schilling & Nichols, Brooklyn, N. Y.
Printed by Mahony & Roese, Inc., New York, N. Y.
Manufactured in the United States of America
Designed by William Meinhardt
Library of Congress catalog card number: 73-111699
International Standard Book Number 0-8065-0014-X

Acknowledgments and Thanks

To Henry Fonda and Jane Fonda Vadim for art and assistance.

To the Publicity Departments and Still Departments of Columbia, MGM, Paramount, 20th Century-Fox, Warner Brothers, Cinerama, National General, Walter Reade-Sterling, RKO Radio, American International, Universal, United Artists; also to Allan, Ingersoll and Weber, Harold Rand, Emily Torchia, Joseph Abeles, Henry Hart *(Films in Review),* and to the Springer/Bettmann Film Archive, for pictorial material.

To Ernest Parmentier, *Film Facts,* for art and research assistance.

To the Theatre Collection, Library and Museum of Performing Arts, Lincoln Center, for research assistance.

Special gratitude to Joshua Logan and Robert Ryan for their contributions and to William Fine and the late John Steinbeck for permission to reprint Mr. Steinbeck's tribute to Henry Fonda, which first appeared in *Harper's Bazaar.*

Contents

The Fondas

Introduction

IN 1967, that celebrated raconteur, *bon vivant* and sometime publisher, Bennett Cerf, phoned Henry Fonda, his voice concerned.

"Hank, I've just read the manuscript of a novel that an affiliate of ours is going to publish. It's just about the most scurrilous thing I've ever read—about an actor and his daughter—and the writer has done everything possible to identify the characters with you and Jane."

"Does it refer to us by name?"

"No, he hasn't gone quite that far—but nobody will have any doubts about with whom he expects the characters to be associated. I wanted you to know we are severing all connections with the publisher, but I think you ought to read the book and see your lawyer."

Fonda, as always, was calm. "I don't want to read the book. I don't have time for crap like that. And there's not much point in seeing my lawyer—there have been enough scandal stories about us all which actually have used our names in connection with all kinds of lies. It used to infuriate me but I don't give a damn anymore. Anybody who knows us—anybody we care about—knows what is true about us. The others—well, if they get their kicks out of thinking those things are true, there's not much we can do except ignore them. We're not about to dignify them with any attention at all."

The novel came out—a wretched thing written by someone safely using a pseudonym, although coyly admitting his real identity when the book achieved some notoriety. We won't advertise author or book by naming them here.

The Fondas made no protest, issued no statements, paid no attention at all. The few column items, which tried to start a controversy, soon ceased.

There are a lot of stories they tell about the Fondas. Some of them were enthusiastically aided by Jane Fonda in her earlier interviews, when she eagerly promoted the image of an unconventional and uninhibited girl, and later by Peter in his era as the "spokesman" for the rebellious younger generation.

Henry has consistently refused to comment on any of them or to answer any of the more outrageous interviews given by his offspring. In spite of those stories you hear, the Fondas could not be closer as a family. Jane and Peter stay at Henry's house when they are in New York and all three are constantly on the long-distance telephone to each other when they are separated. Any estrangement—and there have been a few—is no more serious than a normal family argument, and is over as quickly. A recent magazine article had some pretty rough items about the family in quotes from Peter Fonda. Peter admitted that he had, indeed,

said all of these things but claimed that they had been taken out of context from an interview he had given some years before when he thought it was the thing to turn on that most convenient target of the Establishment, his father. The Fondas were all hurt by the article but neither Henry nor Jane made any public comment about it. Peter did but only to admit his own blame and explain how the situation had changed. But people would much rather hear about a juicy family feud than read about a warm and close family relationship.

Here we deal only with the careers of this present-day first family of Broadway and Hollywood—careers unmatched by any other parent and children in the American theatre.

There have been others, most notably Douglas Fairbanks, senior and junior . . . the well-known character actors, Tyrone Power and Jason Robards, and their even better-known sons . . . Maureen O'Sullivan and Mia Farrow . . . Robert Montgomery and Elizabeth . . . Judy Garland and Liza Minnelli . . . Osgood and Anthony Perkins . . . Maurice Costello and his daughters, Dolores and Helene . . . Bing Crosby, Frank Sinatra, Joan Crawford, Nancy Carroll (Patricia Kirkland), Robert Sterling and Ann Sothern (Tisha Sterling), Helen Hayes (James MacArthur), June Walker (John Kerr), Ruth Taylor (Buck Henry), Joel McCrea, Jennifer Jones and Robert Walker, Loretta Young (Judy Lewis), Lila Lee (James Kirkwood), Mickey Katz (Joel Grey), and others—all of whom have produced children who have been variously successful in the show business world. Perhaps the family closest to the Fondas in celebrity for both parent and progeny are the British Redgraves. And, of course, the successful siblings range all the way from the Barrymores to Warren Beatty and Shirley MacLaine.

But, in America, the family Fonda seems to stand alone. Almost every story about them has referred to them with the same cliché. But why not? It has a nice, lilting, alliterative sound and it's true.

Henry, Jane, Peter—they really do rate the designation of "The Fabulous Fondas."

◆━◆━◆

The careers of the Fondas are covered extensively in the body of this book. Here, then, just a few notes and vital statistics.

Henry Jaynes Fonda was born in Grand Island, Nebraska, on May 16, 1905, son of William Brace and Herberta Jaynes Fonda. His father owned and operated the W. B. Fonda Printing Company in Omaha,

Baby picture and silhouette of Henry Fonda

to which the family moved when Henry was six months old. His younger sister, Harriet, now Mrs. J. B. Peacock, still lives in Omaha, continuing her interest in the Omaha Community Theatre, in which Henry got his theatrical beginning. Another sister, Jayne (Mrs. John Schoentgen) is deceased. Fonda's father died in 1935, his mother a year earlier—too soon for either of them to see him on the screen, but not before they were aware that his acting success was assured.

The name Fonda is Italian in origin, but the family migrated to Holland around 1400 and Fondas were among the early Dutch settlers in upstate New York, where they founded the still-thriving town of Fonda. (Although Franchot Tone and Humphrey Bogart were members of the exclusive Holland Society of New York, Fonda is the only actor to be formally honored by the society.)

As a youngster, Henry planned to be a writer—his first taste of fame came at the age of ten when a story he wrote, "The Mouse," was published in the Dundee (an Omaha suburb) newspaper. Newspaper work had always been his goal and he entered the University of Minnesota as a journalism major.

But the Fonda finances demanded that he work his way through school. So he landed a job directing the sports program at a settlement house. This included coaching all sports and playing on the basketball team. His college work suffered, and he wound up exhausted.

So he dropped out of college after his second year. (He now has an honorary degree, Doctor of Humane Letters, from Ursinus College. Back in Omaha, he got an office boy job with the Retail Credit Company. It was then that he first learned about the theatre and gave up forever any attempts to rise in the business

Henry Fonda's first stage appearance (age five) was at an Omaha Junior League pageant. His leading lady is unidentified.

The Fondas at home in Omaha. Henry, about seven, is between his mother and father. His sisters are at the right; the other child is unidentified.

Henry as a fourteen-year-old Omaha schoolboy.

Teen-age Henry at the beach with his mother (left) and sister.

world. The insistence of Mrs. Marlon Brando, Sr., that he join the Omaha Community Theatre, his experiences there, and the life to which that led are detailed in the chapter on the Fondas of the theatre.

Jane and Peter Fonda were both born of Fonda's second marriage, to the beautiful and socially prominent Frances Seymour Brokaw. Jane was born on December 21, 1937; Peter on February 23, 1940. Fonda's stepdaughter from that marriage, six years older than Jane, is Frances Devillers Corrias, who is married to an Italian diplomat and lives in Rome. Frances Fonda committed suicide in 1950 in a rest home where she was being treated for an emotional breakdown.

Fonda's youngest daughter, Amy, was adopted at birth (November 9, 1953) by the star and his third wife, Susan Blanchard, stepdaughter of Oscar Hammerstein. This marriage, and another to Afdera Franchetti, ended in divorce, as had his first, a very brief union with Margaret Sullavan when they were appearing together on stage before either had ever seen a

Fonda's first paying job in the theatre was to write a vaudeville sketch for the Lincoln impersonator, George Billings. The youthful writer wrote in a part for himself.

movie camera. Fonda remained on very good terms with Miss Sullavan after their marital breakup. Long after their divorce, they co-starred on screen in *The Moon's Our Home.* Fonda's early agent and later producer was Leland Hayward; he was directed in films by William Wyler. Both Hayward and Wyler were married at various times to Miss Sullavan, too. To add to the togetherness, Jane Fonda's best friend as a youngster was Brooke Hayward, daughter of Hayward and Miss Sullavan and former wife of Peter's *Easy Rider* producing partner, Dennis Hopper.

Fonda continues on very friendly terms with Amy's mother Susan—now married to actor-director Michael Wager. Amy, who goes to school in upstate New York and, so far, seems uninterested in following her illustrious relatives into an acting career, spends much of her vacation time with Henry and his present wife, Shirlee.

Fonda married Shirlee Adams on December 3, 1966. She is a bright and bubbling, particularly attractive and extremely popular girl in her mid-thirties. From Aurora, Illinois, she was an airline stewardess and occasional model before her marriage. George Peppard and Elizabeth Ashley were their best man and matron of honor when they married in Mineola, Long Island, be-

In 1933 Fonda worked as an actor and scenic designer at the Mt. Kisco Playhouse.

Fonda and James Stewart first met when they were in the University Players together. They were roommates in the lean days when they were trying to crack Broadway and again during their early Hollywood bachelor days.

tween performances of his Broadway play, *Generation*. Mineola was chosen because it was "off the beaten track" and arrangements could be made for their marriage to be performed with a minimum of cameras and "circus hoopla."

Friends of Fonda (including his children) feel that, in Shirlee, he has finally found the ideal wife. A friendly, happy girl—"completely without the usual phoniness of most stars' wives," says one Hollywood observer— Shirlee Fonda enjoys clothes and parties. And Fonda seems much more socially gregarious since their marriage.

Fonda's favorite recreation is painting. He was always competent at art—there was a time when nobody had much faith in his future as an actor but he knew he could always score as a set designer. And he was always fascinated by art—Andrew Wyeth, for instance, has long been one of his few real heroes. But Fonda never took it up seriously himself until the long years he spent in the New York theatre. His Alvin Theatre dressing room had been full of complicated model airplanes in various stages of construction during the early days of *Mister Roberts*. Fonda and Jimmy Stewart had been model plane addicts when they lived together in their carefree bachelor days—the struggling theatre days in New York, the early days of Hollywood movie stardom. Fonda revived the interest with his young son, Peter, but they soon tired of the planes.

In their early days in Hollywood, Fonda occasionally dated his ex-wife, Margaret Sullavan.

Somebody had given Fonda some pastels, and he idly began to work with them. Soon, what had been something to kill time became a passion. Backstage visitors enthusiastically admired them. The demand for "an original Fonda" became heavy. Fonda had given away his early paintings to members of his family and a few lucky friends—John Swope, for instance, Jimmy Stewart, this writer among them. But then cus-

One of Fonda's best friends, John Swope, took his favorite early Hollywood portrait.

tomers began to bid for them. Richard Halliday commissioned Fonda to do a painting as a Christmas gift for his wife, Mary Martin. Mrs. Robert Preston saw a Fonda painting in a celebrity charity art show and bid $1500 for it—the top price for any painting in the show. (The next day, after Mrs. Preston had bought it as a gift for her star-husband, a picture of the painting appeared in *Time* and many thousands more than Mrs. Preston had paid were offered for it. Fonda was commissioned to do paintings for greeting cards, for advertisements and his work was hung in several exhibitions. He has given up pastels, now paints in oils and watercolors, but his subjects remain still life.

Jane Fonda had once decided to be a painter, too, and had gone to Paris to study. But not understanding French well at that time (although she speaks it as fluently as a native now) and deciding she had no real aptitude for art, she gave it up. She knows now that the "art phase" was just a gesture—a chance to get away from school and parental restraints and have a chance to be on her own.

Jane and Peter spent most of their childhood in an isolated 9-acre farm in Brentwood. Fonda was determined that they be as untouched as possible by the false glamour of being children of a movie star. But the isolation did cut them off from close association with other youngsters of their own age. Around home, Fonda used to dress in work clothes and levis and so did his associates who used to visit and play cards.

A benefit show in Hollywood brought out a group of notables to do "The Cad's Chorus" from Charlot's Revue. Fonda is at extreme right and others, from left, include Reginald Gardiner, Chester Morris, Charles Farrell, George Sanders, Rod La Rocque, Mischa Auer, Alan Mowbray, Sir Cedric Hardwicke, and Henry Wilcoxon.

Long before Barbarella—*Baby Jane Fonda*

Jane remembers that she thought everyone dressed that way and doesn't remember wearing dresses herself until she was eight years old.

From the time she was five, she was riding horseback and she and Peter used to make up their own Western movies, which they would then enact. She remembers that she insisted on playing her father's role in their own version of *Drums Along the Mohawk*.

She was ten when Fonda moved East to play *Mister Roberts* on stage. The family lived in Greenwich, Connecticut, and, after their mother's death, the children lived with their maternal grandmother in Greenwich and with their father in his New York house.

From 13 to 17, Jane attended Emma Willard School in Troy, New York, and there did her first acting—as the male lead in Christopher Fry's *Boy With a Cart* and as Lydia Languish in Sheridan's *The Rivals*. But, although school plays were fun, she gave no thought to acting even after she joined her father for ingenue roles in an Omaha Community Theatre production of *The Country Girl* and in a summer stock *Male Animal*.

She went on to college at Vassar—a good student, as she had been at Emma Willard, but increasingly rebellious at school restrictions. Finally her father agreed to her sojourn in Paris to study art. She lived with a French family but, as noted, wasn't happy with her schoolwork or with life in Paris.

Dad and a couple of the kids—infant Peter and Jane.

Fonda has always been strongly involved in liberal causes. In 1938 he joined other screen personalities in a petition to President Roosevelt, asking that economic relations with Nazi Germany be severed. Left to right, Melvyn Douglas, Gale Sondergaard, James Cagney, Helen Gahagan Douglas, Edward G. Robinson, Fonda, and Gloria Stuart.

She returned to New York to study French, Italian and music. She also began to win some attention as a model. Irving Penn's pictures of her twice made the cover of *Vogue,* and she began to enjoy a considerable flurry of modeling popularity. But she feels the most important event in her acting life was her meeting with Lee Strasberg. That was in 1958.

Jane had been friendly with Strasberg's actress daughter, Susan, and, through Susan, she met the patriarch of the Actors Studio. Lee Strasberg, the Actors Studio, and "the Method" have been major influences in the growth of some of the finest actors of our generation—people like Kin Stanley, Joanne Woodward, Geraldine Page, Paul Newman, Marlon Brando, Montgomery Clift, Maureen Stapleton and many, many more. (Henry Fonda claims he is not a "Method actor"—knows and understands little about it. Strasberg feels that Henry Fonda may act "by instinct," as he claims, but that he is one of the finest "Method actors.") For the first time, Jane Fonda felt that somebody was interested in her as an actress—not just as a girl who happened to be the daughter of a noted star. She studied with Strasberg in his private classes, then joined the Actors Studio. Her career, detailed in upcoming pages, was on its way.

Peter Fonda was still in school when his sister began

A tiny Jane plays leapfrog with Dad.

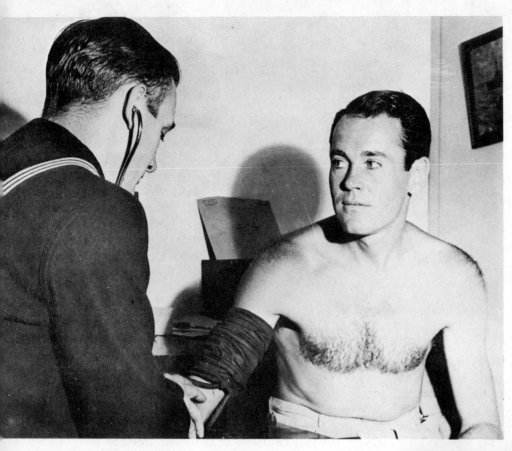

In 1942 Fonda enlisted in the Navy as an apprentice seaman. Here he is having his physical.

to show strong signs of a starry future. He had grown up as she had, at the Brentwood ranch and later in the homes in Greenwich and New York. He has spoken quite freely in interviews of his loneliness and frequent unhappiness as a young boy. When he was ten years old, he was seriously injured in an accident on the rifle range at his Connecticut prep school. He recovered, of course, but it was the "final blow." He hated school, could hardly wait to leave.

Peter always felt he wanted to be an actor. He was attending the University of Omaha when he won the lead in the school play, *Harvey.* His father, always critical when it came to acting, arrived unexpectedly to see him and could not contain his pride. The Omaha newspapers, as well as the school gazettes, praised him. Peter wasn't interested in college after that. He dropped out after his school year, accepted a role in the Broadway play, *Blood, Sweat and Stanley Poole,* and he, too, was off and running.

Peter and his wife, the former Susan Brewer, live off Coldwater Canyon in Beverly Hills with their children, Bridget, five, and Justin, three.

As a Navy officer during the war, with young Jane

The Fonda family at their California home in 1944. Left to right, Mrs. Fonda, Peter, Mrs. Fonda's daughter Frances, Jane and Henry.

Long before he discovered motorcycles—Peter Fonda.

The Fonda child who hasn't yet decided to join the family in the acting world. Schoolgirl Amy visits her father on the set.

A character study of Henry in the beard he grew for War and Peace

Jane visits her father backstage on opening night of Silent Night, Lonely Night.

Mr. and Mrs. Henry Fonda (Shirlee Adams) on their wedding day

With Senator Robert F. Kennedy. Fonda was friendly with, and supported, both Kennedys.

Fonda with one of his paintings

The male Fondas visit Jane on location during the filming of Sunday in New York.

Jane Fonda married Roger Vadim, one of France's most talented and controversial young directors, in Las Vegas on August 14, 1965. Vadim, as colorful in his private life as the characters in his movies (*And God Created Woman, Les Liaisons Dangereuses*) has directed his wife, both before and after their marriage, in several pictures—*La Ronde, The Game Is Over, Barbarella* and *Spirits of the Dead.*

The Vadims live in a farmhouse outside of Paris. Their daughter, Vanessa, was born on September 28, 1968.

Might there be a Vanessa Vadim lighting up marquees a couple of decades from now? A Justin or Bridget Fonda?

At this point, Amy Fonda seems next up, but indications are that she is not interested. Yet one shouldn't forget that Jane Fonda seemed as sublimely indifferent to all that glamour and glory when she was Amy's age.

It seems, though, that there will always be a Fonda on stage, screen or television.

And cheers to Marlon Brando's mother, who started it all.

Fonda surrounded by some of the ladies who paid tribute to him at a L'Etoile party in his honor: Anita Louise, Lauren Bacall, Rita Gam, Susan Kohner, and his wife Shirlee.

The Fondas I Know

by Joshua Logan

THE FIRST sound I heard from Henry Fonda was his laugh. What a laugh he has! It starts with a strangled sob, then soars into a screech played at the wrong speed. You hear it not with your ears but with your bones. But at the time, it was the most beautiful sound I had ever heard, because I was on stage trying to be funny as Huxley Hossefrosse in *The Torchbearers;* this unique laughter was in the audience and he obviously got my message.

We met backstage afterwards. I had no idea who this strange, shy, lanky youth could be as he was being introduced to me in my dressing room. He stood there in sad, skinny white linen knickerbockers. It was the late twenties, the days of the plus-fours; and this Fonda guy was wearing minus-twos. His golf socks and sweater were black, which was either superb taste, or mid-west ignorance. His chest was so caved in and his head and pelvis so pushed forward that I wasn't sure whether he was tall or short, and had to wait until the accordion unfolded to learn that he was well over six feet. But still there was that beautiful male face. (Al Capp once told me that young Fonda's face in the movie *The Trail of the Lonesome Pine* was the prototype of Li'l Abner.) When Fonda smiled, you

were uplifted; when he whinnied out that laugh again and I knew who it had been out there in the darkness, I loved him immediately.

We were in Falmouth, Massachusetts the summer of '28, and I was an actor-member of the University Players. It was the first season of our summer theater company, which was made up of college students who planned to go into the theatrical profession. Fonda had just driven over from Dennis, another Cape Cod town, where he had played a young boy in *The Barker,* and was now headed back home to Omaha. On the way he stopped to visit his friend and our colleague, Bernie Hannighen, to see if there might be a job.

We were rehearsing *The Jest* at the time, and I gladly surrendered to him one of the two parts I was to play. I had been cast in the first act as Tournaquinci, the noble Italian host, and in the third act, I was to play the headsman in black tights and a hood, stripped to the waist. Since I had been doing a lot of push-ups, I chose to keep the part of the headsman, and allowed my new-found laughing friend to play the ageing Tournaquinci. He was disastrous. His Nebraskan drawl in that Florentine setting made the poetic Italianate speeches sound like conversations around a cracker barrel. However, he and I developed an act we did after theater in our tea-room. I transplanted Huxley Hossefrosse to the night club floor, and Fonda, in his skinny knickers, was an idiot boy named Elmer, who shyly imitated fish by wriggling his fingers. Our act kept going for four years, and probably we could still do it, should anybody invite us to the same party and request it. But more than that, our personal and professional relationship, which consisted of deeply felt mutual admiration that could suddenly swerve into violent harangues, went on for many years, and still smokes a bit, especially when we discuss artistic subjects.

In the years that Fonda and I worked together as actors, and later when I was his director, we had many ups and downs and ins and outs. The first "down" was when I was promoted, becoming one of the three directors of the company. In a flash I turned into the Establishment, and he into the prime mover of the Lower Classes. He imitated me outrageously in front of the company, revealing me as the pompous idiot I probably was and probably have never ceased to be when I'm around him.

Fonda had turned out to be a much better actor than he first showed in *The Jest*. Soon I realized that he was a rather strange but special kind of leading man who could play romantic, sexually effective parts and still retain his "cool." He was always real, unactory, and almost, but never quite, inaudible. Henry Fonda has never been a man for the rounded phrase or the pear-shaped tone, and yet by now he has developed a way of speaking that is so especially his own that he represents to many people the true essence of America, a kind of synthesis of all the heroes of Mark Twain, Bret Harte, James Fenimore Cooper, Hawthorne, Poe and Irving. Once he played Abe Lincoln, and again he played Jesse James' brother Frank, and stole the picture from everyone else simply by using that understated technique which he seems to have created by himself out of thin air.

Fonda has a concept of truth in the theater that make those of most of his peers seem pallid. He will never be seduced into overstating a point or a mood. Many actors, when receiving approval from an audience, will give out with just that little bit more, much like throwing the dog an extra bone. Not Fonda. This stringent perfectionist never allows a surreptitious yet grateful look at the laughing audience, never a twist of the hips or a comic crook of the arm or leg to reinforce the laugh. The performance is a sacred rite to Henry Fonda. He speaks with his own special litany of frugality. The chant of his High Mass consists of a single flat melody on a reed instrument. When he is called upon by the author to verbalize or speechify, he screws up his face into a painful grimace as though his cheek muscles were hurting and his voice had reached its breaking point. This may be because he has not developed a really resonant voice through the years, which, perhaps, he has never wanted to. Shakespeare and the classics are not his playing fields. And somehow in the blue flame truth of his quiet portrayals you are apt to apologize for even bringing up the subject of the purple passages of poetic drama. Fonda demands that we write simple American plays for him.

When we first started working together in the University Players, we were fellow rebels fighting shoulder to shoulder against the Establishment. Naturally we always cast an opposing vote to the directors. There was a kind of marvelous anarchy in the University Players. Bretaigne Windust and Charles Leatherbee tried their best to tame us, but it was impossible. We were free souls, and we were all young. There was no one old enough to teach us anything, and anyway we wouldn't have *believed* in anyone that was old enough to dare. Now, looking back, I can see why there was so much feeling. It was because there was so much talent; Margaret Sullavan, Mildred Natwick, Myron McCormick, Barbara O'Neil, Norris Houghton, Kent Smith, Charles Arnt, Leslie Cheek and many others just as passionate were our members.

This all took place during the Depression, and we were lucky to earn enough to live on. Sometimes a member would keep two or three dollars after he'd pay for his laundry at the end of the week. During that time Fonda played many parts and so did I . . . four summers in Falmouth and two winters in Baltimore.

It was Fonda who made me a director. Once when Bretaigne Windust was ill and I was recruited to direct, Fonda led a committee of protest. They bluntly stated that if I, an incompetent, was allowed to remain as director, the entire company would quit. I decided to show them. I worked on the play all night, and by the end of the first day of rehearsal I could see the cast relax and start to cooperate. Fonda even smiled. But he sent in his resignation at the end of the season.

When Fonda left the company, he was replaced by a friend of mine from the Princeton Triangle Club, James Stewart. Later Stewart, Fonda, Myron McCormick (another Princeton friend) and I took a flat in the West 60's, across from the YMCA. We all starved together in a miserable two rooms with a filthy bathroom which stank from a mildewed rubber shower curtain we never thought to throw away. We called it "Casa Gangrene." It was on a street of pimps, gun molls and prostitutes. While we lived there, Jack "Legs" Diamond was shot and killed just down the street. Sometimes we worked out at the West Side YMCA across the street. One horrid time I went there with Fonda. He knew he could annoy me by walking around

Joshua Logan and Jane on the set of her first picture Tall Story, *which Logan directed.*

on his hands, a feat I envied more than anything else he had ever accomplished. So, to prove my own athletic prowess, I said, arrogantly, "Would you like to see me climb that rope?" I pointed to a wide hawser that stretched three floors up into the air. Fonda's snarling Omaha accent caused his "I *certainly* would" to pump me so full of adrenalin that I made it up the three stories of the rope in less than thirty seconds, at which point I froze. My acrophobia took over, and I was a petrified monkey on a string. Finally I willpowered myself into inching down, a procedure that took an agonizing ten minutes. Fonda smirked and walked away. I turned furiously and tried to climb the rope again. I could not lift myself a fraction of a centimeter, which should prove the power of Fonda's special vitriol over me.

But to go back to the University Players, Fonda was married to Margaret Sullavan in the dining room of the Kernan Hotel in Baltimore, Maryland, during our first winter season. The wedding took place at eleven in the morning, just before the matinee of *The Ghost Train,* in which they were to play the roles of young newlyweds. We all drank cheap champagne and Bretaigne Windust played "Ah, Say Not So" from *The Constant Nymph,* which was the show in which they had realized they were in love. When they appeared

on stage that afternoon and Fonda pulled out a handkerchief from his pocket, spilling prop-rice all over the floor, the ushers tried to start a bit of applause, but the small, sparse audience had no idea what the applause was about, and it died. The newlyweds were away for two days, but they became so lonesome for the rest of us, they came back and started rehearsals for J. M. Barrie's *Mary Rose,* which I directed. It was one of the greatest performances either of them ever gave, with the possible exception of *Coquette.* Soon Fonda and Sullavan, in love, inspired fan clubs and autograph hunters began to wait outside the stage door. The marriage didn't last, as they were two positive people who soon disagreed. But there was always mutual respect. They could not make a go of it even though they tried to get together a second time. But we all believed that their love lasted through the many years that they lived apart.

In our early movie days Fonda and I shared several houses with Jimmy Stewart and Johnny Swope in and around Los Angeles. One was called "the house of a thousand cats." Two cats took neighbor cats in, and pretty soon there were grandchildren cats, all called *George.* Eventually we had to move out, and let the cats take over. All through this time Hank and I saw each other a great deal. At one point I directed him in my first motion picture, *I Met My Love Again,* in which he played both the young teenager and the same part eight years older, when he had become a sensitive teacher. Since it was my first picture, and he was getting sick of the average juvenile role he was getting, he was extremely cooperative. The rest of the cast, consequently, treated me with a surprising respect for a neophyte director. I will always be grateful.

Years later when I wrote *Mister Roberts* with Thomas Heggen, Tom and I discovered that, though it had never been mentioned, we both had had the same person in mind while writing the play. It was Hank Fonda. I read *Mister Roberts* aloud to Hank in a hotel room, with Thomas Heggen listening. When I finished it, he said, "I'm going to play it." This meant giving up a lot of Hollywood loot.

There is one bit of *Mister Roberts,* however, that very few people know. About the third day of rehearsal, I gave Fonda a piece of direction, and he turned to me and said, "Are you kidding?" I said, "What's wrong with it?" He said, "What's *wrong* with it? Have you read the script?" I said, *"Read* it, you sonofabitch, I *wrote* it! Do you understand the part of Roberts?" He said, "Do you understand it?" I said, "Come to my house tonight and have dinner with me, and I'll tell you how much I understand it." He said, "I *certainly* will," and that night we dined at the Lombardy Hotel and I talked about Mr. Roberts' background and character until four in the morning. Fonda never opened his mouth, perhaps because I never gave him a chance to. At the end he stood up and said, "I understand." He shook my hand and went away. From then on he worked like the total professional that he always is, the dedicated, priestlike professional. He became Mr. Roberts. His influence on the rest of the cast was enormous. At one point after the play had been playing for several years, I went to see it, and found that they were all trying to underplay Fonda—even to underspeak him. I called a rehearsal and tried to get back some of the vitality I felt it was losing. Hank called me up and said, "I don't feel it's *my* play anymore." I said, "No, you superior bastard, but it's *mine!"*

But I must go back. A year and a bit after his second marriage (to Frances Brokaw) there was Jane, and a year or two after that there was Peter. At the ages of one and two the baby girl was known as "Lady Jane." I don't remember why, but I do know that soon she began to resent the title, and her godfathers, Jimmy Stewart, John Swope and I, were all forced to drop the "Lady" or else she would refuse to answer.

The first time I saw Peter was when I flew in from New York and went to the house on Tigertail Road that Hank and Frances had built and furnished with early American pieces from Vermont. I had met Fran-

ces driving out of her driveway. "Go up and see Peter; he's sitting in the nursery," she said. I remember walking up the stairs and staring into a room where, in a small cage-like pen, sat a tiny child with huge blue-green eyes. It was Fonda staring out at me through those huge eyes. I wanted to say, "You can come out now, Hank. I know where you're hiding."

Jane and Peter grew up along with Leland Hayward and Margaret Sullavan's children. We three godfathers were assigned to them all.

Jane grew more and more beautiful. When she was in her late teens I can remember her sitting on the couch of our home in Stamford, Connecticut saying, "I'm just not interested in the theater, that's all." But one year later, she was under the spell of Lee Strassberg, and he had set her to dreaming. It then remained for me to really start her off. Her first job with with me as the pompom girl in *Tall Story*. She was as calm and cool as a cucumber through all the tests and even throughout all the shooting, doing everything I asked of her, and yet holding on to that mind of her own. She was instant professional. Immediately after that I urged her to play the lead in her first Broadway play. It was Dan Taradash's *There Was a Little Girl*.

Peter was another matter. After a lot of trouble finding himself at school, I learned he was playing the lead in the school's production of *Harvey*. He was about sixteen. I asked why they would cast such a young man in an old part. "It's the star part," said Hank, "and it was Peter's idea." Later I saw Peter when he played the young soldier in the try-out of *Blood, Sweat and Stanley Poole*. It was his first time on the professional stage, and he had all the Fonda aplomb. Then before any of us knew it, he was on a motorcycle and had grown sideburns and a lot of hair and was taking a "trip" in *The Trip*.

I interrupted the writing of this piece today to visit Peter on the picture he is filming now. It is a hippie story conceived and written by Peter in collaboration with Dennis Hopper, who, incidentally, is the husband of Brook Hayward, Margaret Sullavan's oldest daughter. The picture is being produced by William Hayward, Margaret Sullavan's son. I saw lanky Peter today at almost the same age and height as his father was the day we met. He was bronzed and hairy in the hippie tradition. He introduced me to his wife and their little son (who is the same age Peter was when I saw him sitting in that crib on Tigertail Road), and his daughter, who looks like "Lady Jane," but who is named for Bridget, the second daughter of Margaret Sullavan and Leland Hayward. (Margaret Sullavan's children have grown up in close relationship to the Fondas.) Peter introduced me to the two babies as their "great-godfather."

I sometimes think that both Fonda children are flashing some kind of frantic semaphore to the world as if to say "Look at me, I am as big as he is." It must be hard to grow up in the hot reflected light shed from an American symbol. And I am sure that Fonda is as demanding of his children as he is of his authors and his directors.

There have been publicized differences with his collaborators. One play which was well received by the critics did not please its star. The producer had a difficult time getting publicity because everytime Fonda was interviewed, he would insist that the play was no good and that the public should avoid it. Again in *Two For the Seesaw* (perhaps his second greatest success after *Mister Roberts*) we learn from William Gibson's piece that Fonda was dissatisfied with the writing of his role and wasted no tact in dealing with the author. Again, although I did not direct the screen version of *Mister Roberts,* it is well documented that Fonda

was unhappy with the first director and let it be known.

According to theatrical tradition, these should be marks against him. Although I have sometimes been the victim of his invective when things aren't going well, I cannot find it in my innards to object to Fonda's tirades. They come from a huge ego, certainly, but isn't that also what makes him a huge talent? He cares. It matters to him. He is not content to let well enough alone. "Well enough" to Fonda is a cardinal sin. It is a crime against his religion, the theater.

Henry Fonda's mind, his dedication to his art, and his brooding, sad face have always been one of the great influences of my life. No matter what our differences, Fonda is a part of me, and I'm a part of him. He is so intermingled in the interstices of my web, that I cannot ever get free of him. May he live forever, for when Fonda smiles, the theater shines. May this be true also of Peter and Jane . . . and all the fabulous Fondas of the future.

Henry Fonda's most famous stage role was as Mister Roberts, in the play directed and co-written by Joshua Logan.

Henry and Shirlee Fonda and Robert Ryan at the opening of the New York Lincoln Center Film Festival, 1968.

A Letter

from Robert Ryan

London
December 26
1968

Dear John:

I'VE LEARNED that you are doing a book about Henry Fonda and it occurred to me that an actor's contribution might be appropriate and (I hope) welcome. I would like to do this principally because I would like to do it. Also it gives me the chance to say something I would not dare say to his face, since I consider Henry a friend and would like to keep it that way.

It seems unfortunate to me that the highest accolade one actor ever gives another is to call him a "pro." The word means a great deal (when used by an actor), but it doesn't mean enough. It implies discipline and experience, which are honorable attributes indeed. But they could be laid on any performer who for fifteen years or so has minded the store and practiced the necessary (but really minimal) obligations of his craft. Also I feel that the term stops at workmanship and leaves one still short of artistry.

I am working at the moment in a country where an actor is called an artist. Automatically called this without embarrassment or second thought. It is a word that an American would not dare to use, so I will use

it here. I'd like only to say that Henry Fonda is an artist and an artist of the highest order. "Pro," yes, in every sense of the word, but in his case the tools of effort, extraordinary discipline and a constant search have well served him to uncover and refine the essential truthfulness of his art. I doubt very much if Henry has ever rested for one second on the shallow, slick and generally easy technique that any actor can acquire in a short time and use if he wishes to the detriment of his art and very possibly his soul. We are working at a time when the theater is presumed to be "real," but "reality" in acting can become a trick and manner like any other style. When we are brought before the essential reality of Henry's work, we are aware that most actors are obeying a convention and avoiding an art.

What I have said here is perhaps essentially the feeling of an onlooker who might have said the same had we never met. It happens, however, that I have worked with him in the cold, high mountains of northern Spain as well as the even colder reaches of the Mineola Playhouse. At the latter I was struck but not surprised that he brought to a very minor part the same dedication and craft that another performer *might* bring to King Lear.

He is moreover a thoughtful, intelligent and considerate man.

Most sincerely,
Bob

The last public appearance of the late, great John Steinbeck was to pay homage to Henry Fonda at a dinner in Fonda's honor: Mr. and Mrs. Henry Fonda, Mr. and Mrs. John Steinbeck.

gency departs, and this is called "dating." But I did thread the thing on my home projector and sat back to weather it out. Then a lean, stringy, dark-faced piece of electricity walked out on the screen, and he had me. I believed my own story again. It was fresh and happening and good. Hank can do that. He carries with him that excitement which cannot be learned—as many an actor has found to his sorrow—but he backs up his gift with grueling, conscientious work and agony of self-doubt.

Another thing about Fonda that should be obvious is the care he has exercised to keep from being typed. When his name is on the playbill, you have no way of knowing what it will be about. He could go without apparent effort from *The Grapes of Wrath* to *Mister Roberts* to *Point of No Return*. I said apparent effort by design because I know the enormous effort and care and study that go into his easy and relaxed performances.

Once I was working on a short, to me amusing, little novel designed to be translated to the stage. I discussed it with Hank, and he said he would like to

play it. "But it's a musical and I can't sing," he said. "Never mind, I'll take singing lessons." And he did, for a year. Meanwhile, I was praying that he might not learn to sing too well, because I remembered that Walter Huston, who couldn't sing, did "September Song" better than anyone has ever done it since. And Harrison couldn't sing in *My Fair Lady* either.

At the end of a year of singing lessons, Hank auditioned for the part and was turned down by the composer, who was understandably interested in the music. The show flopped dismally and we will never know whether the Fonda kind of magic would have brought it to life. One thing I do know. It would certainly have been believable and consequently better.

I suppose one human never really knows much about another. My impressions of Hank are of a man reaching but unreachable, gentle but capable of sudden wild and dangerous violence, sharply critical of others but equally self-critical, caged and fighting the bars but timid of the light, viciously opposed to external restraint, imposing an iron slavery on himself. His face is a picture of opposites in conflict.

(As Henry Fonda stood in the reception line at the Holland Society dinner in his honor, he greeted celebrated guests in attendance to pay tribute—people like Myrna Loy and Lauren Bacall, Sybil and Jordan Christopher, Leland Hayward. Then, unexpectedly, the eyes of the normally unemotional Fonda misted. Looming up before him—impressive in white tie, tails and full decorations—was the great bearlike figure of John Steinbeck. Fonda had not seen Steinbeck for many months. Nobody had. The great author had been seriously ill. Now, after all that time, he was finally attending a social function. And only, he specified, because he too wanted to honor Henry Fonda. Many people made speeches that night. John Steinbeck did not. But his very presence was the greatest tribute that could be paid to the man who had brought Tom Joad to life on the screen. The Fonda dinner marked John Steinbeck's last public appearance. When he died, Fonda flew in from Los Angeles to New York to deliver the eulogy. And he read these words of Robert Louis Stevenson:

> Bright is the ring of words
> When the right man rings them.
> Fair the fall of songs
> When the singer sings them.
> Still they are carolled and said,
> On wings they are carried
> After the singer is dead
> And the maker buried.

On the screen, Henry Fonda played Tom Joad in Steinbeck's *The Grapes of Wrath*. For television, he narrated Steinbeck's *Travels With Charley* and *America and Americans*. Specifically with Fonda in mind, Steinbeck wrote *Sweet Thursday* from which Richard Rodgers and Oscar Hammerstein II developed the Broadway musical, *Pipe Dream*. Fonda, realizing his singing limitations, reluctantly abandoned that project.

Of everything written and spoken about him, Henry Fonda is most proud of and moved by this tribute from John Steinbeck.)

Henry Fonda
by John Steinb

AFTER I so blithely agreed to write a pie Henry Fonda, and after it was too late to I realized with a certain chagrin, that I d any of the things expected in such a piece sonal, insulting, warm and malicious materia ists thrive on and readers have grown to exp I know about Fonda anyone can know simply ing and seeing him on stage or on film.

Certainly I have heard the gossip by whi reassure themselves that if not better than th they are at least no worse. I have heard moody, introspective, difficult and brooding. I've heard the same things about myself an for a fact that I am easygoing, open, kindly haps a little beautiful, so why should I belie about Hank I know to be false about mysel

I know Henry Fonda as an actor, a devot working, responsible one with a harsh urg perfection. Not long ago a friend loaned me millimeter print of the film *The Grapes* made well over twenty years ago. I was g luctant to look at it. Times pass; we chang

Henry Fonda brought Steinbeck's greatest character—Tom Joad of The Grapes of Wrath—*to life in a well-nigh perfect screen portrayal.*

The last portrait of John Steinbeck, taken by his friend Nathaniel Benchley, on Thanksgiving Day, 1968.

The Fondas

OF THE THEATRE

THERE IS no personality who moves so easily between the theatre and cinema worlds as does Henry Fonda. When such Broadway notables as Helen Hayes, Geraldine Page, Maureen Stapleton, Jason Robards, the latter-day Robert Preston make a film appearance, they are still considered primarily stars of the theatre. Paul Newman, Joanne Woodward, Kirk Douglas, Rosalind Russell, Charlton Heston, Jack Lemmon, Robert Ryan, Katharine Hepburn, and other screen names — even though originally of the theatre—come back to the stage as movie stars still. But Fonda is accepted as a true star of whichever medium is chosen at the moment.

Of course, in the beginning, it was the stage—more specifically the small stage of the Omaha Community Theatre. There was no burning desire for acting. He had literally given it no thought at all. But he had dropped out of college, was jobless, footloose and available when a friend of the family called his mother in distress. The leading man of the next Community play had defected—Henry was physically right for the role—would Mrs. Fonda send him over to read for it? Henry, obedient but not at all interested, went. And so he made his debut in an amateur production of Philip Barry's *You and I*. (The family friend, a Mrs. Dorothy Brando, was to make another contribution to the theatre in the form of a son named Marlon.)

Fonda remembers little about that first play, except that he apparently got through it successfully enough. But he does remember the thrill of discovering the whole theatre atmosphere. He loved the feeling of being part of it, whether he was reading lines, painting scenery or just sweeping up the stage. Basically shy, he quickly became aware that all self-consciousness was gone when he had the "mask" of a role to play. (Even today, Fonda is ill at ease when he must make a public appearance as himself, but that feeling vanishes when he hides his own identity behind the "mask" of a Douglas Roberts or a Tom Joad.)

But there was serious opposition to this theatre life for Fonda, and it came from his father, who was particularly upset that Henry had left a job with the Retail Credit Company, even knowing that there was a chance he would be sent to the company headquarters in Atlanta to train as a supervisor. But the dynamic Playhouse director, Gregory Foley, had given Henry the title role in *Merton of the Movies,* in which Glenn Hunter had scored both on stage and screen. Henry plunged into rehearsals, but he and his father stopped speaking.

The "Merton" opening may have been his most memorable night in the theatre. The audience gave him an ovation, and the Omaha theatre critic would

Mildred Natwick was one of the original University Players with Fonda (and Sullavan, Stewart, Logan, etc.) She also played with him in stock and, much later on Broadway and in films. Here she is in stock in Pursuit of Happiness.

headline his rave review, "Who Needs Glenn Hunter? We have Henry Fonda!"

At home, his mother and sisters waited eagerly, although his father sat silent behind his newspaper. The ladies chattered excitedly about the triumph, but one of his sisters prefaced a comment with "... there *was* one scene in which you didn't quite–."

"Shut up," came the voice from behind the newspaper. "He was perfect!"

Fonda stayed with the Playhouse for three years. Among his roles was one opposite Mrs. Brando in O'Neill's *Beyond the Horizon*. He was also Foley's assistant, and for that he received a salary.

George Billings, the famous old Lincoln impersonator, came to Omaha and let it be known that he was planning to expand his monologue. Fonda wrote a playlet which had a part in it for himself and presented it to Billings. The delighted veteran offered him $100 per week to tour with him in mid-West vaudeville houses.

The three-month tour was the clincher for Henry. The theatre would be his life. And, by now, he had learned that actors actually got paid living salaries in New York. So to New York, in June, 1928, with $100, he traveled.

What he had not realized is that summer was the low point of the theatre season and his money wouldn't last until fall. But, learning of the summer theatres which were beginning to dot Cape Cod, he went to Provincetown and tried to get into the Playhouse there. No luck.

A second attempt, at the theatre in Dennis, was more

Fonda returned to Omaha to do a "guest star" stint with the Community Theatre which had started him off. The play was Barrie's A Kiss for Cinderella–*the leading lady a fourteen-year-old local girl who was to go on to success herself, Dorothy McGuire.*

successful. He met some of the stars of that company—Laura Hope Crews, Peggy Wood, Romney Brent—and they arranged for him to be third assistant stage manager, at no salary. So much for the dreams of high-paying professional theatre in the East.

Then, in true Hollywood fiction style, the actor rehearsing the juvenile lead in *The Barker* had to leave the company and Fonda was given the role. It was while he was thus employed as a working actor with an established company that he met a young group, on summer vacation from college, who had formed their own company in nearby Falmouth and called themselves the University Players. Fonda liked their idea, liked them and accepted their invitation to leave Dennis to join them. They included Joshua Logan, Kent Smith, Charles Leatherbee, Myron McCormick, Bretaigne Windust, Charles Arnt and John Swope, who were later joined by Margaret Sullavan, Mildred Natwick, Barbara O'Neil, James Stewart, Aleta Freel, Logan's sister (now Mary Leatherbee, an editor on Life Magazine) and Norris Houghton (who would eventually write an engaging history of the University Players, called *But Not Forgotten.*)

The University Players stayed together for four years, in Falmouth and in winter repertory in Baltimore. Fonda was the leading man in a majority of their plays, which included *Coquette, Holiday, The Constant Nymph, Mary Rose* and *A Kiss for Cinderella,* in all of which he was teamed with Margaret Sullavan.

Their on-stage romances carried over into their off-stage lives, and they were married on Christmas Day, 1931. But their paths separated after less than two months together as man and wife.

Most of the University Players eventually decided to take on Broadway. There was no immediate demand for their services. Fonda had scenic design to carry him through and he managed to get plenty of work in that field. But acting jobs were not easy to get.

His first Broadway role was as a walk-on and understudy in the Theatre Guild's production of *A Game of Love and Death* (1929) with Alice Brady, Claude Rains and Otto Kruger. He later played bits in plays like *I Loved You Wednesday* and *Forsaking All Others.* He even won the lead in an S. N. Behrman play, *Love Story,* and got good personal notices in the tryout in Philadelphia, which is where *Love Story* folded forever.

During these struggles to get a Broadway toe-hold, he went to Omaha for a visit home. Gregory Foley persuaded him to "guest star" in a play of his own choosing. Having appeared in J. M. Barrie's *A Kiss for Cinderella* with Sullavan in Falmouth, and with Mildred Natwick in a Children's Theatre production in Washington, he suggested that play. The fourteen-year-old youngster in the title role was Dorothy McGuire. Her Omaha triumph was as pronounced as Fonda's had been in *Merton of the Movies.*

(In 1955, Fonda and Miss McGuire returned to Omaha to co-star in a play to raise money for the Community Theatre. Fonda played the alcoholic actor and Miss McGuire his wife in Clifford Odets' *The Country Girl.* Marlon Brando, set to play the director, had to bow out because of movie commitments. This production was responsible for another notable debut when Fonda allowed his daughter, Jane, to play the ingenue role.)

On his return to New York, Fonda obtained a role in the first edition of Leonard Sillman's *New Faces,* (1934). He has a flair for comedy too seldom taken advantage of in screen roles ("Fonda is one of our great clowns," says Joshua Logan) and he used it in some skits with Imogene Coca. Some of the other "New Faces" included Nancy Hamilton, Hildegarde Halliday, Charles Walters, James Shelton, Roger Stevens, O. Z. Whitehead, Alan Handley, Billie Haywood, Gustave Schirmer, and Sandra Gould. Although most of the critics just discussed the show in terms of its ensemble performance, Fonda was singled out for special mention by both John Anderson and Robert Garland.

Leland Hayward, then an actor's agent, saw Fonda in the revue and signed him to a contract. When *New*

After scoring on the screen, Fonda returned to Mt. Kisco where he had played stock to do a production of The Virginian. *With then-"unknown" secondary players, Dan Duryea and Henry Morgan. (1937)*

extraordinarily simple and lustrous characterization."

Now Hollywood beckoned. Fox had bought the play as a movie for its top star, Janet Gaynor. And Fonda repeated his stage role—starting on the screen as a star. The rest is movie history, recounted, picture by picture, in the body of this book, which deals with the films of the Fondas.

The theatre did not come back into his life until 1937, when, now a top screen name, he returned to appear in a summer theatre production of *The Virginian* and then back to Broadway in Arthur Hopkins' production of *Blow Ye Winds* by Valentine Davies.

Richard Lockridge, of the *New York Sun,* spoke of Fonda's "fine, casual assured job," but although he was universally praised, his play was dismissed as listless, loquacious and monotonous.

After *Blow Ye Winds,* there would be almost a decade before the theatre saw Henry Fonda again. There were pictures—some good ones and some bad. There were a couple of years in uniform during the war. (Fonda enlisted, was later commissioned, and, when he was assigned to Washington to direct training films, asked for active duty. He was transferred to a destroyer and spent the rest of the war in the Central Pacific as an assistant operations and air combat intelligence officer on the staff of Admiral John Koover, who commanded the Central Pacific and the Marianas. Fonda received a Bronze Star and a Presidential Citation when he was discharged, as a lieutenant senior grade, in October, 1942.)

Faces finished, Fonda agreed to play leads at the Westchester Summer Theatre and it was while he was doing so that Hayward wired him to fly to Hollywood and sign with Walter Wanger. Fonda, feeling that he was beginning to achieve in the theatre what he had been struggling for, refused, but Hayward persisted. So Fonda made what he thought would be considered an impossible demand—$1000 a week. Wanger agreed, and the astonished Fonda signed.

But there was no picture ready for him, so he returned to Westchester and the role of the tutor in Molnar's *The Swan.* Geoffrey Kerr played the prince, and Kerr's wife, June Walker, was so impressed with Fonda that she suggested him for the title role in her next play, Marc Connelly's *The Farmer Takes a Wife,* (1934). This was the part that made him.

Brooks Atkinson, in *The New York Times,* wrote of his "manly, modest performance in a style of captivating simplicity." Robert Garland called him "a believable Dan Harrow, strong and sweet and silent as a Dan Harrow should be." And Arthur Pollock, in the *Brooklyn Eagle,* declared, "Henry Fonda is perfect. It is an

The original Mister Roberts with two who followed him in the role—John Forsythe, of the national company, and Tyrone Power, who played it in London.

Fonda grills Lloyd Nolan as John Hodiak looks on in The Caine Mutiny Court Martial.

His return to the stage was unplanned. For some time he had been interested in doing two movie roles—the lead in a screen adaptation of John O'Hara's *Appointment in Samarra* and the psychopathic murderer in Marc Brandel's *Rain Before Seven*. But the adaptation of both books presented problems which scriptwriters had not been able to solve. So Fonda sought the advice of his old friend, Joshua Logan, who had become one of the foremost directors in the theatre.

But Logan was about to start his own project—a play, based on Thomas Heggens' story of a Naval officer, *Mister Roberts*. And instead of persuading Logan to take on his film problems, he was persuaded by the director to return to the theatre in the title role of the play.

So, in one of the most popular plays ever presented, Fonda gave one of his most acclaimed performances, making that character the symbol of the decent American fighting a relentless battle against tyranny — and tedium.

(To inject a personal note, I attended that *Mister Roberts* opening night. Fresh out of the Air Force, it was my first opening. There have been hundreds since and many of them have been memorable. But none has ever been more exciting. The literally star-studded audience did not merely give the play an ovation. They shouted themselves hoarse. They stood on seats. The curtain kept going up as the actors took still another

bow. But the audience wouldn't leave. Finally, Fonda made one of his rare curtain speeches: "This is all Tom and Josh wrote for us. If you want, we can start all over again." As John Chapman reported, "I hung around awhile, hoping they would.")

That never-to-be-forgotten first night was at the Alvin Theatre, February 19, 1948. It would go on for years—on Broadway, on tour all over the country, in other countries (although a version for London starring Tyrone Power and Jackie Cooper failed dismally at a time when the Broadway original was at its hottest), and eventually on to the screen and finally in a routine TV series vaguely "based" on the play. Leland Hayward produced it, Joshua Logan directed and, with Thomas Heggen, wrote the play based on Heggens' novel. David Wayne, Robert Keith, William Harrigan, Harvey Lembeck, Ralph Meeker, Steve Hill, Rusty Lane, Murray Hamilton, Marshall Jamison, John Campbell, James Sherwood, Jocelyn Brando, Casey Walters were among other members of the virtually perfect cast.

Brooks Atkinson, in the *Times,* said, "Henry Fonda gives a winning performance. Now that Mr. Fonda is back after eleven years, it would be nice to have him back for good. He has brought quite a lot of good with him. As Roberts, he is lanky and unheroic, relaxed and genuine; he neatly skirts the maudlin when the play grows sentimental and he skilfully underplays the bombastic scenes." And Howard Barnes, in the *Herald Tribune,* reported: "Fonda, returning to the theatre after years of admirable screen acting, plumbs the depths of the play's inner significance. He is every inch the star."

From William Hawkins, in the *World-Telegram,* came the word that "Henry Fonda gives a great performance. He performs with innate simplicity, blending in undertones of charity and anguish that not only make the character a true person but more importantly verify the passionate masculine devotion of the crew."

But every notice was a love letter to the star, and theatre-goers adored him too.

Fonda stayed with *Mister Roberts* for three years on Broadway and on tour.

(Abe Laufe reported in his *Anatomy of a Hit* that "When Fonda left the cast, box-office receipts dropped over ten thousand dollars a week. After Fonda joined the road company, receipts for that company often exceeded the grosses in the same cities where *Mister Roberts* had played previously with another cast.")

He remained in the theatre for several years—first in Paul Osborn's dramatic version of J. P. Marquand's *Point of No Return* (December, 1951) and then in *The Caine Mutiny Court Martial.*

Point of No Return was a highly successful play, its seeming lack of lustre in a list of Fonda plays probably being due principally to its having followed the matchless *Mister Roberts.*

Leland Hayward again produced and H. C. Potter was credited for direction, although Elia Kazan was also involved. Fonda, as Charles Gray, was supported by Leora Dana, Frank Conroy, John Cromwell, Patricia Smith, Colin Keith-Johnson, Robert Ross, Bartlett Robinson, Heywood Hale Broun.

Again the critical bravos for his performance were unanimous. From Atkinson: "Our most ingratiating male star and his effortless, modulated style of acting is a minor miracle. Without throwing anything away, he seems to lounge through a part on a bright current of placid good humor. This is one of his clearest, most honest and winning performances." And Walter Kerr: "Fonda plays with tremendous honesty . . . faultlessly acted. Fonda is convincing, amusing and moving in turn as he struggles for a kind of success he does not really want."

And Whitney Bolton: "I know of no actor of whatever professional stature more consecrated to his profession than Henry Fonda. I know of no more thoughtful and creative actor, no man who gives more to a character or digs deeper into it. The result is always a superbly shaped performance, allowing nothing for chance, nothing for question. He is the master of that most difficult of all things: seemingly casual playing, apparently relaxed, apparently unpestered by the weight of the job that is upon him. In 'Point' he has made a monumental performance, never militant, never thrusting. Quietly, thoroughly and magnificently, he goes about the work of turning himself into Charles Gray."

There are those who feel that Fonda's portrayal of Lt. Barney Greenwald in *The Caine Mutiny Court Martial* belongs with his masterpieces. For the most part, it was an understated performance, with Lloyd Nolan's flashier Captain Queeg garnering much more immediate attention.

But audiences were not deceived, nor were the critics. Said Atkinson: "Henry Fonda's talent for underplaying has never been so apposite or cut so sharply into the veracity of a person. It is the truth of the character of

James Garner (second from left, top) had no lines in The Caine Mutiny Court Martial *but claims he learned about acting from watching Fonda's performance night after night.*

the mournful defending attorney who does not relish his job but never takes it lightly. Relaxed, thoughtful, taciturn, quiet of voice and manner, Mr. Fonda makes a heroic character out of unheroics and his moral summing up in the final scene is all the more penetrating and shocking because he never exploits it."

And Walter Kerr: "It falls to Henry Fonda to turn the tables, to swing our sympathies from the well-meaning but bumble-headed Maryk to the already destroyed Queeg. In a magnificent end-of-the-evening sequence, Mr. Fonda weaves drunkenly into an acquittal party, his eyes glazed and his speech laboriously thick to startle not only a bunch of jubilant recruits but all the rest of us as well with a scalding denunciation of easy and short-sighted patriots. Mr. Fonda is cast as Lt. Barney Greenwald assigned to defend the rebellious Maryk and he has passed most of the earlier sequences in shrewd, restless, low-key maneuvers designed to free his man. Now that he has done it, now that he has performed a given duty with all the skill at his command, he is free to reveal his own personal torment. As he offers his broken, stumbling but heartfelt version of a nation of Goebbels's getting ready to boil their Jewish mothers down to 'useful soap,' as he pays honor to the role the peacetime Navy has played in staving off that terrifying day, he casts a whole new emotional spell over the theatre. We are exhilarated by a ringing, rousing, thoroughly intelligible statement."

Henry Fonda and Barbara Bel Geddes in Silent Night, Lonely Night.

Fonda and Anne Bancroft in Two for the Seesaw.

Paul Gregory produced and Charles Laughton directed the Herman Wouk drama which opened in January, 1954. John Hodiak was Maryk.

(Way down in the cast list, among the bit players and extras without a word to speak was a dark, handsome young man who sat on the court martial board.

His name—James Garner. Garner still tells interviewers that he learned more about acting from months of watching Henry Fonda than he could have *learned* from any dramatic school or coach in the world. "I still use things in my acting that are Fonda's—and I hope he'll forgive me for stealing from him.")

With his three plays, Henry Fonda had spent some seven years away from the movie cameras. The picture that brought him back to the screen was *Mister Roberts.*

Many top actors had played Mister Roberts on the stage by this time—Tyrone Power, Charlton Heston, John Forsythe, Richard Carlson, Robert Sterling, Farley Granger, Howard Keel—and most of them had played it well. But Henry Fonda *was* Mister Roberts.

Even so, since it was the most coveted movie role of its time, it seemed obvious that it should go to the hottest movie male. Warner Brothers, alleging that Fonda was no longer "a screen name," announced that either William Holden or Marlon Brando would do the picture. Holden, it is said, turned it down on the ground that it was Fonda's role. Brando reportedly accepted. Whereupon Fonda's old mentor, John Ford, saved the day. He had been chosen to direct and he was adamant that Fonda should recreate the role on film. And so, with the help of a blast from an outraged press, Fonda was Mister Roberts once more.

Jane Fonda's first stage appearance was as the ingenue in The Country Girl, *when Henry went back to Omaha to star in it for the benefit of his alma mater Community Theatre.*

Tom Hatcher, Jane Fonda, and James MacArthur in Invitation to a March

And he was a "movie name" all over again.

But now he continued to make excursions back to the theatre. In January, 1958, he had another very successful play when he appeared as Jerry in William Gibson's *Two for the Seesaw,* directed by Arthur Penn and produced by Fred Coe. The critics, while taking full notice of the tour-de-force of a young actress named Anne Bancroft who had the other lead in the two-character play, were as enthusiastic as ever for Fonda.

"Mr. Fonda is a wonderfully straightforward actor who plays at low pressure," reported Brooks Atkinson.

"As Jerry in Mr. Gibson's play, he gives his most limpid and moving performance. What he does not say in the dialogue, he says with the silent eloquence of a fine actor."

And John McClain, in the *Journal-American:* "Henry Fonda has never given a poor performance but this may be one of his best. The role of a disillusioned attorney, his marriage a failure as he faces loneliness and desolation is hand-tailored to his talents. It is, of course, an exhaustive part and he takes full advantage of even the most minute pantomime. (He has to: he's never off the stage for more than a minute.)"

Henry Fonda, Eddie Hodges, and Mildred Natwick in Critics Choice.

Peter Fonda's first stage appearance was in a college production of Harvey.

John Beaufort, in the *Christian Science Monitor:* "Fonda is giving the kind of solid, deft and unobtrusively resourceful portrayal without which Mr. Gibson's lengthy conversation piece would quite easily founder."

But Walter Kerr put his finger on the problem that troubled Fonda. "William Gibson has a deft, buoyant, rapid-fire flair for dialogue and his eye for accurately observed detail is excellent. What he hasn't quite mastered at the moment—and this seriously involves the earnest and accomplished Mr. Fonda—is the business of sustaining a psychology, a troubled and uncertain state of mind through all of its possible dramatic complexities."

Fonda himself was miserable with *Two for the See-*saw. Jerry, he felt, was a one-dimensional role while Gittel, the girl, was full-bodied. Fonda considered himself betrayed by the writer who had assured him that he would work on the role, add dimension to it. In spite of his notices, Fonda believed that Gibson never kept his word. (Gibson has given a striking picture of the situation from his point of view in his book, *The Seesaw Log.*)

Fonda's next Broadway venture, Robert Anderson's *Silent Night, Lonely Night,* (December, 1959) was a lovely bittersweet drama. But critics found it slight and reminiscent and, even though they gave their usual accolades to Fonda and to Barbara Bel Geddes, the play was a disappointment.

Atkinson, for instance, commented: "Since Fonda

Peter Fonda's Broadway debut—in Blood, Sweat and Stanley Poole, with Darren McGavin (left) and others.

and Bel Geddes are golden people with persuasive voices, it is easy to believe what they say is true. Never a false note in their areas of words. But after an act and a half of recollections and rationalizations, a theatregoer cannot be blamed if he wishes that Mr. Anderson and his actors would please change the subject." But, in a final tribute to the stars, he added, "Although they are skillful actors, they have also been abundantly gifted by nature. They can magnetize an audience by standing on a stage."

Boston's Elliot Norton found fault with the play, too, but it gave him an opportunity for a tribute to Henry Fonda: "When he walks half across the stage and back, Henry Fonda drops his own personality without altering his appearance and by some kind of magic becomes John Sparrow, who is desperately eager for companionship, yet at the same time, reasonably reserved. He is, also, a kindly man and a considerate one; he has a sense of humor, and a gentleman's eye for a charming woman. He is not diffident, but he is sensitive to trouble. All this in a dozen sentences and a minute or two of elapsed time. This kind of acting, devoid of trickery, self-effacing and supremely honest, is rare and wonderful. That it wins instant acceptance probably is reward enough, but it deserves something more. What both of these exceptional players do in *Silent Night, Lonely Night* deserves more praise than they are likely to get in a play that, for their sakes and for everyone else's sake, should be a good deal better than it is."

Silent Night, Lonely Night was a Playwrights Company presentation, directed by Peter Glenville and also featuring Lois Nettleton, Bill Berger, Eda Heinemann and Peter De Vise.

But now another Fonda came to the theatre. In 1955, Jane Fonda had first stepped on a stage with her father and Dorothy McGuire in Omaha's Community Theatre benefit production of *The Country Girl* and, in 1956, had appeared as the ingenue lead with Fonda in a stock production of *The Male Animal* at his old stamping grounds, Dennis and Falmouth. But, she explained, these appearances were made as a lark. She wasn't interested in the theatre at all. Instead she spent two years in college, a winter in Paris and had a fling as a fashion model.

It was Lee Strasberg—first her neighbor, then her teacher—who convinced her that the theatre was indeed for her. Fonda had always shied away from pushing her toward acting, well aware of the problems that faced offspring of the famous when they were almost forced to take up that life "because it was expected of them." Jane, on her side, was absolutely determined not to try for success on the basis of being her fathers' daughter.

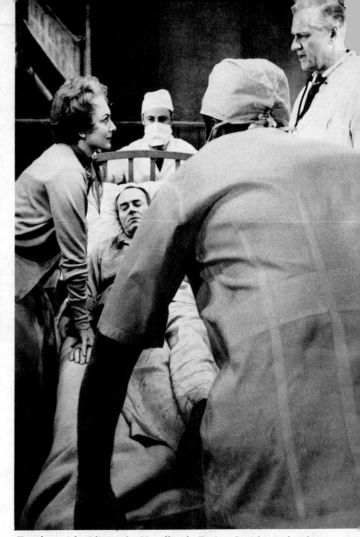

Fonda, with Olivia de Havilland, Rufus Smith, and other players, in A Gift of Time.

But, as a member of Strasberg's Actors Studio, she *was* an actress. And, insisting that it was because she was an actress completely right for the role and not because she was a Fonda, she was cast in her first Broadway play by her father's old friend and her own godfather, Joshua Logan. (Logan had already given her the lead in her first movie, *Tall Story,* and she was the best thing about that picture too.)

In the first big magazine story about her, Tom Prideaux, of *Life,* repeated that "Any suspicion that Jane is riding to fame on her father's shoulders is unfounded. Fonda never gave Jane any help or even encouragement in getting on the stage and she never traded on his name. But, by inheritance, he did give her a tipped-up nose, blue eyes, a sudden smile—and talent . . . Jane displays her best theatrical asset—an unspoiled authority and a natural magnetism that draws attention to whatever she does. 'Jane has made more progress in one year,' says her surprised and immensely pleased father, 'than I have in thirty.'"

There Was a Little Girl, by Daniel Taradash, opened in New York on March 1, 1960. Logan directed it,

Robert Fryer and Lawrence Carr produced and the company included Dean Jones, Whitfield Connor, Ruth Matteson, Joey Heatherton, Sean Garrison, Gary Lockwood and others. But the play, a cliché-ridden melodrama about wild youth, was a disaster.

It was obvious, however, that Jane Fonda was a new star. The demanding Mr. Atkinson had this to say: "For his leading lady, he [Logan] has an attractive and talented young actress who is the daughter of a respected actor. Although Miss Fonda looks a great deal like her father, her acting style is her own. As the wretched heroine of an unsavory melodrama, she gives an alert, many-sided performance that is professionally mature and suggests that she has found a career that suits her."

John Chapman, in the News added, "With the budding talent that she displayed, she might become the Sarah Bernhardt of 1990. But she'd better find herself a more genuine play than this one between now and then." And John McClain hailing her "personal triumph," called her "a resplendent young woman with exceptional style and assurance. Jane Fonda has a fine future but not, regrettably, in this play."

Even so, Jane Fonda emerged at the end of the season as the New York Critics Award choice for the most promising actress of the year.

Her next play, Arthur Laurents' *Invitation to a March,* (October, 1960), was an improvement, receiving moderate notices rather than the vicious panning given to "Little Girl." Laurents directed the Theatre Guild production, which had an exceptional cast (Celeste Holm, Eileen Heckart, James MacArthur, Madeleine Sherwood, Tom Hatcher, Richard Derr, Jeffrey Rowland).

Whitney Bolton, in the *Telegraph,* called her "by 87 statute miles the handsomest, smoothest and most delectable ingenue on Broadway," while Walter Kerr found her "delectable" too. And George Oppenheimer, of *Newsday,* said she had a "glow that almost dims the moonlight. Here is surely the loveliest and most gifted of all our new young actresses."

Father Fonda was back in the theatre at this point, too. He had found a comedy, *Critic's Choice,* and while it doesn't rank as one of his major contributions, it kept his theatre-going fans very happy for a season.

Otto Preminger produced and directed the Ira Levin play and Mildred Natwick, Eddie Hodges, Virginia Gilmore, Murray Hamilton and Georgeann Johnson were helpful. But again it was all Fonda.

Walter Kerr, himself a critic with a playwright wife, was happier with the star than with the play, although he confessed in the *New York Herald Tribune* that he realized he himself was the inspiration. But when it came to the star who, in a sense, was playing a critic who could be Kerr, the real critic couldn't have been more pleased. "As for Mr. Fonda, he is a critic to the life. He is handsome, he is nattily dressed, he is so full of integrity he should be Secretary of State, and when he kisses a girl the girl says, 'They don't make them like that any more.' I cannot praise this performance highly enough. (Aside to Mr. Fonda: pay no attention, it's beautiful work; and, as Keats said, beauty is truth.)"

Critic's Choice opened in December, 1960.

And October, 1961, brought still another Fonda to the Broadway stage. Outside of playing the lead in a University of Omaha production of *Harvey* (his father found him "amazingly believable"), Peter Fonda had given no indication of acting aspirations. But suddenly

Jane Fonda, with Ben Piazza, Dyan Cannon, Brad Dillman, in The Fun Couple.

José Quintero (left) directing stars Jane Fonda, Geraldine Page, Pat Hingle, Ben Gazzara in Strange Interlude.

here he was in a leading role opposite the old pro, Darren McGavin, in the James and William Goldman play, *Blood, Sweat and Stanley Poole.*

Howard Taubman, of *The New York Times,* observed that "Young Peter Fonda behaves as if he will grace a famed name" and John McClain in the *New York Journal-American* called him "brilliant and uncommonly assured." Walter Kerr, in the *New York Herald Tribune,* wrote that "This is no doubt the very last morning in which Peter Fonda will have to be identified as Henry Fonda's son. Hereafter dad can dig up his own publicity. The appealing and already thoroughly skilled young Mr. Fonda is in the moment he's on." But Kerr found the play thin, contrived, a little mechanical and "sometimes amusing and fortunate in finding Mr. Fonda. *Blood, Sweat and Stanley Poole* hasn't a firm enough stride to see it all the way home."

The play had a brief run and then young Peter was off to Hollywood and the movies where—except for a couple of routine television drama appearances—he has remained.

1962 was hardly a happy year for the Fondas in the theatre. Later in the year, Jane was to have a complete Broadway disaster. And Henry, on February 22, opened in his first failure since he had returned to the theatre with *Mister Roberts. A Gift of Time* was Garson Kanin's play based on Lael Tucker Wertenbaker's biography of her husband, the novelist, Charles Wertenbaker. William Hammerstein produced, Kanin directed, Olivia de Havilland played the wife and Joseph Campanella stood out in a good supporting cast.

A shaken Paul Newman spoke for a whole theatre of stunned first-nighters when he came back to the Fonda dressing room after the play. "It's just the God damndest, greatest performance I've ever seen!"

The critics echoed him, and so did audiences—the few who came to see the play. For its study of a man dying of cancer, who in his final agony persuades his wife to bring him a razor and stand over him while he cuts his veins, was just too harrowing for the ordinary theatre-goer. Richard Watts, Jr., for example, began his review by stating, "The fact may as well be faced at the outset that *A Gift of Time* is one of the most depressing plays ever written." And, for the first time, Fonda found himself frequently being stopped in the street by people who told him that, although they had never before missed a Fonda performance, they could not bring themselves to see *A Gift of Time.* There were too many theatre-goers who felt that way. *A Gift of Time* closed after a disappointingly short run and Fonda, disillusioned and unhappy, went back to Hollywood with the cynical idea that, if that's how audiences felt, he'd give them *Spencer's Mountain.*

But these nervous play-goers missed a Fonda performance of overwhelming beauty. Walter Kerr, in the *New York Herald Tribune,* wrote, "It would be difficult to offer enough respect to Henry Fonda's plain, unblinking, straightforward and unbelievably controlled performance. In some way, he has managed to look out at the vanishing world with his pale blue eyes as though sight were streaming from a skull. Without so much as wasting a catch in his throat, he can grin—sheepishly but grimly—to say that an electric typewriter is out of the question for him; he will have nothing to do with a machine that is smarter than he is. As he begins to show the unpredictable effects of more and more medication, the opportunity for random violence rears its head. Mr. Fonda delivers the violence, seizing Olivia de Havilland by the shoulders and hurling her from him in manic anger. Yet within the brief flashes of delirium, a steady sense of rueful affection keeps ringing its small alarm-bell. The actor can ride two opposed impulses at once, without losing either speed or rein, just as he can make of a moment in which he tries to sing down his pain a clear assertion of power, and will, and surrender."

And for Jane Fonda, in October of that year came the aforementioned disaster. Its official title was *The Fun Couple,* a play by Neil Jensen and John Haase, and Bradford Dillman, Ben Piazza and Dyan Cannon were also in the cast. The comments of Watts in the *Post* were typical of the reviews: "The most incredible thing about the play is that two such talented young performers as Jane Fonda and Bradford Dillman were willing to appear in the title roles. Even the sight of Miss Fonda in a bikini doesn't rescue *The Fun Couple* from being an epic bore."

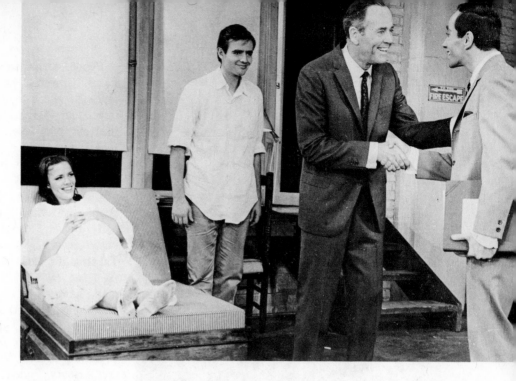

Fonda, with Holly Turner, Richard Jordan, and Sandy Baron, in Generation

The Fun Couple stopped playing after three performances.

There was one more for Jane Fonda before she, too, forsook the theatre completely. The all-star Actors Studio revival of Eugene O'Neill's *Strange Interlude*, directed by José Quintero, opened on March 12, 1963. Jane played Madeline Arnold, the girl with whom the son of Nina Leeds, played in this production by Geraldine Page, falls in love. The impeccable company also included Betty Field, Ben Gazzara, Pat Hingle, Geoffrey Horne, William Prince, Franchot Tone and Richard Thomas. Howard Taubman, in the *Times,* called it a "brilliant revival" and declared that "Jane Fonda happily contributes her vivacity and beauty to the final two acts."

In spite of his disappointment over the failure of *A Gift of Time,* and his shock over finding that his agents had turned down *Who's Afraid of Virginia Woolf?* for him without letting him know (see page 109), Henry Fonda eventually, as always, would return to his first love, the theatre. The next play, on October 6, 1965, was William Goodhart's *Generation.* Gene Saks directed, Frederick Brisson produced and A. Larry Haines, Richard Jordan, Don Fellows, Sandy Baron and Holly Turner all showed up well in support.

Its comedy about the generation gap dates quickly and, even then, it was inclined to be quite superficial in its treatment of the subject. But it was warm and engaging in contrast to, say, such a cheapjack farce as *The Impossible Years* and all of its imitations to come. And again Fonda was the Rock of Gibraltar.

Watts, for instance, dismissed the play but noted "its interest arose chiefly from Mr. Fonda's deft, captivating and deceptively effortless characterization of the tolerant father of the childbearing bride. My own impression was that the winning honesty of his brilliant performance also underlined the essential flatness of the vehicle he brightened." And Walter Kerr's notice began, "First I'd like to tell you how good Henry Fonda is in *Generation* and then I'd like to tell you why Henry Fonda shouldn't be in *Generation.*"

But even though it was dismissed like this by many critics, *Generation* had charm and it was just the right thing at that point to show off Mr. Fonda beautifully.

One of the best summations of the Fonda theatre personality was given in an unsigned review of *Generation* in *Newsweek.*

"The physique is tall, slender, erect, slow-moving but absolutely sure of where it is going. The face is strong, planed, complete, a fusion of boyishness and irreversible maturity. The hands imply both enormous competence and sensitive concern for self; clasped in front of him they express pensive deliberation, jammed into his pockets they register a provisional withdrawal from combat and society. The voice is Midwestern, but with an edge of the sophisticated East, its flat earnestness modulated by sudden rises and falls—the voice of a man who has not run after experience but to whom experience has nevertheless fully come. At the age of sixty, Henry Fonda looks a transcendent forty-five; after thirty-five years on the stage and screen he is beyond recall from his almost mythical position as an archetype. Fonda is an archetype, the kind of actor that the great Russian film director Pudovkin described as a receptacle, a container for the emotions and dreams of the audience. This quality makes his presence on any stage nearly irresistible. Needless to say, this is a boon to his co-workers; like nearly every stage piece he has

Henry Fonda in the first Plumstead Playhouse production of Our Town, *with Katharine Winn and Mark Bramhall*

been in, his new play, *Generation,* is a banal work which would not survive for a moment without his gifts. . . . Why Fonda should lend himself to such trivial proceedings is a riddle. Yet perhaps the answer lies in another remark of Pudovkin's, to the effect that the archetype-star is entirely independent of his material, that in a sense the more trivial it is the more his mythic personal status grows. This time Fonda is not the age-lessly active lover who promises youthful ardor plus maturity, but the temporarily retired lover who places his reassuring presence at the service of others. In any case, he shines as brightly as ever. Slim, shy, bemused or baffled by turns, easygoing as milk yet indestructible as diamonds, he is a testament not to drama but to those dreams of human perfection into which no conflict is ever allowed to enter."

After getting well ahead on movie roles (Fonda usually managed to have several films opening during the course of a stage run), he was ready to return to the theatre. But he couldn't find a new play which pleased him.

Instead he joined a dedicated group, headed by Martha Scott and Alfred deLiagre, whose aim was to establish a national American repertory company somewhat in the manner of the Olivier-Tynan National Theatre Repertory of England. For its first season (two plays running for two weeks each in September and October of 1968), the Plumstead Playhouse presented the thirtieth anniversary production of Thornton Wilder's *Our Town* and the fortieth anniversary production of the Ben Hecht-Charles MacArthur *The Front Page.*

Fonda starred in *Our Town* in the role created by Frank Craven, The Stage Manager. (He had once agreed to alternate *Our Town* and *The Glass Menagerie* in a State Department-sponsored tour of Europe, but the tour had fallen through.) Because Robert Ryan took a secondary role in the Fonda *Our Town,* Fonda returned the favor by playing one of the reporters in Ryan's Plumstead starring vehicle, *The Front Page.*

Others in *Our Town* included such distinguished people as John Beal, John McGiver, Estelle Parsons and Jo Van Fleet. Edward Hastings, who had previously staged *Our Town* for the American Conservatory Theatre, directed and brought in a couple of young ACT actors, Mark Bramhall and Katharine Winn, to play George and Emily. (Producer Martha Scott, the first Emily, refused to make even a token appearance in this production, preferring to work from behind the scenes.)

Writing in *The New Yorker,* Edith Oliver reported that "Henry Fonda just became the Stage Manager, unassuming in manner but always in charge. His playing of the drugstore proprietor is perfect and so is his wedding sermon." And Clive Barnes, in *The New York Times,* decided that "Henry Fonda might have been born to play the Stage Manager. Although his manner and even his accent seemed a little farther West than New England, he does have to perfection that home-spun elegance and dignity the part requires. Mr. Fonda is one of our few great—not to be confused with good—actors. Like all great actors, he has a style of his own; even more, an image of his own. With Mr. Fonda, it is a much imitated but inimitable way of watching visions in the middle distance of his inner mind.

About his minor role in *The Front Page,* Barnes wrote, "There is a kind of pleasure in seeing Henry Fonda in the tiny cameo role of a minor reporter, and my respect for him grew to watch the way he so unobtrusively, yet still decisively, went about his business." And Jerry Tallmer, in the *New York Post* called Fonda "simply superb in a small part into which he has drilled his whole long, loose being. Doing nothing, he is doing everything."

Ryan received raves, too, in *The Front Page* and a season later repeated his triumph in a Broadway version produced by the trio of Richard Barr, Edward Albee and Charles Woodward. Besides Fonda, Ryan's Plumstead cast included most of the stars who had already appeared in *Our Town,* plus such additional starters as Anne Jackson, Anthony George, Charles White, Robert Milli and Harold J. Kennedy, who also directed the Broadway version. The Plumstead production was directed by Edward Hastings.

The extraordinary casts and superlative notices led both Plumstead productions to break the house record at the theatre in Mineola, Long Island, which was their

Henry Fonda in the Broadway-Plumstead Our Town, *with John Beal and Mildred Natwick.*

temporary home. But house records at Mineola could be broken without the theatre being full. Fonda, Ryan and Miss Scott, disenchanted with their first theatre, postponed any further Plumstead Playhouse productions until the fall of 1969.

Fonda returned to Broadway in November, 1969, in another Plumstead Playhouse production of *Our Town,* which, after a limited New York run, moved to Los Angeles. Mildred Natwick, Elizabeth Hartman, John Randolph, John Beal, Harvey Evans and Irene Tedrow appeared in both of these productions, with Jim Backus and Doro Merande replacing New York's Ed Begley and Margaret Hamilton for the Coast show. Fonda himself took over the directorial reins for the latter company. (Donald Driver had directed in New York). Both productions received strong critical reaction with Fonda's direction lauded as, of course, was his performance.

Fonda had been eager to do another play for his Plumstead Playhouse return and William Saroyan's *Time of Your Life* had been set, with Gene Kelly to direct. (Kelly's first major Broadway role was in the original production of *The Time of Your Life* as the hoofer, which was to have been played in the Plumstead Playhouse production by Joel Grey.)

After all plans were made for *The Time of Your Life* the rights were withdrawn by its author without any apparent reason, according to Producers Scott and de-Liagre. They and Fonda, understandably bitter about the withdrawal, next considered John Steinbeck's *Of Mice and Men,* but gave that up when it proved impossible to cast Lennie.

So they settled for a return engagement—actually a "first" for Broadway—of Fonda's *Our Town,* to the delight, incidentally, of its playwright, Thornton Wilder, who considers Fonda "the theatre's consummate actor."

Fonda has other projects in mind for the Plumstead

Playhouse—among them *Ethan Frome,* to co-star Joanne Woodward and Martha Scott. He may also direct *Merton of the Movies,* the play in which he made his own first stage hit back in Omaha, possibly with Peter Fonda in the Merton role. Ryan and most of the other original members of the company are expected to return and such other stars as Robert Preston, Lauren Bacall, Ethel Merman, Paul Newman, Jack Lemmon, Charlton Heston, Warren Beatty, Jordan Christopher, Richard Benjamin, Paula Prentiss, Myrna Loy and many others have expressed their eagerness to participate in future projects.

Away from the Plumstead Playhouse, there are always many plays dangled hopefully before Henry Fonda. But with a TV series in the offing, he is concentrating on a one-man show which can be done in individual dates, concert-style, dropped when he has other activities, and then picked up again. Put together by Syd Steibel and tentatively called *Henry Fonda—With a Little Help From His Friends* and subtitled "Fathers Against Sons," it comprises a session of readings and scenes from the works of Socrates, Shakespeare, Thoreau, Arthur Miller, John Steinbeck, Eugene O'Neill, and Bob Dylan, among others. Broadway and a TV special are expected after a tour.

There was some talk about Peter Fonda's taking over the Dustin Hoffman role in *Jimmy Shine* on tour but his *Easy Rider* triumph opened new and more exciting opportunities than replacing another actor and he withdrew from this assignment. Roger Vadim is to produce a Paris duplicate of Kenneth Tynan's erotic revue, *Oh! Calcutta!,* but Jane Fonda's plans are indefinite at this writing.

The Fondas have just about settled on a movie life. But you can usually count on Henry making periodic returns to the theatre. He confesses the stage is still his first love.

The Fondas

ON TELEVISION

JANE AND PETER FONDA each did an appearance or two on dramatic television shows in the early stages of their careers but these days their appearances are pretty well confined to the talk shows on which they are both easy and articulate.

Henry Fonda is not a relaxed talk show guest, although he is in such demand for these appearances that he occasionally gets trapped into doing such a spot with Johnny Carson, Joey Bishop, Merv Griffin or Barbara Walters. Fonda, who has no nerves at all when he is hiding behind what he calls "the mask" of a characterization, is painfully shy when he has to appear before the public as just Henry Fonda. He has developed a technique of disarming his interviewer and audiences by confessing this self-consciousness at the outset. He invariably turns out to be an ingratiating and occasionally even somewhat loquacious guest. Miss Walters still considers his filmed appearance with her on the "Today" show to be one of the two or three best interviews with an entertainment personality ever presented on that show. (Fonda, incidentally, has become a fan of Dick Cavett, the bright young commentator on whose show both Jane and Peter were particularly sparkling. Although Cavett is also a devout Fonda admirer, they have never been able to do a show together since Fonda was filming on the Coast all during the period that the Cavett show was taped in New York. David Frost is another television personality Fonda admires and,

chances are, he will have done an interview spot with Frost by the time you read this.)

But if he considers himself somewhat ill at ease as a talk show guest, he is the ideal television personality as an actor, a narrator and even a comedian. With the same ease with which he moves from stage to screen and back, he can also invade every area of television drama.

Nobody is more wanted as a narrator for documentaries (and he has narrated theatre films, too—Fred Zinnemann's Academy Award-winning *Benjy* being a notable example.) The voice of Henry Fonda, completely individual, sincere, unemotional but expressive, gives a particular meaning to any project, whether it be a one-minute charity appeal or a major network special, like the John Steinbeck *Travels with Charley* and *America and Americans,* the two which meant most to Fonda himself. And he has been the ideal host for musical and variety shows ranging from such as a "Bell Telephone Hour," in which he introduced musical numbers and read dramatic passages, to big splashy specials in which he also performed.

Among the latter were "The Good Years," in which Fonda, Lucille Ball and Mort Sahl traced in song, dance, comedy skits and dramatic vignettes the pattern of American life from 1900 until the beginning of World War I. That 1962 show followed a much more elaborate revue—Leland Hayward's "The Fabulous Fifties," a two-hour CBS special presented in February, 1960. This gave us the brilliant and then comparatively new team of Mike Nichols and Elaine May at the top of their form, along with a delightful bit by another two-some, Betty Comden and Adolph Green, and others contributed by Rex Harrison, Julie Andrews and Suzy Parker. Cecil Smith in the *Los Angeles Times* reported that "The program, under Norman Jewison's steady directorial hand, shifted easily from the solemn to the ridiculous, from entertainment to history with Henry Fonda and Eric Sevareid carefully controlling the great unyielding mass of material as masters of ceremony." Smith also selected as a high point of the show "wonderfully moving solemn moments like Henry Fonda's restrained reading of a letter from Captain Robert Scott at Antarctica." Jack O'Brian called Fonda, "the show's catalyst; he was absolutely right and his narration brilliantly, modestly devised" and Jack Gould, in the *Times,* reported that "Henry Fonda and Eric Sevareid made an interesting combination, a refreshing departure from the usual masters of ceremonies."

One other such appearance was the inaugural gala at Washington's Ford's Theatre, recreated almost exactly as it had been at the time of the assassination of Abraham Lincoln. Fonda, who had once been young Abe Lincoln himself, was a natural choice to host the televised program which also featured such stars as Harry Belafonte, Richard Crenna, Carmen DeLavallade, Helen Hayes, Fredric March, Odetta, Robert Ryan and Andy Williams. Stewart L. Udall, Secretary of the Interior, wrote, "You have made a contribution to history . . . not to the history of Ford's Theatre as it was, but to the history of this place as it will be in the years ahead."

And then, for television, too—just as for stage and screen—there is Henry Fonda, the great actor. As far back as the earliest Ed Sullivan show, he was the magnet with his recreation of a scene from his then-current Broadway sensation, *Mister Roberts*. And, at this writing, he is already scheduled to transfer at least one of his repertory performances—probably *Our Town*—to television for the Xerox-Metromedia series of Plumstead Playhouse dramatic specials.

There was one depressing television experience— "The Deputy," a series into which he went with high hopes. Fonda frankly admits that he was partly motivated by the fact that his agents had arranged an extremely lucrative deal. Furthermore, all rights in the series would revert to him in several years. And, finally, a schedule was worked out which made it possible for him to film the episodes during the summer and early fall, which meant the rest of his time was available for stage and screen work. On a limited number of episodes, he took the lead as Marshal Simon Fry, but on

Henry Fonda (left) as Emmett Kelly, with Kelly himself, in Clown.

most of them he appeared in character at the opening but then disappeared after a few establishing moments when the story line then would concentrate on his reluctant young deputy. But, with no disrespect to capable Allen Case who had that title role, audiences who tuned into a Henry Fonda show wanted to see Henry Fonda. Allen Case just wouldn't do. Also, "The Deputy," with all of its promise of being an adult Western television series, suffered from the urgencies of scheduling so that scripts could not be polished and production was hurried.

So the series, after two seasons, went off the air. Fonda has vowed that he would never do a television series again. He was briefly tempted when it seemed that John Steinbeck's delightful *Travels with Charley* would be turned into just such a series. But it became a documentary special instead and Fonda narrated and appeared in it.

Among the most notable of the Fonda dramatic performances on television were in adaptations of *The Petrified Forest* and *Arrowsmith*.

The latter was only a half-hour version, on the short-lived CBS "Medallion Theatre" series, of an episode

Humphrey Bogart recreated his Broadway and screen role in the television version of The Petrified Forest. *Henry Fonda and Lauren Bacall had the leading roles, originally played by Leslie Howard and Peggy Conklin/Bette Davis.*

from the lengthy novel. As John Crosby described it, "The particular chunk of the book was the crisis in the West Indies where Dr. Arrowsmith is trying to find an inoculation against the bubonic plague. In the long-range interest of humanity, he inoculates two out of three, throwing each third person to the germs, in order to prove with scientific precision whether or not his serum is any good. This sort of agonizing choice—his compassion for a small, uninoculated boy warring against his instincts as a scientist—is the sort of thing a good actor can really get his teeth into. And Henry Fonda is a very good actor indeed. It's a joy to watch Fonda finger a test tube or handle a syringe as if he had been up to his hips in medicine all his life. He brings an imposing authority to every role he does."

CBS also presented the "Producers Showcase" on which *The Petrified Forest* was revived. Jack Gould's *New York Times* notice was typical of the acclaim: "The Robert E. Sherwood play about the disillusioned idealist who meets both his love and a gangster killer in an Arizona roadside restaurant packs power and intensity after twenty years. The TV interpretation successfully caught most of the poignancy and the melodrama of the original. . . . Not only were the finer shadings of Mr. Sherwood's characterizations preserved but there was an opportunity to include in adequate detail the idealist's philosophical discourse on the vanishing race of intellectuals. (*The Petrified Forest* is not with-

out contemporary pertinence.) What emerged was a production that had its dimension-in-depth of a Broadway play, not a harried TV narrative. The cast was both box-office and extremely good. *The Petrified Forest* is really the idealist's play and Mr. Fonda contributed to it with a magnificent performance. He fully conveyed the writer's haunting sensitiveness, his lean humor and his perceptive understanding of himself and the world. As the frustrated dreamer, Lauren Bacall was most effective. Her scene with Mr. Fonda in the opening act, when the daughter of the owner of the bar-b-q stand recognizes a kindred soul in the hitch-hiking writer, was most moving. Humphrey Bogart, who created the role of Duke Mantee, the killer, on the stage and in the film version, has been so identified with the part that he virtually has made it his own. Last night, in what was his debut on a live TV drama, he was cold, vicious and convincingly peremptory. Few actors can suggest so much evil so quietly. Delbert Mann's direction was uncommonly good."

Fonda's own particular favorite of any of his television appearances was *Clown* based on the autobiography of Emmett Kelly and presented on the CBS "General Electric Theatre." It won one of the top ratings of any dramatic show in television history and the critics threw around words like "triumph" and "masterpiece" to describe Fonda's recreation of Kelly and his Weary Willie. *Life* noted that "Henry Fonda in

A major Fonda TV venture—but a disappointment to him—was his Western series, "The Deputy," with Allen Case.

makeup is a spitting image of Kelly. Fonda lowers his eyes with the same hangdog look and ambles around with the same air of epic lassitude. The plot sticks fairly close to Kelly's real life from the days when he did an aerial act with his wife, but broke with her because she insisted on staying in trapeze work while he went on to create his little tramp act. To coach Fonda in the fine points of his role, Kelly, in Hollywood, went through all his clown routines. He remained resolutely gloomy until Fonda began to imitate him. Then, for about the first time on public record, Kelly let slip a chuckle."

Fonda had bought the rights to Kelly's autobiography, planning to produce and star in a film version. When his own film production of *Twelve Angry Men,* although a top critical winner, proved something less than that in financial returns, Fonda shelved his plans to produce any more films personally. But *Clown* remains a notable example of Henry Fonda on TV.

Early in her career (1960), Jane Fonda gave a sensitive performance in a television drama, *A String of Beads,* playing opposite George Grizzard. But, outside of quite a dazzling appearance as one of the set of top stars selected to present Academy Awards in 1969

as well as the aforementioned talk shows, she has been a comparative stranger to TV. Peter, though, did a number of guest appearances in dramatic shows and series segments after he was well established in movies and returned in 1968 for a co-starring role with Van Heflin in a drama special. These days, as noted, he turns up frequently as a panel guest who always has a great deal to say—and says it well.

Henry Fonda has agreed to star in a new television series for ABC-TV. In spite of his disenchantment with his former series, "The Deputy," he agreed to the new one for several reasons: he likes the money involved; he likes the working conditions which tie him down to a maximum of fifteen weeks in any year; and, most importantly, he likes the scripts, which offer dramatic and comedy opportunities in their study of the life of a big-city officer who is also a family man.

Many television producers—like those of the screen and theatre—have the dream of coralling all the Fondas in one production. It would seem only a dream. Where is the drama that would provide three worthy roles for actors of such contrasting styles?

The Fondas

OF THE FILMS

THERE ARE the Fonda eyes—still electric-blue, although he is in his sixties and a grandfather . . . the quick, embarrassed smile—the grin of a kid caught stealing a forbidden cigarette puff behind the barn. There is the Fonda walk—the most graceful lope in the world and as inimitable as the Fonda voice (none of the impersonators ever get that voice quite right—or the walk either).

(In France and England, the most respected critics write paeans to the Fonda walk and the Fonda voice. When Noël Coward had to play an American, he begged Fonda to record his lines so that he could study them. "Nobody," said Coward, "Has a more American voice." Yet Fonda despairs of it. "When I have to read poetry, I know the voice is all wrong. And, God knows, I could never attempt Shakespeare.")

Jane Fonda has her father's eyes and smile. Peter, an inch taller at 6'2", reminds you of Henry when he walks. But both of them have their own thing going for them; neither of them depends on their father to be honest-to-God movie stars in their own right. You can surround Jane with the great beauties of the day and she's the one from whom you won't be able to take your eyes. And Peter—at last with something to do on screen other than look sensitive and tortured—joined the slim ranks of major youthful movie stars with *Easy Rider*.

But it is their father who remains the consummate and extraordinary screen star. Of the actors who were as prominent as he when he made his first film in 1935— and he had the star role in that very first picture—only a handful are still active. John Wayne and Fonda's old friend Jimmy Stewart are still very much around, of course, but, back in 1935, they were playing secondary support roles while Fonda was already a star. Fredric March has made another of his infrequent returns to the screen in a character role while Charles Boyer and Fred Astaire also make an occasional movie return. Fred MacMurray is primarily of his television series and Bing Crosby seems content with an occasional TV guest shot. Cary Grant apparently has decided on the business world, Jimmy Cagney and William Powell retired after their last *Mister Roberts* roles in support of Fonda, and the lustre of other survivors of that particular movie era is considerably dimmed.

But Fonda remains, according to Wanda Hale, of the New York *Daily News,* "the most sought-after actor in the business." And *The New York Times,* a couple of years ago, followed the careers of two "super-stars" from the point when they arrived in Hollywood over thirty years before as happy-go-lucky youngsters sharing an apartment. James Stewart, the article found, is now settled, conservative, middle-aged. But for his ex-roommate, Henry Fonda, the *Times* used such descriptions as "slender . . . handsome . . . taut . . . emotional

Young Mr. Lincoln

. . . dynamic . . . a fiery liberal." (Stewart, characteristically, did not complain, but Fonda and others who know the admittedly conservative Stewart well were furious with the description, insisting that it made Stewart sound stuffy, which he certainly is not.)

Although *Variety,* in 1967, listed Fonda among the top twenty all-time box-office draws among actors, he has never been an automatic box-office draw of the proportions, say, of Abbott and Costello or Deanna Durbin, nor a "fan idol" like, for example, Van Johnson or Farley Granger. Fonda himself downgrades the *Variety* poll. Helping to make up his grand total were films like *The Longest Day* and *How the West Was Won,* in which he played only cameo roles, or pictures like *Spencer's Mountain,* which he loathed. Some of his most successful films, at the box office as well as with critics, were not considered because they were released before the period recorded by *Variety.* (In the same year, 1967, Jane Fonda was named one of the four top female stars. She is constantly high in box-office and popularity polls. And, certainly, Peter, with "Easy Rider" has made one of the most spectacular forward leaps in both box-office ratings and personal prestige—a rise comparable in recent years only to those of Dustin Hoffman in *The Graduate,* Warren Beatty in *Bonnie and Clyde,* and Clint Eastwood in the *Dollars* films.)

More serious to fervent Fonda admirers is the fact that he has never won an Academy Award (although

this puts him in the class with Chaplin, Garbo, John Barrymore, Cary Grant, Orson Welles, Richard Burton, Montgomery Clift and other players of more distinction than the majority of Oscar-winners). But awards are usually won by characterizations of some flamboyance and Fonda's abiding horror is that anything theatrical might turn up in his acting. He has worked unremittingly to perfect an acting style of deceptive ease, which eschews personal mannerisms and traits and acting tricks. Foreign critics have repeatedly cited him as representative of the finest in American acting. Kenneth Tynan leads an impressive group of Britishers who consider him the best American actor. And a couple of years ago, a delegation of visiting Russian filmmakers selected him as one of the three or four American film figures whose work seemed to them of special value.

There has always been, for Hollywood and its fans, a sense of not really knowing Fonda as a person. Most Hollywoodians, in real life, live up to their movie-created image. Gable, Stewart, Gary Cooper, John Wayne, Marlon Brando, Errol Flynn, Humphrey Bogart, Montgomery Clift—all of them are, or were, pretty much like the characters they played on screen, or at least worked hard to give that impression.

Fonda, though, could never be so easily pigeonholed. In his acting, he could be a naive innocent . . . a fierce young idealist . . . a sensitive and brooding intellectual . . . a bitter cynic . . . a suave sophisticate. Off screen,

The Grapes of Wrath

he may be all of these (with the definite exception of the first), but he is also a man of complexity not suggested by any of his stage and screen roles.

Warm and outgoing with friends, he has a strong reserve with strangers, particularly if he feels he is "on exhibition." An articulate and witty man when discussing people or projects in which he is interested, he becomes taciturn when conversation turns to his own life and career. He will hold forth at length on his admiration for, say, Warren Beatty's performance in *Bonnie and Clyde,* but praise of his own work makes him obviously uncomfortable.

He can, when cornered, comment on his pride at the strides made by his son and daughter, but misguided attempts to probe more deeply into the life he considers private cause him to retreat almost immediately into a shell.

So it is true that Henry Fonda is largely known to the public for his work—not for any publicizable private life. He is, and has been since he first discovered the magic of the theatre, a serious, indeed a dedicated, actor.

Richard Burton says, "When I see Fonda, whether on the stage or screen, he completely involves me in whatever he is doing. I can't believe he's anything but the part he is playing. You might call him the super-realistic actor. He ought to play Iago."

James Garner was one of the silent judges in *The Caine Mutiny Court Martial* and used to watch Fonda and learn from his performance night after night. He

Barefoot in the Park

Mister Roberts

realize when it is important not to be noticed. I learned that first from Henry Fonda, when I was in *Mister Roberts*. When it is somebody else's moment, this man knows it! 'Look,' he'd say, 'in this scene, the play lives with you. I have to *listen* to you here. I could move or do something here, but if I do, we're dead.'" Mr. Fonda's artistry leads him to another long theatre discourse—about acting style . . . and about the construction of a stage laugh ("Fonda would rather sacrifice a laugh than lie to get it.")

And although Fonda has never been associated with the Actors Studio, Lee Strasberg, the dean of the current "Method" of American acting, says of him, "He is an actor who represents very characteristically the American approach to acting with sincerity, honesty, and directness. He is capable of roles of the most enormous challenge." Richard Watts, Jr., the critic, says, "He has a unique capacity for throwing away a line, for going in for the most casual understatement, and still offering a characterization that is complete, detailed and filled with insight."

Perhaps Fonda's friend Jimmy Stewart says it best: "When people start analyzing a successful acting career in the theatre or in movies, the 'analyst' many times attributes the success to great good fortune or the whole success was an accident—or the actor had this great, consuming ambition and, therefore, success was his; or he liked to face a challenge—or he just worked his little old heart out. I don't think any of this applies to Hank Fonda. Hank is one of the really fine successful actors of our time because **he** deserves to be. He has made

confesses he has "borrowed" Fonda touches for his own performances when he could fit them in.

Larry Blyden is another good actor who has proclaimed his debt to Fonda. In a *New York Times* interview with Tom Burke, Blyden said, "As a young actor, you have to be hit in the mouth a few times before you

Barbarella

amazing use of his talents and, what is perhaps most important of all, he has a deep, sincere love and respect for acting."

Charlton Heston has gone further. In addition to his admiration for Fonda's acting, Heston says, "Henry Fonda has the most typically American face of any actor." (But then, of course, there is an interview given by the irrepressible Michael J. Pollard to Joyce Haber: "I think I really look like Henry Fonda. In fact, I *am* Henry Fonda.")

"Typically American" describes every major performance he has ever given—with the exceptions of the tormented Latin American priest in *The Fugitive* and Pierre in *War and Peace,* performances that were effective in spite of his seeming miscasting. (He was also a Russian type in a picture called *The Dirty Game*—but everything was wrong with that one.)

But, as "typically American," he has played the President of the United States twice (in *Fail Safe* and in *Young Mr. Lincoln),* a Presidential candidate in *The Best Man* and a Presidential appointee in *Advise and Consent.*

The Wild Angels

Each of the Fondas is a star. Yet, superficial family resemblances aside, each is a complete individual. How long has it been since you have heard anyone feel the need to identify Jane as "Henry Fonda's daughter?" She has steadily moved into the rarefied atmosphere occupied by only a few other ladies of the movies. She has always, from the beginning, been considered a particularly capable actress [see critical quotes on all of her plays and films later in this book]. But she has also been a consistently provocative personality—and more and more she makes news. When you look for the most

exciting stars of the day, those with the charisma of the Marilyns, Avas, Ritas of the past, only Jane Fonda and a very few others are even contenders.

And long before he became accepted with his own enormously successful movie, Peter Fonda stood for much more than just another youthful movie actor. The Peter Fonda motorcycle poster hung on the same walls that displayed everybody from Dean to McQueen to Dylan. He already had great magnetism even without the major movie to point it up. Now he has that, too. So it is of all of them and of all of their films that we now deal—the films of the fabulous Fondas.

They Shoot Horses, Don't They?

The Farmer Takes a Wife

Fox. 1935. Directed by Victor Fleming. Produced by Winfield Sheehan. Screen play by Edwin Burke. Adapted from the play by Frank B. Elser and Marc Connelly, based on *Rome Haul* by Walter D. Edmonds.

HENRY FONDA played *Dan Harrow* and the cast included: Janet Gaynor, Charles Bickford, Slim Summerville, Andy Devine, Roger Imhof, Jane Withers, Margaret Hamilton, Siegfried Rumann, John Qualen, Kitty Kelly, Robert Gleckler.

THE PICTURE: Almost alone among his contemporaries—Stewart, Grant, Wayne, Cooper, Gable, Power, Milland, McCrea, Bogart, etc. first played secondary roles or less—Henry Fonda was a star in his very first picture. Fonda's initial film role was as the leading man in *The Farmer Takes a Wife*. Even more remarkable was the fact that he was repeating a role he had originated on stage. Rare it was then for a stage actor, particularly a relatively unknown example of the breed, to be given a chance to re-enact his performance in

the movies—not when all the real movie stars were desperate for really juicy roles.

Actually, Gary Cooper and Joel McCrea were two who were first wanted for the lead here. When they were unavailable, Fonda had his chance. He had not been too eager about forsaking the footlights where, after a long period of virtual apprenticeship, he had just begun to become established. When Walter Wanger beckoned with a screen contract, Fonda asked "the enormous sum of $1000 a week," certain that would cancel negotiations. Wanger accepted the terms immediately. It was as a loanout from Wanger to Fox that Fonda recreated the role of Dan Harrow.

Fonda gives a great deal of the credit for the fact that his screen debut was successful to director Victor Fleming. "I had been playing it as I did on stage—'projecting' to the audience. After the first day, Fleming took me aside. 'Hank,' he told me, 'you're hamming.' Well, that was a dirty word to me. He made me see the difference between playing to an audience and playing for the camera." Fonda never confused the two again.

Henry Fonda and Janet Gaynor

Although Janet Gaynor's box-office importance had faded considerably since her heyday in the early thirties, she was still Fox's biggest female star. The Molly Larkins character suited her long-established "little girl breathlessness" and yet was appropriate to her growing maturity, to give her one of the best roles she had had in some time. One of those famous Fox supporting casts—full of such actors as a burly Charles Bickford, along with Slim Summerville, Andy Devine, John Qualen, Margaret Hamilton, Roger Imhof, right to a bit moppet named Jane Withers—was well chosen.

But the big news of the movie was Henry Fonda, and the bright blue eyes, the engaging grin, the loping stride—all of the things that characterize his screen image—were immediately established.

THE CRITICS
"A good deal of what delighted us so hugely in the stage version of *The Farmer Takes a Wife* has found its way into the photoplay. If some of the saltiest humors of the original have evaporated, the film still is able to recapture the sentimental warmth and the pun-gent charm of the most lovable of recent American folk plays. A kindly history of those great days when the Erie Canal was the biggest thing that had ever happened to New York, it is a rich and leisurely comedy of American manners and its roots are deep in our native soil. For comparative purposes the photoplay suffers chiefly from the circumstances that only Henry Fonda (of the Broadway cast) and Charles Bickford manage to approximate the superb performances of those stage players who caused Brooks Atkinson, in his excitement, to cry, 'Jeepers Cripers.' . . . Mr. Fonda, in his film debut, is the bright particular star of the occasion. As the virtuous farm boy, he plays with an immensely winning simplicity which will quickly make him one of our most attractive screen actors. . . . If you can forget Herb Williams and June Walker, you will find pleasant performances by Slim Summerville and Janet Gaynor. . . . As a comedy of customs, *The Farmer Takes a Wife* recaptures something that was very endearing in American life. Here is an affectionately amusing photoplay."

Andre Sennwald, *The New York Times*

Henry Fonda and Janet Gaynor

"Charm and atmospheric color are two qualities that it is difficult for the screen to capture successfully and because *The Farmer Takes a Wife* manages both of them attractively, it deserves approval as an excellent motion picture. . . . In the case of the new film, both charm and atmosphere are so sanely manipulated that you forget the unnecessary length of the picture, the absence of a sturdy story and the excessive amount of dialogue employed. . . . The producers of the film were wise enough to retain Henry Fonda, of the stage cast, in his original role of the young man who was working on the canal just long enough to make enough money to buy a farm. Mr. Fonda is that rarity of the drama, a young man who can present naive charm and ingratiating simplicity in a characterization and yet never fail to seem both manly and in possession of his full senses. His is a delightful portrayal in a role that might easily have seemed the type of thing Buddy Rogers used to strive for helplessly. Miss Janet Gaynor has the role that Miss June Walker played in the theatre, and by employing some of Miss Walker's vocal mannerisms she achieves a good deal of convincing charm."

Richard Watts, Jr., *New York Herald Tribune*

"If *The Farmer Takes a Wife* is a satisfactory film, then the screen debut of Henry Fonda seems something more than that. Mr. Fonda is a tall, lanky young man with a boyish face, a low voice and a quiet manner particularly effective. One of Mr. Fonda's most outstanding assets is his appearance of sincerity."

Eileen Creelman, *New York Sun*

"Henry Fonda's day dawns. . . . He dominates the scene and emerges from his film debut a certain film success and one of the really important contributions of stage to screen within the past few seasons."

New York American

Way Down East

Fox. 1935. Directed by Henry King. Produced by Winfield Sheehan. Screen play by Howard Estabrook and William Hurlbut, from the play by Lottie Blair Parker.

HENRY FONDA played *David Bartlett* and the cast included: Rochelle Hudson, Slim Summerville, Edward Trevor, Margaret Hamilton, Andy Devine, Russell Simpson, Spring Byington, Astrid Allwyn, Sara Haden, Al Lydell, Harry C. Bradley, Clem Bevans, Vera Lewis, Seymour and Corncob, Phil LaToska, William Benedict.

THE PICTURE: With *The Farmer Takes a Wife* a success, Fox wanted another teaming of its leads. Way back in 1920, when D. W. Griffith had made *Way Down East,* with Lillian Gish and Richard Barthelmess as the lovers, it had been regarded as something of a screen classic. It must have been badly dated even then, but with Miss Gish's beautifully tragic face, the old melodrama was moving. The new picture had no such

redemption. Janet Gaynor, who did have sensitivity, left the film, whether because of illness or as the result of a personal disagreement is uncertain. To replace her, Fox brought in a lissome dark ingenue with fabulous eyes but no discernible acting ability. Probably no other actress could have made the old chestnut palatable but Rochelle Hudson's earnest attempts were only pathetic. Again there was the Fox stock company— Slim Summerville, Andy Devine, Margaret Hamilton, Russell Simpson, Spring Byington, Sara Haden—in support, all doing their usual things. And Fonda was, at least, a manly and upstanding hero.

THE CRITICS
"When you see Miss Rochelle Hudson in her great comedy scene hopping about on the prop ice floes in the new film edition of *Way Down East,* your first impulse is to applaud the production as a sly and uproarious burlesque of the celebrated tear-drama. Calmer reflection, however, obliges me to regard the rich, satiric qualities of the photoplay as a product of the same

Henry Fonda and Rochelle Hudson

kind of unplanned dramatic genius that evolved the famous nut-cracking motif in *Once in a Lifetime*. The drama turns out to be surprisingly good fun, but the chances are that you will like it for all the wrong reasons.... But the film possesses genuine charm in its earlier pastoral scenes on the New England farm. In large measure this is the personal triumph of Henry Fonda, whose immensely winning performance as the squire's son helps to establish an engaging bucolic mood for the drama in its quieter moments.

"Russel Simpson struggles earnestly to make the squire seem impressive instead of just a howling caricature of New England piety, but his performance is chiefly important as dead-pan comedy. Margaret Hamilton is vastly amusing as the venomous gossip. As the mistreated heroine, Miss Hudson is less than convincing when she is tearfully telling the world about her innocence. There is an astringent quality in her that ought to result in some effective performances in the termagant department, but she is temperamentally unfitted for the business of manufacturing treacle."

Andre Sennwald, *The New York Times*

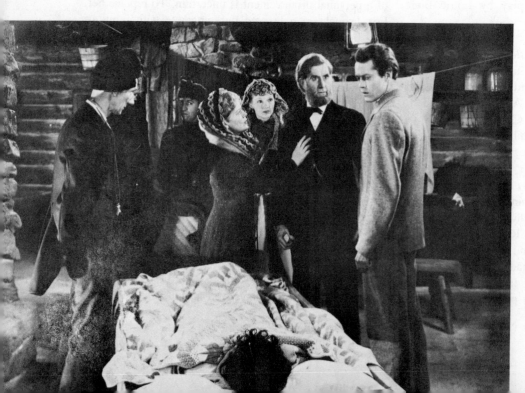

Clem Bevans, Slim Summerville, Margaret Hamilton, Spring Byington, Astrid Allwyn, Russell Simpson, Henry Fonda, and (on bed) Rochelle Hudson.

I Dream Too Much

RKO-Radio. 1935. Directed by John Cromwell. Produced by Pandro S. Berman. Screen play by James Gow and Edmund North. Adapted from story by Elsie Finn and David G. Wittels. Score by Jerome Kern and Dorothy Fields.

HENRY FONDA played *Jonathan* and the cast included: Lily Pons, Eric Blore, Osgood Perkins, Lucien Littlefield, Esther Dale, Lucille Ball, Mischa Auer, Paul Porcasi, Scott Beckett.

THE PICTURE: Columbia had made something of a splash by bringing opera to the screen with Grace Moore and so, of course, the other film companies followed suit. Divas were in demand. It was RKO who lured the best known of them all at the time, Lily Pons, and they celebrated this coup by giving her nothing but the best for her first movie. Jerome Kern and Dorothy Fields wrote the score, Pandro S. Berman produced with the same elegance that characterized his Astaire-Rogers musicals, and Miss Pons was surrounded by a

Henry Fonda and Lily Pons

top-drawer cast. For her leading man, she won Henry Fonda, most popular of the new young screen stars. With all of this, it would be nice to say that the picture was a triumph. Actually, it was considerably less than that—a light little comedy with Miss Pons singing the Bell Song from *Lakme* and "Caro Nome" from *Rigoletto,* along with the current Kerns. Her acting was adequate enough for her undemanding role but she made no super-splash and, after a couple of less well received follow-up pictures, she returned to the world where Lily Pons *was* a big star—not just a small French girl who sang.

THE CRITICS

"Lily Pons makes a graceful cinema debut in the pleasant if somewhat minor operatic comedy called *I Dream Too Much.* Designed pretty candidly as a vehicle for Miss Pons, *I Dream Too Much* suffers from inaction and a limited sense of humor. But it is amiably managed, admirably played and provides a reasonably painless setting for the gifted soprano.... Miss Pons has the excellent assistance of Henry Fonda, the most likable of the new crop of romantic juveniles; Osgood Perkins, as the frenetic opera impresario, and Eric Blore, the perfect comedy butler."

Andre Sennwald, *The New York Times*

"Opposite Miss Pons is the likable Henry Fonda, who makes the part of the disgruntled husband considerably more pleasant than it might have been in less skillful hands."

Richard Watts, Jr., *New York Herald Tribune*

Henry Fonda and Lily Pons

"Lily Pons has the advantage of splendid support that approaches the brilliant, especially on the part of Henry Fonda whose performance is absolutely stellar. Such simplicity, directness and ability to create living character is a talent that cannot be analyzed and certainly not dismissed as accidental."

New York American

Osgood Perkins, Lily Pons, and Henry Fonda.

Henry Fonda and Sylvia Sidney

The Trail of the Lonesome Pine

Paramount. 1936. Directed by Henry Hathaway. A Walter Wanger production. Screen play by Grover Jones. Adapted by Harvey Threw and Horace McCoy from the novel by John Fox, Jr.

HENRY FONDA played *Dave Tolliver* and the cast included: Sylvia Sidney, Fred MacMurray, Fred Stone, Beulah Bondi, Fuzzy Knight, Robert Barrat, Spanky McFarland, Nigel Bruce, Ricca Allen, Margaret Armstrong, Powell Clayton, George Ernest, Frank McGlynn, Jr., Alan Baxter, Ed LeSaint, Hank Bell, Fred Burns, Richard Carle, Bud Geary, Jim Welch, John Beck, Bob Cortman, Jim Corey, William McCormick.

THE PICTURE: In his first two films, Henry Fonda had been a shy and peaceful rural type who turns to violence only as a last resort. In *The Trail of the Lonesome Pine,* he was a mountaineer—loving and even poetic with his womenfolk, but already completely embroiled in one of those blood feuds that had flourished in fiction, theatre and films from generations back.

The Trail of the Lonesome Pine, though, didn't seem old hat in the same way as had *Way Down East.* To begin with, it was the first outdoor picture in the new Technicolor—a very big selling point—and the greens, browns, blues of nature had never been shown off quite so well on the screen.

And the picture was exceptionally well acted, par-ticularly by Fonda and the principal women. Sylvia Sidney used well her customary alternating radiance and emotional intensity as the spitfire who leaves the hills for an education but who reverts to screaming savagery when her young brother is killed. And there was Beulah Bondi, in a lovely characterization of Melissa Tolliver, the mother who cries out against bloodshed. There were other effective performances, too—by

Henry Fonda and Sylvia Sidney

it was very contemporary as the result of Henry Hathaway's vigorous direction, Wanger's meticulous production, the exceptional cast, and the sweeping panorama of the Technicolored outdoors. Brought back in recent tributes to Fonda, it proved one of the least dated of his early films.

THE CRITICS

"Of the story, John Fox, Jr.'s well-known novel speaks for itself. Published in 1908 and twice before used as a basis for a film—once with Charlotte Walker and once with Mary Miles Minter—it tells of the feud between the Tollivers and the Falins of Kentucky . . . This is no turgid, drawing room drama with a superabundance of dialogue and a minimum of action. It is none too generously endowed with story values. For all its gunplay and fist-swinging, its plot—considered alone—would be unimpressive and little more meaningful than the elemental fodder on which most Class B melodramas feed. But when, to that story, is added a cast of unusual merit and a richly beautiful color production, then it becomes a distinguished and worthwhile picture, commanding attention no less for its intrinsic entertainment value than as another significant milestone in the development of the cinema."

Frank S. Nugent, *The New York Times*

"Henry Fonda contributes another fine cinematic portrait to the galaxy he has given in the role of the sombre mountaineer whose heart, filled with murderous tradition, is sometimes warmed by sunnier emotions."

Regina Crewe, *New York American*

Fred Stone, Robert Barrat, Alan Baxter and young Spanky McFarland.

Fonda had the more rewarding role as the hot-tempered, yet idealistic, boy of the hills. Al Capp has said that Fonda's Dave Tolliver, was the inspiration for Li'l Abner and, indeed, in the early Capp drawings, they looked remarkably alike.

The Trail of the Lonesome Pine had been filmed before (in 1916 and in 1923), had been a popular book, and as a stage play had been a favorite trouping vehicle. But the 1936 movie was the first of its kind in a long time and, instead of seeming like a throwback,

MacMurray, Sidney, Beulah Bondi, Robert Barrat, and Fred Stone with the dying Fonda.

*Margaret Sullavan and
Henry Fonda.*

The Moon's Our Home

Paramount. 1936. Directed by William A. Seiter. Produced by Walter Wanger. Adapted by Isabel Dawn and Boyce DeGaw from the novel by Faith Baldwin. Additional dialogue by Dorothy Parker and Alan Campbell.

HENRY FONDA played *Anthony Amberton* and the cast included: Margaret Sullavan, Charles Butterworth, Beulah Bondi, Margaret Hamilton, Henrietta Crosman, Dorothy Stickney, Lucien Littlefield, Walter Brennan, Brandon Hurst, Spencer Charters, John G. Spacey, Margaret Fielding.

THE PICTURE: Shirlee Fonda, catching up on the movies of her husband, perched before the television set one night in 1967, while her groom sat, buried in a book, in another room. She giggled at the comedy of the thirty-year-old movie and, at first commercial, called out, "Come and watch this with me—I think its adorable!"

"I had pretty well forgotten *The Moon's Our Home,*" says Fonda. "But Shirlee was right—it was fun. It had pace and charm and I found myself laughing and enjoying it, too. It has held up so much better than a lot of those pictures of the thirties."

At the time of its release, *The Moon's Our Home* was well-received but there were so many gay, slightly screwball, comedies of its type in those days that it

didn't get as much attention as it perhaps deserved. Too, it was adapted from a Faith Baldwin novel and Miss Baldwin, no matter how prolific and well-selling, was hardly a favorite of the critics.

And, of course, the very casting of Henry Fonda and Margaret Sullavan together gave the picture a publicity angle that rather obscured the fact that they were also delightfully right for the roles of the tempestuous movie star (who might have been modeled after Katharine Hepburn) and the adventurer-writer (a Richard Halliburton type). For Sullavan and Fonda were the first romantic movie team to win a great deal of attention from the fact that they had once, in real life, briefly been man and wife. (William Powell and Carole Lombard, also once wedded, came along later in the year as co-stars in *My Man Godfrey* but, by that time, the edge was off the idea and it was easier to accept them in their screen roles and forget that once upon a time these loving characters had in fact been married and divorced.)

The Moon's Our Home was a highly enjoyable trifle about a couple of world-famed celebrities who meet, fall in love and marry, even though neither realizes who the other is. To Miss Baldwin's credit, she provided the original story line which was considerably helped by a bright screen play by Isabel Dawn and Boyce DeGaw and, undoubtedly, by the "additional

Margaret Sullavan and
Henry Fonda.

dialogue" supplied by Dorothy Parker and Alan Campbell. Sullavan and Fonda, both of them much more familiar in much more serious things, were extremely bright and attractive with sparkling comedy senses. Charles Butterworth contributed one of his funnier bits. And some of the most competent character actresses on the screen—Beulah Bondi, Henrietta Crosman, Margaret Hamilton, Dorothy Stickney—helped a great deal, too.

THE CRITICS

"An authority on recent Faith Baldwin has assured us that the film edition of her *The Moon's Our Home* is considerably more sprightly than the novel itself. The picture, certainly, is about the most likable of the many screen entertainments inspired by Faith, produced in hope and not always received with charity. Comedy romance is the heading under which the new film roughly would fall, and roughly is the way most of the comedy romance is handled. One step more and we should call it slapstick; one step to the side and it would have been farce. Producer Walter Wanger and his current company have had the wisdom to avoid either step; the picture stands its amiable ground, and

Henry Fonda, Margaret Sullavan,
Beulah Bondi, and unidentified
actor.

Margaret Sullavan and Henry Fonda, with Walter Brennan.

merely bobs up and down with ingratiating animation and an occasional spout of dialogue which justifies the hiring of Dorothy Parker for the rewrite job. . . . Miss Baldwin or her adapters have spiked this unimportant little concoction with half a dozen ponies of rowdy humor, and Miss Sullavan and Mr. Fonda—not to mention the blank-faced Charles Butterworth, the hatchet-nosed Margaret Hamilton and the rubber-jawed Walter Brennan—have served it with spirit and zest. . . . Above all, we endorse that moment of the wedding night when Mr. Fonda, about to embrace his bride, is suddenly assailed by the scent of her perfume—musk always makes him deathly sick. In the contemplation of such enjoyable bits, one can forgive many things—even the boy meets girl, loses girl, formula."

Frank S. Nugent, *The New York Times*

"The temperamental pyrotechnics that illumine *The Moon's Our Home* are more likely to fascinate than amuse you. . . . The film takes leave of plausibility without getting a foothold in the realm of fantasy. . . . Margaret Sullavan and her quondam real-life husband, Henry Fonda, engage in the series of premarital and marital bouts that constitute what might be called the plot of the work. Particularly does Miss Sullavan succeed in creating an arresting characterization of a spoiled heiress and screen star, tossing lamps, perfume

bottles and bric-a-brac about in tiny crises. . . . As an explorer writer, in the Richard Halliburton tradition, Mr. Fonda is engaging, although not very persuasive. The motivation of the piece is so tenuous and so much a matter of incredible coincidence that his part would tax the ingenuity of far more experienced cinema troupers."

Howard Barnes, *New York Herald Tribune*

Henry Fonda and Margaret Sullavan, between scenes of **The Moon's Our Home.**

Spendthrift

Paramount. 1936. Directed by Raoul Walsh. Produced by Walter Wanger. Screen play by Raoul Walsh and Bert Hanlon. Based on Eric Hatch's story.

HENRY FONDA played *Townsend Middleton* in a cast that also included: Pat Paterson, Mary Brian, June Brewster, George Barbier, Halliwell Hobbes, Spencer Charters, Richard Carle, J. M. Kerrigan, Edward Brophy, Jerry Mandy, Greta Meyer, Miki Morita.

THE PICTURE: Into the career of every actor comes something like *Spendthrift*—slick and silly, easy to for-get. Fonda says he has virtually no recollection of having made it and is quite sure he never saw it.

THE CRITICS
"A slight and superficially diverting fable of a polo-playing Cinderella. Fonda is probably as morose a play-boy as you would care to meet."
Frank S. Nugent, *The New York Times*

"Mr. Fonda is, as usual, an engaging actor."
Richard Watts, Jr., *New York Herald Tribune*

Pat Paterson, Henry Fonda, and Mary Brian.

Annabella masquerades as a boy for unsuspecting Henry Fonda.

Wings of the Morning

20th Century-Fox. 1937. Directed by Harold Schuster. Produced by Robert T. Kane. Screen play by Tom Geraghty. Based on stories by Donn Byrne.

HENRY FONDA played *Kerry* in a cast that also included: Annabella, Leslie Banks, Stewart Rome, Irene Vanbrugh, Harry Tate, Helen Haye, Teddy Underdown, D. J. Williams, Philip Sydney Frost, Mark Daly, Sam Livesey, E. V. H. Emmett, Capt. R. C. Lyle, John McCormack, Steve Donoghue.

THE PICTURE: Now it was England's turn to try out Technicolor and, for the first British film in that medium, we had *Wings of the Morning,* in which the settings ranged all the way from the lakes and meadows of Killarney to Epsom Downs on Derby Day. And the story had gypsy princesses and gypsy curses, a horse that must win the Derby, a handsome Canadian trainer, and a girl who gets into all sorts of mischief in a masquerade as a boy. For the latter part, as well as the prologue role of the princess, they brought over the bewitching French star, Annabella, who had been attracting a great deal of attention in such René Clair films as *Le Million.*

Because Annabella was not a well-known name out-side of France, the producers insisted on backing her up with a popular leading man. Henry Fonda, who had made the first American outdoor Technicolor picture, was asked to repeat the pioneering step for England. More because he wanted the trip and the experience of filming in Ireland and England than because he was interested in the routine leading man role, Fonda accepted. While the part made no remarkable demands on his talent, he was particularly attractive and the romance with Annabella, who masqueraded quite believably as a boy through a good part of the film, was charming. The color had that quality that, even now, seems more typical of British films than American—softer, muted tones, never harsh or garish—and was, by all odds, the most beautiful movie in the medium to that date.

THE CRITICS
"On at least three counts *Wings of the Morning* deserves commendation. It has the best color compositions yet devised by the screen in its prismatic researches and backs them up with a comparatively solid narrative. It introduces the utterly captivating French star, Annabella, in her first English-speaking role. Finally, it proves a generally disarming and amusing romance,

potent to capture and hold your attention, hues or no hues. First and last, this is a delightful entertainment. Annabella gives an enchanting performance. Playing the dual role of a gypsy princess who marries an Irish nobleman in 1889 and that tragic beauty's great granddaughter, circa 1937, masquerading in boy's clothes, she combines grace and subtlety to a remarkable degree. In the latter part, particularly, she gives the work a fresh vitality which is one of its chief distinctions. She handles the farcical episodes which find her unwillingly attending the hero in a tub, passing a night with him in a haymow or stubbornly refusing to take off her trousers for a morning plunge, with exquisite assurance. . . . Henry Fonda plays the hero in a brashly effective manner. . . . It seemed rather absurd to bring on John McCormack for a few vocal numbers, but the principals are competent to rescue the plot from these interruptions."

Howard Barnes, *New York Herald Tribune*

"*Wings of the Morning* is a visual delight. More than that, it is a wholesome, refreshing and altogether likable little romance. *Wings of the Morning* is quaintly old-fashioned but the picture takes a deep and invigorating breath and plunges into a pleasantly unimportant romance."

Frank S. Nugent, *The New York Times*

John McCormack, Henry Fonda, and Annabella.

You Only Live Once

United Artists. 1937. Directed by Fritz Lang. Produced by Walter Wanger. Original screen play by Gene Towne and Graham Baker.

HENRY FONDA played *Eddie Taylor* in a cast that also included: Sylvia Sidney, Barton MacLane, Jean Dixon, William Gargan, Jerome Cowan, Chic Sale, Margaret

Hamilton, Warren Hymer, Guinn Williams, John Wray, Walter De Palma, Jonathan Hale, Ward Bond, Wade Boteler, Henry Taylor, Jean Stoddard, Ben Hall.

THE PICTURE: One of the most stunning dramas of the thirties was Fritz Lang's *You Only Live Once,* a study of a young ex-convict, hounded and persecuted

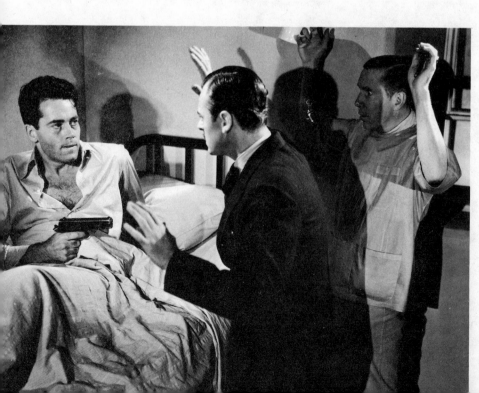

Henry Fonda, Jerome Cowan, and Stanley Mack

and finally sentenced to death for a murder of which he is innocent; of his escape from prison and his flight through the countryside with his wife to their killing just before they reach the state line. A relentlessly grim and tragic film, it found little favor with the fans who had palpitated to the lyric romance of Sylvia Sidney and Henry Fonda in *The Trail of the Lonesome Pine*. In the Lang picture, Fonda and Sidney were doomed from the start, and the box office just didn't approve.

In later years, *You Only Live Once* was to become a much more popular item in television and theatre revivals and critics still consider it as a milestone movie of its era. At the time, their flight from the law—living at night and in cars, stealing to live but being blamed for any crime in their area—was likened to the real-life story of a couple of recent Texas outlaws, Bonnie Parker and Clyde Barrow. When Pauline Kael, in *The New Yorker,* and Stephan Kanfer, in *Time,* wrote their extensive analyses of Warren Beatty's *Bonnie and Clyde,* they reached back thirty years to point out analogies to *You Only Live Once.*

Some hold out for *Fury,* but, to many other ob-

The shattering finish of You Only Live Once *(Sidney, Fonda)*

The ironically idyllic honeymoon of You Only Live Once *(Sidney, Fonda)*

servers, *You Only Live Once* is Fritz Lang's American masterpiece. Certainly it was brilliantly conceived on every level—the tender, bittersweet romantic passages ... the headlong rush into melodramatic excitement with the staging of the crime, the capture and the escape from prison ... and the agonizing, desperate final flight. (Fonda, incidentally, dislikes Lang more than any director with whom he has ever worked, claims he treats his actors like puppets and has "no human communication" with them. Yet Fonda, too, realizes that the picture has the unmistakable touch of a great director and that the result, at least in this instance, may have justified the means.)

Credit for *You Only Live Once* must go to so many besides Lang—to Gene Towne and Graham Baker for their tight, tense screen play ... to Walter Wanger, for the uncompromising courage of his production ... to excellent actors like Jean Dixon, Barton MacLane, William Gargan, Jerome Cowan, Warren Hymer, Guinn Williams, Ward Bond, Margaret Hamilton, Chic Sale. And it would go particularly to its stars. In a lifetime of performances of heartbreaking perfection, Sylvia Sidney has never been more poignantly lovely. Fonda's quiet sensitivity eventually explodes in bitter anguish. Together, they made the study of a boy and girl, caught in forces they cannot control, a devastating screen experience.

THE CRITICS

"Fonda is flawless. Skilled in the impressive art of representing the befuddled and confused, he puts on a show which resounds with sincerity and integrity."

Bland Johaneson, *New York Mirror*

"In *You Only Live Once,* Fritz Lang again demonstrates his talent for achieving significant suspense and terror on the screen. The new offering is a harrowing story of physical and spiritual violence. Holdups, prison breaks, man hunts and sudden death are its stock in trade. Mr. Lang has used these conventional situations to make a powerful production that is acted with terrifying honesty by Henry Fonda, Sylvia Sidney and the other players. ... It is a photoplay that will shock and move you and make you aware that our handling of criminals is far from perfect ... Miss Sidney plays the heroine with splendid understanding and emotional depth. The portrait is stamped with tragedy almost from the first, but it is human and always in character. In his performance of the ex-convict, Mr. Fonda achieves a fine balance between the romantically engaging and desperate aspects of the role. He does a brilliant acting job."

Howard Barnes, *New York Herald Tribune*

Henry Fonda as Slim

Slim

Warner Bros. 1937. Directed by Ray Enright. Produced by Hal B. Wallis. Screen play by William Wister Haines, based on his novel.

HENRY FONDA played *Slim* in a cast that also included: Pat O'Brien, Margaret Lindsay, Stuart Erwin, J. Farrell MacDonald, John Litel, Dick Purcell, Joe Sawyer, Harlan Tucker, Carlyle Moore, Jr., Henry Otho, Max Wagner, Craig Reynolds, Jane Wyman, Joseph King, James Robbins, Dick Wessell, Alonzo Price, Ben Hendricks, Maidel Turner, Walter Miller.

THE PICTURE: Warner Brothers had been presenting a series of action program pictures, many of which starred Pat O'Brien, usually with James Cagney. In the case of *Slim,* a paean to the dangers of the lives of the linemen, they needed a more youthful, idealistic actor vis-á-vis Mr. O'Brien. And who, among the younger stars, could be a more idealistic, slimmer "Slim" than Henry Fonda? It was an exciting and entertaining film, not one that has gone into the annals as a major movie

but a lot more likable than most. O'Brien teamed well with Fonda as the tough, old hand to whom the naive kid looks up. And there were high-tension moments on the high-tension wires.

THE CRITICS
"The performers in *Slim* are so engaging that they make the new offering a fair to middling entertainment. It has to do with the fellows who string high tension electric wires across the landscape. With Henry Fonda, Pat O'Brien and Stuart Erwin impersonating the linemen and groundmen, the proceedings are generally instructive and often exciting and amusing. The show has a natural tendency to become repetitious and the plot goes haywire to achieve a melodramatic-romantic climax, but it is always steadied by first-rate acting. Mr. O'Brien and Mr. Fonda are exceedingly good. The former plays a veteran lineman who inducts a farm boy into the mysteries of the job. He is a past master at this sort of thing and keeps the part plausible and intriguing. Mr. Fonda is shyly aggressive as the neo-

mortalize the commissioned stalwarts of the army, the navy, the marine corps and the Department of Justice, have discovered—to their delight and ours—that there are peacetime heroes, too. They are celebrating them, with their customary eye to the dramatic chance, in *Slim,* which William Wister Haines adapted from his novel for the Brothers' vigorous use. . . . The very romanticization of the genus lineman raises *Slim* above mere melodramatic classification. For the picture does grope, not always too subtly, toward the major truth that there is a nobility inherent in labor from which sparks may be struck and take lodging in the soul of even an ordinary little man. The narrative flashes along dramatically, treating in a series of heart-pounding sequences the successive stages of the lad's apprenticeship, his first trip up a skeleton steel tower, his increased mastery of the rueful art of defying the laws of gravity; going on from there to the pleasantly subordinated romance with the anxious nurse and building tensely to a tragic and somehow inspiring climax. It is a swift and engrossing photoplay, admirably performed straight down the cast line."

Frank S. Nugent, *The New York Times*

phyte and plays the awkward love scenes with laudable restraint. Together they give the piece a persuasion which isn't in the script."

Howard Barnes, *New York Herald Tribune*

"The Fréres Warner, who have done so much to im-

"Fonda is better than good. When he climbs his first high tension wire tower and stands there hanging on and Red asks, 'How do you like it?', his dry-throated 'Yeah' is fright itself."

Archer Winsten, *New York Post*

Henry Fonda, with Stuart Erwin and Jane Wyman

That Certain Woman

Warner Bros. 1937. Directed, written, produced by Edmund Goulding.

HENRY FONDA played *Jack Merrick* in a cast that also included: Bette Davis, Ian Hunter, Donald Crisp, Anita Louise, Hugh O'Connell, Katherine Alexander, Mary Phillips, Minor Watson, Ben Welden, Sidney Toler, Charles Trowbridge, Herbert Rawlinson, Norman Willia, Tim Henning, Dwane Day.

THE PICTURE: Bette Davis confesses in her auto-biography that when she was a young actress in summer stock, she had an enormous crush on a young actor playing leads in her company. He scarcely noticed her existence. But she was to have her revenge on Henry Fonda.

As the biggest star on the Warner lot, she was in a position to *demand,* and what she wanted was Henry Fonda as her leading man. So, in two pictures—*Jezebel,* which was good, and *That Certain Feeling,* which was very bad—Fonda played the conventional leading man to a woman's star in woman's pictures.

Dwane Day, Bette Davis, and Henry Fonda

That Certain Woman, which came first, was Edmund Goulding's remake of an earlier film he had made, *The Trespasser,* which was Gloria Swanson's first talking picture. The 1938 version, though, brought laurels to nobody—not to Goulding, not to Davis, and certainly not to Fonda.

THE CRITICS
Howard Barnes, of the *New York Herald Tribune,* berated the picture and the Davis performance in terms that are now better left in the files. And he added, "The other players make a brave attempt to give the production a conviction that is missing in the script. Henry Fonda has the worst time of it as the father-ridden playboy who deserts the heroine on their wedding night, leaving her to struggle with a growing boy, an amorous employer who inconsiderately dies in her apartment, the memories of her early life as a gangster's wife, and cruel reporters."

Henry Fonda, Bette Davis, and Donald Crisp

I Met My Love Again

United Artists. 1938. Directed by Arthur Ripley, Joshua Logan. Produced by Walter Wanger. Screen play by David Hertz from Allene Corliss' novel, *Summer Lightning*.

HENRY FONDA played *Ives Towner* in a cast that also included: Joan Bennett, Dame May Whitty, Alan Marshal, Louise Platt, Alan Baxter, Tim Holt, Dorothy Stickney, Florence Lake, Genee Hall, Alice Cavenna.

THE PICTURE: If Henry Fonda were to play one conventional leading man opposite Bette Davis in a woman's picture at Warners, there seemed no reason to Walter Wanger, who held his contract, that he should not do another of the same. Particularly when the lady involved was Mr. Wanger's favorite actress and soon-to-be off-screen wife. So Joan Bennett got him for *I Met My Love Again,* in which she, as an unconventional type, returns home and proceeds once again to disrupt the life of her ex-love, now a staid young professor. The stars played it as well as possible and there was an especially good supporting cast. It reunited Fonda with his old friend of the University Players, Joshua Logan, who was co-director on this picture.

Henry Fonda as a young professor, with players

Henry Fonda as a young professor, with players

THE CRITICS

"A film about serious thinkers up Vermont way—Lynboro, Upton or some such place. The most serious thinker of all is Ives Towner (Henry Fonda) whose girl has jilted him for a writing chap and Bohemia in Paris. Ives takes it hard, stops reading the Song of Solomon and winds up—after ten years—in a small-town college as an embittered lecturer on the polymorphism of ants. Then the girl comes back, a widow with a shoulder-high daughter, but otherwise completely age-resistant. And there's quite a muddle. For one of Professor Towner's students threatens to kill herself unless he marries her and Miss Bennett's daughter hates him and his folks are leagued against the widow from Paris and the professor himself seems to be of several minds. Everything is resolved finally to the cast's satisfaction, if not to mine, because, not knowing what was going on behind Mr. Fonda's Indian-like façade, I didn't know whether to hope for his return to Miss Bennett or encourage him to accept the frank offers of Louise Platt."

Frank S. Nugent, *The New York Times*

Henry Fonda and Joan Bennett

Henry Fonda

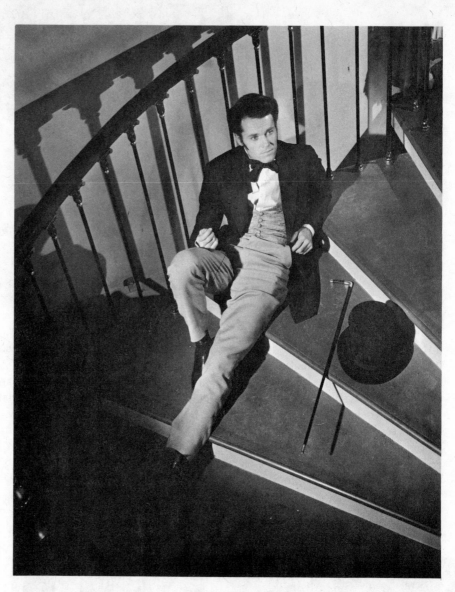

Jezebel

Warner Bros. 1938. Directed by William Wyler. Produced by Henry Blanke. Screen play by Clements Ripley, Abem Finkel, John Huston from the play by Owen Davis.

HENRY FONDA played *Preston Dillard* in a cast that also included: Bette Davis, George Brent, Margaret Lindsay, Fay Bainter, Donald Crisp, Richard Cromwell, Henry O'Neill, Spring Byington, John Litel, Gordon Oliver, Janet Shaw, Theresa Harris, Margaret Early, Irving Pichel, Eddie Anderson, Stymie Beard, Lou Payton, George Renevant.

THE PICTURE: Again Henry Fonda played leading man for Bette Davis in a "woman's picture," but *Jezebel* was one of her best, and Fonda scored strongly, too. In 1967, at the San Francisco Film Festival tribute to his work, the festival officials scheduled a scene from *Jezebel* over Fonda's objections. He felt it was Bette Davis' picture, not his.

But the scene—the one in which Miss Bette perversely decides to wear a red dress to a white gown ball "like a woman from Gallatin Street"—is played brilliantly. And Fonda's poker-faced ferocity as he escorts her, forces her on to the dance floor, stares down anyone

Bette Davis and Henry Fonda

who would appear critical, won cheers and applause from the students and festival buffs.

Jezebel had been a mildly successful Owen Davis play with Tallulah Bankhead and, later, Miriam Hopkins. In the days of excitement over the forthcoming *Gone With the Wind,* it was hurriedly dusted off to give Miss Davis her own Scarlett O'Hara-type Southern belle. She won an Academy Award for her performance. And the picture, directed with style by William Wyler, with screenwriting that strengthened the Davis play and with a really outstanding cast was, and remains, one of the best of its year.

Bette Davis, and Henry Fonda at the famous white ball

Bette Davis, with Fay Bainter, Henry Fonda, and Henry O'Neill

THE CRITICS

"The straggling story demands acting pyrotechnics and extraneous excitement. It has received both on the screen. You will be more interested in the various characters which Miss Davis assumes—from hussy through to self-sacrificing angel—than in the events which make her an intriguing chameleon. She contributes steady power to a badly outlined character and her supporting players stand her in good stead. . . . There are first-rate interludes in the production. The ballroom scene, in which Miss Davis is forced to dance in her red dress with her disgusted fiancé, is brilliantly staged and played to get all the emotional evocations out of film images. . . . It is Miss Davis' show, but she has valiant aid from other performers. Henry Fonda makes an adequately disgusted hero. No amount of sincere acting would turn *Jezebel* into a sincere tragedy, though. The story is still bad, even if it is persuasively enacted and resourcefully staged."

Howard Barnes, *New York Herald Tribune*

"Henry Fonda performs up to the high Fonda standard, adding a bit of stiffening to the more willowy character he has made."

Archer Winsten, *New York Post*

Bette Davis, Fonda, and Margaret Lindsay

Henry Fonda and Madeleine Carroll

Blockade

United Artists. 1938. Directed by William Dieterle. Produced by Walter Wanger. Screen play by John Howard Lawson.

HENRY FONDA played *Marco* in a cast that also included: Madeleine Carroll, Leo Carillo, John Halliday, Vladimir Sokoloff, Reginald Denny, Robert Warwick, William B. Davidson, Fred Kohler, Peter Godfrey, Carlos de Valez, Katherine DeMille, George Byron, Lupita Tovar, Nicl Thompson, Rosina Galli, Roman Ros, Dolores Duran, Guy d'Ennery, Edward Brady, Murdoch MacQuarrie, Harry Semels, Baby Maria de la Paz, Demetrius Emanuel, Hugh Prosser, Arthur Aylesworth, George Lloyd, Allan Garcia, Herbert Heywood, Roger Drake, Paul Bradley, Carl Stockdale, Skins Miller, Evelyn Selbie, Mary Foy, Belle Mitchell, Cecil Weston, Ricca Allen.

THE PICTURE: *Blockade* was banned in some cities preached against from the pulpits of churches, and altogether won a notoriety too important for it. It was a contrived and synthetic spy story, supposedly happening during the Spanish Civil War. But the sides were very carefully not identified and, if the agitators against the picture chose to identify the villains as Loyalists, it was not because the picture gave the villains such a label.

Madeleine Carroll may have been the most beautiful woman of her time and, with a darkly handsome Fonda, they made a pictorially impressive couple. But, outside of a stinging denunciation of war in a final monologue by Fonda and some scenes of well-chosen extras as starving villagers looking helplessly to sea for a boat that will come with provisions, there was very little to believe in *Blockade*.

Henry Fonda, Madeleine Carroll, and bit players

THE CRITICS

"That *Blockade* is a straddling job of motion picture exposition does not keep it from being an engrossing and provocative film. It is badly out of focus with a romantic spy story thrown up against the terrifying realities of the Spanish Civil War. Moreover it works so hard to maintain a purportedly impartial view of that conflict that it is constantly being drained of dramatic power. . . . The pity is that *Blockade* could not have been the stirring, impassioned film that it is forever on the verge of being. The writing is there in the eloquent cinematic passages which John Howard Lawson has prepared. The staging, by William Dieterle, is pictorially splendid and points up the muted thesis of the show. The acting is resolute and compelling. The fact is that the background of the photoplay, even though the combatants are presented in as anonymous a manner as possible, is far too strong for a fable of spies and love triumphant. No matter how much you may sympathize with the plight of Henry Fonda, playing a peasant militiaman, and Madeleine Carroll, portraying an unwilling secret agent for the side that bombs civilians, their particular destinies are badly dwarfed by the civil war itself. Mr. Fonda does a creditable job of acting; Miss Carroll is attractive as the spy. But even with Mr. Dieterle's expert direction, the personal drama remains singularly unimportant. *Blockade* has touched on far more moving stuff than a hackneyed romance. In doing so, it takes on a significance which rarely attaches to Hollywood offerings, although it does not keep its central theme from seeming incredibly banal."

Howard Barnes, *New York Herald Tribune*

Henry Fonda and Madeleine Carroll

Spawn of the North

Paramount. 1938. Directed by Henry Hathaway. Produced by Albert Lewin. Screen play by Jules Furthman. Adapted from the novel by Barrett Willoughby.

HENRY FONDA played *Jim Kimmerlee* in a cast that also included: George Raft, Dorothy Lamour, Louise Platt, John Barrymore, Akim Tamiroff, Lynne Overman, Fuzzy Knight, Vladimir Sokoloff, Alex Woloshin, Duncan Renaldo, Richard Ung, Archie Twitchell, Michio Ito, Lee Shumway, Stanley Andrews, Wade Boteler, Guy Usher, Henry Brandon, Egon Brecher, Harvey Clarke, Galan Galt, Monte Blue, Irving Bacon, Robert Middlemass, Rollo Lloyd, John Wray, Eddie Marr.

THE PICTURE: *Spawn of the North* was a big adventure drama of Alaska on just about as epic scale as could be imagined in that day of movie-making. Here the story, though it was serviceable melodrama, was

George Raft, Henry Fonda, and Akim Tamiroff

Dorothy Lamour, Lynne Overman, Henry Fonda, Louise Platt, George Raft, and John Barrymore

not the thing and, although the cast was impressive, their roles were conventional.

There had been action movies about Alaska before—*The Spoilers* and *Call of the Wild* being two that come immediately to mind—and there would be many, many more to come including the Robert Ryan remake of *Spawn, Alaska Seas*. But the first one had sweep and magnitude, authentic backgrounds (much of it was actually filmed there and showed it), as well as the kind of all-out action that is director Henry Hathaway's forte.

The story revolved around the war between Alaska fishermen working for the canneries and salmon pirates.

Fonda, of course, was properly heroic, with George Raft cast in one of those good-bad roles as his long-time friend who joins Fonda in his cannery business in Alaska. But conflict develops as Raft goes along with the pirates. Obviously, upstanding Hank is not going to stand for that. And, obviously, right will triumph, with Raft redeeming himself at the end. (He was now too much a star at this point to be a thorough bad man.) People like Akim Tamiroff, Lynne Overman and even John Barrymore showed up impressively in support.

THE CRITICS

"Told in Henry Hathaway's habitually direct and vigorous cinematic style, *Spawn of the North* is a satisfactorily wild-eyed tale of the Alaskan salmon fisheries in the days, now dead we trust, when Russian pirates raided the fish traps and looked as mean as Akim Tamiroff with a stubble of whisker. Handwrought for

Akim Tamiroff, George Raft, Dorothy Lamour, and Henry Fonda

the masculine trade, up to and including the appearance of Dorothy Lamour in a sweater instead of a sarong, the film finds a surprising store of red meat in the tinned salmon industry. Director Hathaway has built excitement steadily in the two-man and free-for-all battles between the pirates and the honest fishermen. Scorning such effeminacies as fists or marlin spikes, the picture's huskies go at it with harpoon guns, sealing knives, lengths of chain and gaffs. The bloodshed is beautiful; in technicolor it would have rivaled Remington. But the battles are not all of it, although they happen to be the best parts. There are some impressive shots of crumbling icebergs, of the salmon run and of Henry Fonda's puzzled brow."

Frank Nugent, *The New York Times*

"In *Spawn of the North*, Paramount has discovered a new American frontier and used it as backdrop for a rousing old-fashioned spectacle. The film deals with the Alaskan salmon fishing industry and is vaguely historical in its references to that remote peninsular territory. Nevertheless the action is the same compound of melodrama and romance which has gone into most of the screen's frontier epics. The scenic stuff is fresh from salmon catching to icebergs cracking up but first and last the production is a show. You are likely to be more interested in what happens to those old frontiersmen, Henry Fonda and George Raft, and an engaging seal called 'Slicker' than in the building of Alaska."

Howard Barnes, *New York Herald Tribune*

Henry Fonda and Barbara
Stanwyck

The Mad Miss Manton

RKO-Radio. 1938. Directed by Leigh Jason. Produced by P. J. Wolfson. Screen play by Philip G. Epstein, based on a story by Wilson Collinson.

HENRY FONDA played *Peter Ames* in a cast that also included: Barbara Stanwyck, Sam Levene, Frances Mercer, Stanley Ridges, Whitney Bourne, Vicki Lester, Ann Evers, Catherine O'Quinn, Linda Terry, Eleanor Hansen, Hattie McDaniel, James Burke, Paul Guilfoyle, Penny Singleton, Leona Maricle, Kay Sutton, Miles Mander, John Qualen, Grady Sutton, Olin Howland.

THE PICTURE: This was a routine little farce about a batch of debutantes on the trail of murder. Screwball society girls were very much in movie fashion at the time and *The Mad Miss Manton* gave Barbara Stanwyck her turn at bat. As the ringleader of a whole group of harebrained debs, poor Stanwyck was merely incongruous. And Henry Fonda will never look back upon his role of their particular antagonist with any particular pride. It was all harum-scarum, determinedly wacky and relentlessly unfunny in its attempt to combine a *Thin Man* kind of melodrama with a *My Man Godfrey* type of madcap heiress.

Stanwyck played that role, with Sam Levene as the police lieutenant who has been the butt of the escapades of her crowd before and doesn't believe them when they insist they have discovered a murder. Fonda, a newspaper columnist, raps them sarcastically in print. So the girls set out to make the police and the newspaper man look silly and wind up, of course, proving the murder and exposing the murderer.

THE CRITICS
"The romance in the hands of Henry Fonda and Barbara Stanwyck is refreshingly natural, considering the

*Henry Fonda, Barbara Stanwyck,
and bit player*

unnatural background it moves against. . . . The Wilson Collison-Philip Epstein script is dredged with bright lines and cheerfully absurd situations."

Frank Nugent, *The New York Times*

"If you can take your screen entertainment piecemeal, you are apt to find *The Mad Miss Manton* moderately diverting. As far as I am concerned, it is too piecemeal to make for more than a meretricious comic melodrama. The fact is that the nonsense in the motion picture almost never mixes with its hair-raising interludes."

Howard Barnes, *New York Herald Tribune*

*Henry Fonda, Barbara Stanwyck,
and Stanley Ridges*

Jesse James

20th Century-Fox. 1939. Directed by Henry King. Produced by Darryl F. Zanuck. Screen play by Nunnally Johnson.

HENRY FONDA played *Frank James* in a cast that also included: Tyrone Power, Nancy Kelly, Randolph Scott, Henry Hull, Slim Summerville, J. Edward Bromberg, Brian Donlevy, John Carradine, Donald Meek, John Russell, Jane Darwell, Charles Tannen, Claire DuBrey, Willard Robertson, Harold Goodwin, Ernest Whitman, Eddy Waller, Paul Burns, Spencer Charters, Arthur Aylesworth, Charles Middleton, Charles Halton, George Chandler, Harry Tyler, Virginia Brissac, Ed Le Saint, John Elliott, Erville Alderson, George Breakston, Lon Chaney, Jr.

Henry Fonda, Tyrone Power, and Harry Tyler

Tyrone Power and Henry Fonda

THE PICTURE: Jesse James, whether he is played by Robert Wagner or Fred Thomson or Christopher Jones on TV or any of the numerous others who have taken on the part, is always a pretty conventional Western hero. He is open-faced, likeable, an outlaw only because of circumstances.

In the best version of the Jesse James legend ever filmed, Tyrone Power was, of course, a Tyrone Power kind of hero every step of the way. He was very good indeed in the role as presented—but that was exactly how it was presented.

This left the real performing to Jesse's brother, Frank, and Henry Fonda had a field day in this role, one of the classic characterizations of Western movie history. Fonda's Frank was a laconic, tobacco-chewing sod-buster. You believed his metamorphosis from Kansas City farm boy into dangerous man with a gun. In a quite extraordinary supporting cast the performances of Nancy Kelly, Henry Hull, Donald Meek and John Carradine—the latter as "the dirty little coward who shot Mr. Howard and laid poor Jesse in his grave"—were of particular note.

John Carradine, Nancy Kelly, Tyrone Power, Henry Fonda, and Spencer Charters

Tyrone Power, Nancy Kelly, and Henry Fonda

Nunnally Johnson's script had Jesse and Frank as farm boys, whose mother is shot by a representative of the Midland Railroads, which has been trying to swindle the farmers out of their land. That sets Jesse and Frank off into the world of outlaws and the picture follows their exploits until Frank finally escapes the law and Jesse is killed.

THE CRITICS

"The legend of Jesse James has come to the screen about as one might have expected. Produced expensively in Technicolor, the cinema's saga of the Ozark outlaw is a glittering and generally exciting cops and robbers show. In the sequences of straight action, *Jesse James* makes stunning capital of train and bank holdups, wild horseback riding and gunplay. When it introduces romantic and sentimental interludes or attempts half-heartedly to analyze its hero's character it is no more dramatically effective than most of Hollywood's historical reconstructions. Few resources have been spared in making the film an impressive spectacle. Under Henry King's knowing direction, the account of post-Civil War banditry has considerable flavor and suspense. . . . Henry Fonda, as the tight-lipped Frank James who delivers Jesse from a jail surrounded by soldiers and accompanies him on the breathtaking escape from the Midland Missouri Bank ambush, does by far the best job in the show, to my mind. Mr. Power, in the title role, strikes me as badly cast. Neither in

appearance nor manner does he suggest the role convincingly. . . . There is a lot of color . . . and a lot of excitement, but one is forced to take a good deal of conventional nonsense along with the effective spectacle."

Howard Barnes, *New York Herald Tribune*

"Henry Fonda, as the tobacco-chewing Frank James, in a beautiful characterization."

Bosley Crowther, *The New York Times*

Tyrone Power, Henry Fonda, and Ed Le Saint

Henry Fonda and Alan Baxter

Let Us Live

Columbia. 1939. Directed by John Brahm. Produced by William Perlberg. Screen play by Anthony Veiller and Allen Rivkin, based on a story by Joseph F. Dineen.

HENRY FONDA played *Brick Tennant* in a cast that also included: Maureen O'Sullivan, Ralph Bellamy, Alan Baxter, Stanley Ridges, Henry Kolker, Peter Lynn, George Douglas, Philip Trent, Martin Spellman.

THE PICTURE: As he had in *You Only Live Once* and as he would again in *The Wrong Man,* Henry Fonda played an innocent man railroaded to prison and the shadow of execution by circumstantial evidence. While Director John Brahm missed the Fritz Lang genius which made *You Only Live Once* an overwhelming motion picture experience, he directed *Let Us Live* with solid authority. Brahm's direction, the sensitivity of Fonda's performance and a tight-knit screen play made *Let Us Live* of much more importance than its Grade B production and distribution would have indicated. Maureen O'Sullivan, normally never given a chance to do much more than look extremely pretty in ingenue roles, had a stronger leading lady role here and was thoroughly up to the challenge. *Let Us Live* was a much better picture than its studio,

which rushed it through routine bookings without special exploitation or hoopla, seemed to be aware.

In the story line—the basis for the story was a real-life situation (see *New York Times* review excerpt)—Fonda played a taxi driver, arrested as a suspect and trapped by circumstantial evidence and mistaken identification. Only the last-minute reprieve seemed false and too pat.

THE CRITICS
"In 1934, two Boston taxicab drivers were identified by seven of eight witnesses as having been among the three men who held up a Lynn (Mass.) theatre and shot and killed a bill-poster in making their getaway. Their trial for murder was entering its third week when the Millen brothers, Irving and Murton, and their accomplice, Abraham Faber, were arrested in New York and confessed to the Lynn crime. The cab drivers were exonerated. Faber and the Millens were executed. This is the factual basis for *Let Us Live,* a taut and strongly played drama which Columbia presented with such anonymity that the credits refer only to 'a story by Joseph F. Dineen' not even mentioning its title, 'Murder in Massachusetts.' The unofficial explanation from Hollywood was that the Commonwealth preferred not to

Henry Fonda, Maureen O'Sullivan
and Charles Lane

be reminded of its near-miscarriage of justice and had threatened action of a vague but unpleasant nature if the film so much as implied any inefficiency or harshness to its police, its prosecutor or its courts in the case of the unfortunate cabbie. . . . At this late date it could hardly be called a daring theme or an indictment of anything or any one—except, usually, of the scriptwriters and players for the routine treatment the plot normally gets. But *Let Us Live* is a notable exception. . . . Although it is the film's direction that has made it good, if not great, Mr. Brahm must share his credit with Allen Rivkin and Anthony Veiller for a splendidly turned script, and to Henry Fonda, Maureen O'Sullivan, Ralph Bellamy, Alan Baxter and the others for the incisive performances all good directors seem able to extract from their players. *Let Us Live* is not exactly a novel theme, but it is news when so old a theme has been handled so well."

Frank S. Nugent, *The New York Times*

"Sound script construction and imaginative direction have made *Let Us Live* something more than a run of the mill melodrama . . . There is little distinctive drama at the core but what there is has been fully realized . . . Mr. Fonda is extremely persuasive and Maureen O'Sullivan and Ralph Bellamy give staunch supporting portrayals. *Let Us Live* is a definitely superior Class B motion picture in addition to being an entertaining melodrama."

Howard Barnes, *New York Herald Tribune*

Henry Fonda and bit players

The Story of Alexander Graham Bell

20th Century-Fox. 1939. Directed by Irving Cummings. Produced by Kenneth Macgowan. Screen play by Lamar Trotti from an original story by Ray Harris.

HENRY FONDA played *Thomas Watson* in a cast that also included: Don Ameche, Loretta Young, Charles Coburn, Gene Lockhart, Spring Byington, Sally Blane, Polly Ann Young, Georgianna Young, Bobs Watson, Russell Hicks, Paul Stanton, Jonathan Hale, Harry Davenport, Elizabeth Patterson, Charles Trowbridge, Jan Duggan, Claire du Brey, Harry Tyler, Ralph Remley, Zeffie Tilbury.

THE PICTURE: And this is how Don Ameche invented the telephone. Actually, *The Story of Alexander Graham Bell* was a good, forthright, uninspired movie biography with a good, forthright, uninspired performance by Ameche. There was nothing startling here—nothing to blaze movie biography trails in the manner, for instance, in which some of the Paul Muni films had made biography extremely dramatic. But the picture was well made, told its story effectively enough. Loretta Young played his deaf wife, with Fonda as Bell's assistant, Thomas Watson. The screen play detailed the struggle of Bell, a teacher of the deaf, to perfect a

Henry Fonda and Don Ameche

Henry Fonda and Don Ameche

telegraphic invention. The discovery, its success and then a conflict with a rival company, with a court trial and final victory were covered.

THE CRITICS

"Seldom have the bitter struggles and meager joys of a great man been intermingled with such cumulative and forceful effect . . . Behind the eloquence of a film that never loses momentum is the splendid playing of Don Ameche, who must have caught some of Bell's genius to interpret him so admirably . . . If one were inclined to find fault, one might reason that the comedy contrast of Thomas Watson, who is a loyal but unimaginative soul, is a bit too finely drawn. However, one would have to admit that these strains of levity, furnished by the increasingly capable Henry Fonda, are welcome safety valves when the situations are most tense."

R. W. D., *New York Herald Tribune*

Henry Fonda, Loretta Young, and Don Ameche

Young Mr. Lincoln

20th Century-Fox. 1939. Directed by John Ford. Produced by Darryl F. Zanuck. Screen play by Lamar Trotti.

HENRY FONDA played *Abraham Lincoln* in a cast that also included: Alice Brady, Marjorie Weaver, Arleen Whelan, Eddie Collins, Pauline Moore, Richard Cromwell, Donald Meek, Dorris Bowdon, Eddie Quillan, Spencer Charters, Ward Bond, Milburn Stone, Cliff Clark, Robert Lowery, Charles Tannen, Francis Ford, Fred Kohler, Kay Linaker, Russell Simpson, Edwin Maxwell, Charles Halton, Harry Tyler.

THE PICTURE: Henry Fonda's very first professional job was as an assistant to George Billings, the famous old impersonator of Abraham Lincoln, on a vaudeville tour. Fonda played a young Army officer, his presence on stage being solely for the purpose of "feeding" lines to the old actor.

He may have been thinking of Billings when he so vigorously resisted John Ford's attempts to persuade him that he should play the young Abe in a new film. But Ford is a persuasive man, and he persuaded Fonda right into the great nose and wart makeup and stove-pipe hat for a screen test, and assured him that the

Fonda voice was far better suited to a young Lincoln than were the elocutionary tone expected of most actors who played the character.

As everyone knows, Henry Fonda did indeed play *Young Mr. Lincoln* and gave the definitive characterization of the great man as a young man in a picture which remains one of the most frequently revived on television and in film society and classroom showings. It also began his association with Ford, with whom he was to make a string of notable pictures.

THE CRITICS
"Henry Fonda's characterization is one of those once-in-a-blue-moon things: a crossroads meeting of nature, art and a smart casting director. Nature gave Mr. Fonda long legs and arms, a strong and honest face and a slow smile; the make-up man added a new nose bridge, the lank brown hair, the frock coat and stove-pipe hat (the beard hadn't begun to sprout in those days) and the trace of a mole. Mr. Fonda supplied the rest—the warmth and kindliness, the pleasant modesty, the courage, resolution, tenderness, shrewdness and wit that Lincoln, even young Mr. Lincoln, must have possessed. His performance kindles the film, makes it a moving unity, at once gentle and quizzically comic.

Henry Fonda

And yet, while his Lincoln dominates the picture, Director John Ford and Scriptwriter Lamar Trotti never have permitted it to stand out too obviously against its background—the Midwestern frontier. Scene and minor character have their place, and an important one. The prairie types have been skillfully drawn. One knows, somehow, that they are Lincoln's kind of people, that they think as he does, laugh at the same jokes, appreciate the same kind of horseplay. Had they been less carefully presented, Abe himself would have seemed less natural, would have been a stranger in his own community. Alice Brady's frontier mother, Donald Meek's spellbinding prosecutor, Spencer Charter's circuit judge, Eddie Collin's Efe—they all fit into the picture, give Mr. Fonda's colorful Lincoln the protection of their coloration.

The result of it, happily, is not merely a natural and straightforward biography, but a film which indisputably has the right to be called Americana. It isn't merely part of a life that has been retold, but part of a way of living when government had advanced little beyond the town meeting stage, when every man knew his neighbor's business and meddled in it at times, when a municipal high spot was a pie-judging contest, the parade of the Silver Cornets and a tug of war on the principal thoroughfare. Against that background and through events more melodramatic and humorous than nationally eventful, Twentieth Century's *Young Mr. Lincoln* passes; and is a journey most pleasant to share."

Frank S. Nugent, *The New York Times*

"You will not forget, I hope, the lank, eager, common-man sweetness of Henry Fonda, whose Abe Lincoln was so high and far above the studied caricature of Raymond Massey that it is not to talk."

Otis Ferguson, *The New Republic*

Henry Fonda, Alice Brady, un-billed bit player, and Eddie Quillan

Henry Fonda

"Henry Fonda has the great chance of his acting career as the boyish Abe Lincoln. He makes the most of that chance. The make up department has deepened his eyes, drawn in a few lines, enlarged his nose, given him an extra three inches of height. He looks startingly like Lincoln without the deep grooves tragedy and years had drawn upon his face. Unless he had looked like Lincoln, even Mr. Fonda's quiet, forceful performance might not have counted. It counts now for a great deal. Neither he nor Mr. Ford nor the scenarist, Lamar Trotti, have let themselves become overly sentimental or theatrical. The film remains, in spite of the excitements of a murder, a near lynching and a crackerjack trial, a character study."

Eileen Creelman, *New York Sun*

"With the forceful staging of John Ford, it adds the strongest kind of action to reinforce Henry Fonda's understanding and wholly convincing portrayal. It will be no small task in Lincoln films still to come to match the work of Henry Fonda. His Lincoln might have stepped out of a picture gallery and come alive to stride through the streets of Springfield. Fonda's Lincoln is physical as well: a tall, gaunt, clean-shaven fellow with sunken eyes and a protruding brow and a misplaced clump of hair—a thin gangling fellow in a stovepipe hat who loved to stretch his long legs down by the river. We can't remember when Fonda has been better."

Herbert Cohn, *Brooklyn Eagle*

Marjorie Weaver and Henry Fonda

Drums Along the Mohawk

20th Century-Fox. 1939. Directed by John Ford. Produced by Darryl F. Zanuck. Adapted by Lamar Trotti and Sonya Levien from the novel by Walter D. Edmonds.

HENRY FONDA played *Gilbert Martin* in a cast that also included: Claudette Colbert, Edna May Oliver, Eddie Collins, John Carradine, Dorris Bowdon, Jessie Ralph, Arthur Shields, Robert Lowery, Roger Imhof, Francis Ford, Ward Bond, Kay Linaker, Russell Simpson, Spencer Charters, Si Jenks, J. Ronald Pennick, Arthur Aylesworth, Chief Big Tree, Charles Tannen, Paul McVey, Elizabeth Jones, Beulah Hall Jones, Clarence Wilson, Lionel Pape, Edwin Maxwell, Robert Grieg, Clara Blandick.

THE PICTURE: Fonda and John Ford joined forces to make a colorful and lusty screen version of Walter D. Edmonds' study of frontier skirmishes in the Revolutionary War when a rabble-at-arms fought to protect their farms and families. Again the association was rewarding for them both. Readers of the book may have found that the screen writers sacrificed some of the wealth of detail, felt perhaps that the screen play had a sketchiness, an episodic treatment. But Ford put it all on film so stunningly and Fonda's performance had such quiet force—there was a long moment in which he described the horrors of a battle which is as notable a

piece of performance as anything he has ever done—that *Drums Along the Mohawk* was quite a film experience. Claudette Colbert and Edna May Oliver were particularly effective, too, as indeed were all the long list of actors—most of the inevitable Ford company.

THE CRITICS
"Walter D. Edmonds' exciting novel of the Mohawk

Claudette Colbert and Henry Fonda

Valley during the American Revolution has come to the screen in a considerably elided, but still basically faithful, film edition bearing the trademark of John Ford, one of the best cinema story-tellers in the business ... A first-rate historical film, as rich atmospherically as it is in action ... Mr. Ford has been fortunate in finding such externals to play his Mohawk people as those which go under the names of Henry Fonda, Claudette Colbert, Edna May Oliver, Eddie Collins, Arthur Shields, Ward Bond and Roger Imhoff. Mr. Fonda and Miss Colbert have done rather nicely with the Gil and Lana Martin who saw their cabin destroyed, their precious wheat burned, yet fought to hold the valley. They've matched the background excellently, all of the actors, and the background, paradoxically, is the dramatic foreground of the film."

Frank S. Nugent, *The New York Times*

"John Ford has brought all of his wizardry as a director to the making of *Drums Along the Mohawk* and the result is a singularly satisfying film. The adaptation of Walter D. Edmonds' novel has taken the form of a rambling and episodic narrative, but it is an honest and faithful script and it has been blessed with truly brilliant handling. With the striking gallery of portraits which the excellent cast has contributed, the offering deserves to be placed among the best historical reconstructions to be seen on the screen.... 'Drums' has had consum-

mate staging; it has also had splendid acting. Henry Fonda is perfectly cast.... Claudette Colbert brings warmth and depth ... there is a brilliantly balanced performance by Edna May Oliver ... *Drums Along the Mohawk* lacks unity but, thanks to its direction and its playing, it is a genuinely distinguished historical film."

Unsigned Critic, *New York Herald Tribune*

Henry Fonda and Claudette Colbert

Henry Fonda and Russell Simpson

The Grapes of Wrath

20th Century-Fox. 1940. Directed by John Ford. Produced by Darryl F. Zanuck. Screen play by Nunnally Johnson based on the novel by John Steinbeck.

HENRY FONDA played *Tom Joad* in a cast that also included: Jane Darwell, John Carradine, Charley Grapewin, Dorris Bowdon, Russell Simpson, O. Z. Whitehead, Eddie Quillans, John Qualen, Zeffie Tilbury, Frank Sully, Frank Darien, Darryl Hickman, Shirley Mills, Roger Imhof, Grant Mitchell, Charles D. Brown, John Arledge, Ward Bond, Harry Tyler, William Pawley, Arthur Aylesworth, Charles Tannen, Selmar Jackson, Charles Middleton, Eddie Waller, Paul Guilfoyle, David Hughes, Cliff Clark, Joseph Sawyer, Frank Faylen, Adrian Morris, Hollie Jewell, Robert Homans, Irving Bacon, Kitty McHugh.

THE PICTURE: The Great American Novel made one of the few enduring Great American Motion Pictures. John Steinbeck's saga of the dispossesed was brought to the screen in a production that was without flaw. Nunnally Johnson's screen play may well be the definitive job of novel-to-film adaptation. John Ford's direction was of such sweep and magnitude—tough, un-

compromising, almost completely without those touches of sentiment and broad comedy, usually so dear to the heart of Ford—that it may well stand as his masterwork. Gregg Toland's camera work was revolutionary, dramatic in its impact, documentary in its approach. But then, every element in Darryl F. Zanuck's production, right to the sparse, yet beautifully appropriate, musical score of Alfred Newman, was completely and perfectly right.

Certainly the casting was so correct that you could have felt that every individual, down to the most fleeting faces, could have been chosen by Steinbeck himself. (To me, there was one exception, one piece of miscasting—but I quickly add that nobody I have known, no critic I have read has ever indicated agreement on this point. My feeling is that Jane Darwell, physically, was too much the comfortable, motherly landlady type for Steinbeck's spare, tough Ma Joad. Beulah Bondi, first announced, was closer to my personal picture of Steinbeck's Ma. Having indicated this, I can only say that Miss Darwell's performance was unforgettable.) But every cast member—John Carradine's Casey, John Qualen's Muley, Charley Grapewin's Grampa, Zeffie Tilbury's Granma, Russell Simpson's Pa. O. Z. Whitehead's Al, Eddie Quillan's Connie, Dorris Bowdon's Rosasharn, right down to the bits played by such actors as Paul Guilfoyle, Charles D. Brown, Kitty McHugh, John Arledge, Joseph Sawyer, Irving Bacon and every one of the others—made his moment count importantly.

It is inconceivable to think of any one but Henry Fonda in the role of Tom Joad. With that shining honesty that is his hallmark—Fonda was never an actor playing a part—he *was* Tom Joad. He was the immediate choice of Ford and of Steinbeck. But it was 20th Century-Fox's big picture of the year and the studio felt that the part should go to one of its major stars—Tyrone Power or Don Ameche. Fonda was a free-lance. (For the same reason, contract player Jane Darwell won out over free-lance Beulah Bondi for the Ma Joad role.) Fonda was finally persuaded to sign a term contract with 20th Century-Fox in order to be given the Tom Joad role. Whatever it cost, no matter how many "Lillian Russells" and "Magnificent Dopes" were forced on him, was little enough. Tom Joad was Henry Fonda, Henry Fonda was Tom Joad.

Henry Fonda has never won an Academy Award. When Award time comes, the winner is almost always somebody who has given a bravura performance in a big successful film. Fonda's understated style, his horror of "seeming to be acting," are recognized as the epitome of great acting by critics and directors all over the world. But, when awards are given, the Fonda performance—"he makes it all seem so easy, as if he's not acting at all"—is apt to be passed by in favor of the actor who has created some fireworks in a role.

Still, he was nominated for Tom Joad in 1940, along

Henry Fonda and Jane Darwell

with Charles Chaplin (for *The Great Dictator*), Raymond Massey (for *Abe Lincoln in Illinois*), Laurence Olivier (for *Rebecca*) James Stewart (for *The Philadelphia Story*.) Everybody was certain that he would

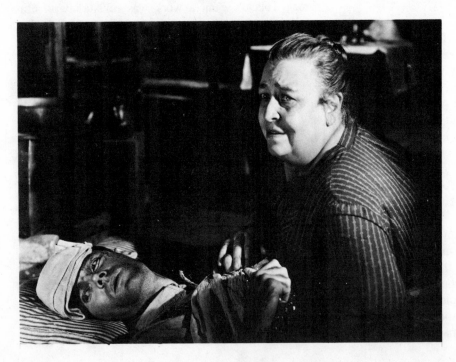

Henry Fonda and Jane Darwell

Henry Fonda, Jane Darwell, Dorris
Bowden, and Russell Simpson

be the winner. One of the other nominees, Stewart, even gave interviews in which he acknowledged that the winner should be Fonda and that he (Stewart) himself had voted for Fonda. The night came. The winner was James Stewart. Stewart couldn't have been much better than he was as the young reporter, but *The Philadelphia Story* was Katharine Hepburn's picture. (She didn't win either.) Explanations seem to indicate that Stewart was making rapid popularity strides in Hollywood and that a good segment of the Academy felt that he had been "done out" of the Award the year before when he was up for *Mr. Smith Goes to Washington.*

THE CRITICS

"The Grapes of Wrath is the first picture made in Hollywood since 1929 that deals with a current social problem, that has faithfully kept the intent of an author who stirred the country; that has reproduced the bloody violence that has accompanied an economic upheaval; a violence that has been reported in the press from many parts of the country besides California but never on film—a picture that records the story of a tragic American migration into slavery. It is quite a movie. . . . Ford did have in Henry Fonda an actor who gave him one of the finest performances I have ever seen; in fact, you may forget Fonda is in the company—his performance is so tough, undeviating and simple you may think

he is one of the extras, or one of the actual migrants. . . . There is a scene in the book that made me cry and it is the best scene in the picture; here the author, director, cast and producer all recreated to the letter and the spirit the work of a great writer; the simple incident in the hot dog stand where Pa Joad buys ten cents worth of bread. There, in one simple, dignified sequence is the story of a great people. If it had been much better I wouldn't have been able to discuss it."

Pare Lorentz, *McCall's*

"A great film has come out of Hollywood called *The Grapes of Wrath.* Based on John Steinbeck's account of the 'Okie' hegira from the dust bowl to California, it is an honest, eloquent and challenging screen masterpiece. Great artistry has gone into its making and greater courage, for this screen tribute to the dispossessed not only has dramatized the large theme of Mr. Steinbeck's novel in enduring visual terms—it has demonstrated beyond any question that the cinema can take the raw stuff of contemporary living and mold it to a provocative photoplay pattern. For once in a long, long time the screen has made electric contact with the abiding verities of existence in *The Grapes of Wrath,* and the result is a heart-shaking and engrossing motion picture. . . . John Ford, who has few peers among directors, has staged the work with extraordinary skill,

*John Carradine, Henry Fonda, and
unbilled bit players*

*Eddie Quillan, Dorris Bowden,
Henry Fonda, Jane Darwell, Rus-
sell Simpson, Frank Darien, O. Z.
Whitehead, and John Carradine.*

Henry Fonda

understanding and feeling. The players, from Henry Fonda as the embittered Tom Joad to Dorris Bowdon as the bewildered Rosasharn, act their parts like figures in the main stream of history rather than puppets in a shallow bit of make-believe. For my part I would give Gregg Toland, the cameraman, special commendation for the way he has photographed scenes of this modern Odyssey in the stark terms of the documentary film. In every case, *The Grapes of Wrath* is a film which should mean for nearly everyone an exciting and enriching emotional experience. . . . Ford has directed a large company with brilliant knowledge of their capabilities. Mr. Fonda, for example, has never been better on the screen than he is as the surly but reasonable Tom. . . . It is a genuinely great motion picture which makes one proud to have even a small share in the affairs of the cinema."

Howard Barnes, *New York Herald Tribune*

"In the vast library where the celluloid literature of the screen is stored there is one small, uncrowded shelf devoted to the cinema's masterworks, to those films which by dignity of theme and excellence of treatment seem to be of enduring artistry, seem destined to be recalled not merely at the end of their particular year but whenever great motion pictures are mentioned. To that shelf of screen classics Twentieth Century-Fox has added its version of John Steinbeck's *The Grapes of*

Wrath. . . . Its greatness as a picture lies in many things, not all of them readily reducible to words. It is difficult for example, to discuss John Ford's direction, except in pictorial terms. His employment of camera is reportage and editorial and dramatization by turns or all in one. . . . Direction, when it is as brilliant as Mr. Ford's has been, is easy to recognize, but impossible to describe. It's simpler to talk about the players and the Nunnally Johnson script. There may be a few words of dialogue that Steinbeck has not written, but Mr. Johnson almost invariably has complimented him by going to the book for his lines. . . . And if all this seems strange for Hollywood—all this fidelity to a book's spirit, this resoluteness of approach to a dangerous topic—still stranger has been the almost incredible rightness of the film's casting, the utter believability of some of Hollywood's most typical people in untypical roles. Henry Fonda's Tom Joad is precisely the hot-tempered, resolute, saturnine chap Mr. Steinbeck had in mind. Jane Darwell's Ma is exactly the family-head we pictured as we read the book. . . . We could go on with this talk of the players, but it would become repetitious, for there are too many of them, and too many are perfect in their parts. What we're trying to say is that *The Grapes of Wrath* is just about as good as any picture has a right to be; if it were any better, we just wouldn't believe our eyes."

Frank Nugent, *The New York Times*

Henry Fonda and unidentified
punchee

Lillian Russell

20th Century-Fox. 1940. Directed by Irving Cummings.
Produced by Darryl F. Zanuck. Screen play by William
Anthony McGuire.

HENRY FONDA played *Alexander Moore* in a cast that
also included: Alice Faye, Don Ameche, Edward Arnold, Warren William, Leo Carillo, Helen Westley,
Dorothy Peterson, Ernest Truex, Nigel Bruce, Claude
Allister, Lynn Bari, Weber and Fields, Una O'Connor,
Eddie Foy, Jr., Joseph Cawthorn, Diane Fisher, Elyse
Knox, Joan Valerie, Alice Armand, William Davidson,
Hal K. Dawson, Charles Halton, R. E. Keane, Harry
Hayden, Frank Darien, Frank Sully, Richard Carle,
Ottola Nesmith, Ferike Boros, Frank Thomas, Robert
Homans, C. Cunningham.

Alice Faye and Henry Fonda

Edward Arnold, Don Ameche,
Alice Faye, Henry Fonda, and
Warren William

THE PICTURE: In order to play *The Grapes of Wrath* Henry Fonda had to sign a 20th Century-Fox contract and it was a steep price to pay. He was shoved into one routine film after another—his high spots of the period coming only with such loanouts as *The Lady Eve* and *The Male Animal*. The shape of things to come was evident in his first studio assignment after *The Grapes of Wrath*. The man who had just played one of the great roles in film history was given a routine romantic lead—one of many—opposite a singing cutie trying to cope with one of those interminable "life story" movies about a star of another era. About Fonda, Howard Barnes, of the *New York Herald Tribune*, reported that he "wastes a lot of intensity in the role of Alexander Moore."

Leo Carillo and Henry Fonda

The Return of Frank James

20th Century-Fox. 1940. Directed by Fritz Lang. Produced by Darryl F. Zanuck. Screen play by Sam Hellman.

HENRY FONDA played *Frank James* in a cast that also included: Gene Tierney, Jackie Cooper, Henry Hull, John Carradine, J. Edward Bromberg, Donald Meek, Eddie Collins, George Barbier, Ernest Whitman, Charles Tannen, Lloyd Corrigan, Russell Hicks, Victor Kilian, Edward McWade, George Chandler, Irving Bacon, Frank Shannon, Barbara Pepper, Louis Mason, Stymie Beard, William Pawley, Frank Sully, Davidson Clark.

THE PICTURE: Jesse James was killed off at the end of the picture which bore his name. But the movie was an enormous success—and Henry Fonda's portrayal of the subordinated, but better characterized, brother, Frank, was so well received that a successor to the original was hardly unexpected. The great German director Fritz Lang may have been an odd choice and perhaps Lang sacrificed some normal Western action to

mood but the result was head and shoulders above the typical melodrama of the species. (Fonda disliked working with Fritz Lang on *You Only Live Once,* considering him not so much a director as a "manipulator" in his relationship to actors. Lang, aware of Fonda's feelings, promised to have more respect and regard for the actor if he were allowed to direct this film. The association, however, became almost as unpleasant as before.) Fonda's characterization had all of the same virtues of that in the first picture and other actors from *Jesse James*—Henry Hull, John Carradine, Donald Meek, J. Edward Bromberg—repeated their roles. Gene Tierney, (billed "Miss" so that there would be no question about the gender of her unusually spelled Christian name), made her screen debut and Jackie Cooper had grown up to the point where he could take on the part of a youthful sidekick.

THE CRITICS

"It was a wise move to continue the saga of the James brothers in *The Return of Frank James.* Here was an

Jackie Cooper and Henry Fonda

opportunity to capitalize on one box-office success with another of its kind without having to rely on the imagination alone. There were records to show that the story of the less romanticized Frank also was worth chronicling in celluloid. That the producers of the picture were able to do so, and splendidly, is a tribute to shrewd research, fine writing and consummate direction and acting. Fritz Lang's methodical direction may exasperate those who look for a faster tempo in a drama of the outdoors, but its emphasis on small things like gestures and shadows and sounds of nature reveal the Western in a new and interesting light. Two other factors that make *The Return of Frank James* a superior picture are its abundance of humor, which is never forced, and just enough feminine interest to keep it from becoming lopsided. . . . Henry Fonda contributed a great deal to the success of *Jesse James,* even though his role was subordinated to the Jesse of Tyrone Power. In the sequel he is the top hand and, whether he is calmly chewing tobacco on his farm in the Ozarks, talking patiently to a pretty woman reporter, answering courtroom questions in a matter-of-fact way or galloping relentlessly up and down a mountain terrain in pursuit of his brother's murderers, he is convincingly Frank James. The final scene in which he stalks the cowardly Bob Ford in a livery stable, has the kind of deadly suspense that made the climax of *Stagecoach* so noteworthy."

Robert W. Dana, *New York Herald Tribune*

Henry Fonda and Jackie Cooper

Chad Hanna

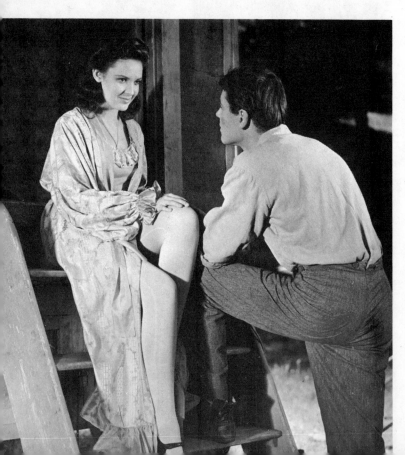

20th Century-Fox. 1940. Directed by Henry King. Produced by Nunnally Johnson. Screen play by Johnson from *Red Wheels Rolling* by Walter D. Edmonds.

HENRY FONDA played *Chad Hanna* in a cast that also included: Dorothy Lamour, Linda Darnell, Guy Kibbee, Jane Darwell, John Carradine, Ted North, Roscoe Ates, Ben Carter, Frank Thomas, Olin Howland, Frank Conlan, Edward Conrad, Edward McWade, Edward Mundy, George Davis, Paul Burns, Sarah Padden, Leonard St. Leo, Elizabeth Abbott, Tully Marshall, Almira Sessions, Virginia Brissac, Si Jenks, Victor Kilian, Louis Mason, Charles Middleton.

THE PICTURE: It probably was inevitable that Henry Fonda be cast in the title role of *Chad Hanna*, a film version of Walter D. Edmonds' *Red Wheels Rolling*. Fonda had played in two other adaptations of Edmonds' historical sagas of upstate New York, *Rome Haul*, which became *The Farmer Takes a Wife* on

Linda Darnell and Henry Fonda

*Henry Fonda, Linda Darnell and
Dorothy Lamour*

stage and screen, and *Drums Along the Mohawk*. This time he was a country boy who joins a small traveling circus after he becomes infatuated with its star, a bareback rider. But the story was familiar and episodic and the 1840's upstate New York atmosphere seemed synthetic and straight from the back lot. Fonda was likeable in one of his standard country boy roles but *Chad Hanna* was minor and mild.

THE CRITICS

"Of all Hollywood actors, Henry Fonda was the most natural selection and he carries the role perfectly."

The New York Times

"Once again, Mr. Fonda demonstrates he is an actor of great stature. While his voice is still definitely his own familiar one, his portrait of Chad is something else, the something that proves an actor can be somebody else if he is good enough. Fonda makes Chad terribly ingenuous, almost stolid. It is the one clear-cut aspect of the film, perfect in every respect."

Robert Dana, *New York Herald Tribune*

Henry Fonda and friend

Director Preston Sturges shows Henry Fonda and Barbara Stanwyck how to do it.

The Lady Eve

Paramount. 1941. Directed by Preston Sturges. Produced by Paul Jones. Screen play by Preston Sturges, based on a story by Monckton Hoffe.

HENRY FONDA played *Charles Pike* in a cast that also included: Barbara Stanwyck, Charles Coburn, Eugene Pallette, William Demarest, Eric Blore, Melville Cooper, Martha O'Driscoll, Janet Beecher, Robert Grieg, Dora Clement, Luis Alberni.

THE PICTURE: In the bleak period of Henry Fonda's contract days at 20th Century-Fox, at least there were loan-outs. Thank the Lord—and Preston Sturges—for *The Lady Eve*.

It remains Sturges' wittiest, wackiest, most brilliantly polished picture. Here, for instance, was Barbara Stanwyck in a welcome respite from all of those hysterical, snarling females she usually played in what were called "women's pictures." She was the very model of the sophisticated temptress, at her most wise and knowing, and with tongue planted firmly in cheek. Here, too, were such pros as Charles Coburn, Eugene Pallette, Eric Blore, William Demarest in roles obviously written to give them opportunities to do the things they do best.

And here is Fonda in his first real all-out comedy effort—a performance that would lead critic Andrew Sarris to describe Fonda as "the funniest deadpan comedian since Buster Keaton." He was, if you can believe such a thing, a shy, naive Howard Hughes kind of character—the richest and most eligible of all rich, eligible bachelors. He was also the most thorough innocent since Mr. Deeds played the tuba. His shipboard adventures with a predatory Stanwyck . . . his disillusionment just when it is turning to love on her part . . . her masquerade as a mythical "Lady Eve" to entrap him again . . . culminating in the most hilarious honeymoon in movie history—all of this was grist for the mill. That it was anything but surefire material was proven when it turned up some years later as a hopeless vehicle for George Gobel and Mitzi Gaynor. But the original, re-released even after the Gobel disaster, proved to be as bright and sparkling and completely undated as on its first time around—one of the screen's few real comedy classics.

THE CRITICS

"Barbara Stanwyck is a bit abrasive for comedy under normal conditions and her partner, Henry Fonda, is seldom associated with unrestrained merriment. Fortunately, Preston Sturges' films qualify as special situations. Fonda, particularly, emerges in *The Lady Eve* as the funniest deadpan comedian since Buster Keaton. When Fonda erupts hilariously in *The Lady Eve*, Sturges wittily tosses in everything from 'Lohengrin' to D. H. Lawrence. The sheer density of Sturges' dialogue is even more staggering today [1964] than it was at

Barbara Stanwyck and Henry Fonda

Henry Fonda, William Demarest, and Robert Grieg

the time. He wrote more funny lines for his bit players than contemporary jokesmiths can write for their leads."

Andrew Sarris, *The Village Voice*

"With *The Lady Eve,* Preston Sturges is indisputably established as one of the top one or two writers and directors of comedy working in Hollywood today. A more charming or distinguished gem of nonsense has not occurred since *It Happened One Night.* Superlatives like that are dangerous, but superlatives like *The Lady*

Eve are much too rare for the careful weighing of words. And much too precious a boon in these grim and mirthless times. For this bubbling and frothy comedy romance, which Mr. Sturges has whipped up for Paramount, possesses all the pristine bounce and humor, all the freshness and ingenuity, that seem to have been lacking from since away back—we don't know when . . . The screaming honeymoon sequence which Mr. Sturges has devised for two in a flower-decked Pullman compartment is one of the most de-

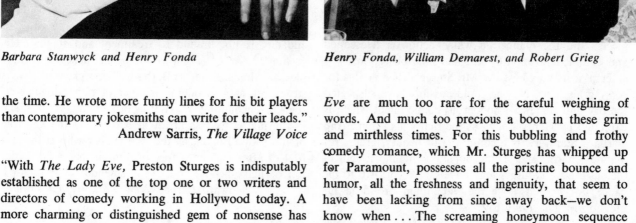

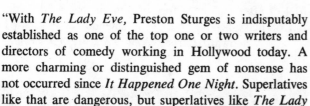

Eugene Pallette, Janet Beecher, Henry Fonda, Barbara Stanwyck, and Eric Blore

liciously funny scenes ever put into a motion picture. . . . No less than six flat falls are taken by the hero in this piece. And the manner in which action is telescoped and commented upon by fast and hilarious glimpses is cinema at its very best. . . . Mr. Sturges has a genius for picking his casts. No one could possibly have suspected the dry and somewhat ponderous comic talent which is exhibited by Henry Fonda as the rich young man. And Barbara Stanwyck is a composite of beauty, grace, romantic charm and a thoroughly feminine touch of viciousness. . . . Sturges may have sacrificed a rib to the cause but he has done the old Adam proud in his creation of The Lady Eve."

Bosley Crowther, The New York Times

"For a third time Preston Sturges has demonstrated that a fresh and imaginative treatment can work wonders in making an entertaining screen show. The Lady Eve is the brightest sort of nonsense, on which Sturges' signature is written large. As in the case of The Great McGinty and Christmas in July he has doubled on script and direction and the result is triumphant. For the offering has a sustained comic flavor and an individual treatment that are rarely found in Hollywood's antic concoctions. Played to breezy perfection by Barbara Stanwyck and Henry Fonda, who are not usually associated with sly clowning, it is a captivating movie farce. . . . When it is not overly familiar, the story is preposterous, but it is not the story that counts in The Lady Eve. It is the bright Sturges dialogue and the deft articulation of witty exchanges with arrant slapstick. It

is the human, recognizable quality of the proceedings, no matter how cockeyed they become. . . . Sturges' audacity is not limited to treatment and staging. His casting of The Lady Eve is one of the most surprisingly pleasant things about it. Barbara Stanwyck, who always struck me as a wooden portrayer of rather lugubrious roles, is enchanting. In a series of stunning get-ups, she is alluring as well as artful in performing the key role of the show. Fonda, as the rich sucker who is made a fool of after making a fool of himself, has a far easier job of make-believe, but he is splendid in any case."

Howard Barnes, New York Herald Tribune

Henry Fonda and Barbara Stanwyck

Wild Geese Calling

20th Century-Fox. 1941. Directed by John Brahm. Produced by Harry Joe Brown. Screen play by Horace McCoy, based on a novel by Stewart Edward White.

HENRY FONDA played *John Murdock* in a cast that also included: Joan Bennett, Warren William, Ona Munson, Barton MacLane, Russell Simpson, Iris Adrian, James C. Morton, Paul Sutton, Mary Field, Stanley Andrews, Jody Gilbert, Robert Emmett Keane, Michael Morris, George Watts, Charles Middleton.

THE PICTURE: With critics and public still singing

Joan Bennett and Henry Fonda

Henry Fonda and Ona Munson

the praises of *The Lady Eve,* Fonda returned to his home studio, which had nothing better for him than a tired melodrama in which he suspects (wrongly) that his wife has returned to her shady ways of the past, but is reconciled when she has a baby. *Wild Geese Calling,* as a novel by Stewart Edward White, may have read better than it played, but its pace was too measured for action melodrama, its characters and incidents too trite for a serious psychological study of a young man with wanderlust.

THE CRITICS

"The action is studied and believably counterfeit for the most part but some good acting by the principals is submerged by the excess weight of mood and thought . . . Henry Fonda, splendid as always, plays with as much reality as possible the strong-armed dreamer . . . Joan Bennett isn't able to do much with the role of the wife."

Robert W. Dana, *New York Herald Tribune*

Henry Fonda, Iris Adrian. and Warren William

You Belong to Me

Columbia. 1941. Produced and directed by Wesley Ruggles. Screen play by Claude Binyon based on story by Dalton Trumbo.

HENRY FONDA played *Peter Kirk* in a cast that also included: Barbara Stanwyck, Edgar Buchanan, Roger Clark, Ruth Donnelly, Melville Cooper, Ralph Peters, Maude Eburne, Renie Riano, Ellen Lowe, Mary Treen, Gordon Jones, Fritz Feld, Paul Harvey.

THE PICTURE: Every comedy can't be a "Lady Eve," even when it's tailored to the abilities of the same cast-toppers. *You Belong to Me* was like one of those book-length novels at the back of a popular magazine—flimsy, full of marital misunderstandings, but with everything turning out well in the end. That it was more pleasant than it might have been was due to bright lines in the Claude Binyon script, well-paced directed by

Wesley Ruggles and the ingratiating charm of Fonda and Stanwyck in what, played by other actors, could have been stereotyped roles. This was Fonda's third picture with Stanwyck and, like such other actors as Robert Preston and William Holden, he considers her his favorite leading lady—professional, considerate and fun to work with.

THE CRITICS

"The felicitous combination of Barbara Stanwyck and Henry Fonda in *The Lady Eve* was much too successful not to warrant a soon-as-possible repeat. So it is really by virtue of fiat that the two are playing together again in a lightweight but pleasant Columbia picture entitled *You Belong to Me* . . . These tensile marital comedies, strung out on a very thin line, have a way of snapping in the middle unless written and acted to the hilt. This one is fortunate in having a smart script as foundation—

Henry Fonda and Barbara
Stanwyck

bright and easy dialogue and cute situations. It is directed by Wesley Ruggles in a brisk and amiable style and it is well supported by a cast including Fritz Feld, Edgar Buchanan and Melville Cooper. But the best thing about it is its principals, Mr. Fonda and Miss Stanwyck. He, with his loose-jointed blunderings and charming diffidence, and she with her forthright manner and ability to make a man forget, are a right team for this sort of dalliance. *You Belong to Me* is a bit of well-turned fun."

Bosley Crowther, *The New York Times*

"Lightweight and second-rate even with such popular stars."

Howard Barnes, *New York Herald Tribune*

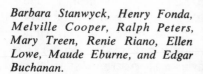

Barbara Stanwyck, Henry Fonda, Melville Cooper, Ralph Peters, Mary Treen, Renie Riano, Ellen Lowe, Maude Eburne, and Edgar Buchanan.

The Male Animal

Warner Bros. 1942. Directed by Elliott Nugent. Produced by Hal B. Wallis. Screen play by Julius J. and Philip G. Epstein from the play by James Thurber and Elliott Nugent.

HENRY FONDA played Tommy Turner in a cast that also included: Olivia de Havilland, Jack Carson, Joan Leslie, Eugene Pallette, Herbert Anderson, Ivan Simpson, Don DeFore, Minna Phillips, Regina Wallace, Jean Ames, Hattie McDaniel, Frank Mayo, William B. Davidson, Bobby Barnes.

THE PICTURE: Loan-out luck still worked for Henry Fonda. Before returning to the 20th Century-Fox inani-

Henry Fonda and Jack Carson (the famous "Statue of Liberty" play)

ties of *The Magnificent Dope* and *Rings on Her Fingers,* he went to Warners to recreate, for the screen, the role originated by Elliott Nugent in *The Male Animal.* This was one of Broadway's better plays of the era—an irresistible comedy with, not at all incidentally, something very meaningful to say. Nugent, co-author (with James Thurber) as well as star of the stage version, directed the film. He led the chorus which insisted that Fonda was the ideal Professor Tommy Turner and that the film, if anything, surpassed the play. Here the villains were college trustee reactionaries—very funny as led by

a pompous Eugene Pallette—but no less sinister for that.

In a film that had such comic highlights as an intellectual drunken brawl and the re-enactment by a blustering Jack Carson—the very picture of a hotshot football star beginning to turn to blubber and Babbitt—of his famous "Statue of Liberty play," there was one unforgettable climactic scene that still stands in the gallery of great movie moments. You could have defied a Senator Joe McCarthy to remain unmoved when Fonda read the letter of Bartolomeo Vanzetti.

The Male Animal is hardly foolproof. There have

Eugene Pallette, Joan Leslie, Olivia de Havilland, Henry Fonda, Regina Wallace, and Jack Carson

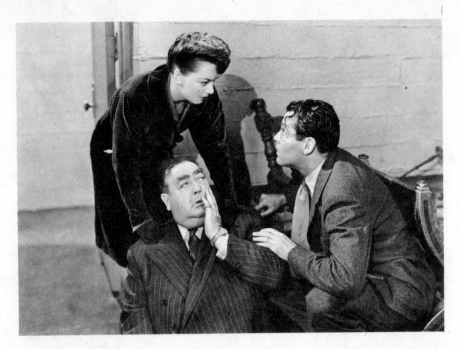

Olivia de Havilland, Eugene Pallette, and Henry Fonda

been disastrously dull stock productions of it and there
was a movie remake, something called *She's Working
Her Way Through College*, that is better left unde-
scribed. But here everyone was just right—the aforementioned Carson and Pallette, a glowing Olivia de
Havilland, a fresh Joan Leslie, a couple of well-cast
youngsters, Herbert Anderson and Don DeFore, along
with such capable people as Hattie McDaniel and Ivan
Simpson. And, above all, there was Henry Fonda.

(In the 1950's accepted an invitation from his old
stock company at Dennis to repeat his role in a summer
stock presentation of *The Male Animal*. He was heralded, of course, and so was a youngster making her
stage debut. Her name was Jane Fonda.)

THE CRITICS

"Here, at last, is a college comedy in which the fellow
who scored the touchdown doesn't get the girl, in which
the pre-game football rally is beautifully satirized and
the hero turns out to be a young, bespectacled, married
prof. Heaven only knows what this picture will do to
the old formula. The Warners are flaunting tradition in
a most entertaining way. . . . The Messrs. Thurber and
Nugent wrought a jaunty play which has been considerably improved in the retelling—and in the performance, too. The Epstein brothers, Julius J. and Philip G.,
and Stephen Morehouse Avery have reconstructed the
original along much more practical lines, retaining the
best of the boiling and putting the climax where it
should be—at the end. . . . Along the way have been
scattered, in logical and well-ordered form, some highly
amusing reflections upon homo sapiens—especially the
sapiens who fit into the classification of rah-rah college
grads. And here has also been developed a deeply pro-
voking dissertation upon masculine psychology. Henry
Fonda plays the young professor with a floppy dogged-
ness which is comically pat, still conveying a sense of
integrity which gives his character more than comic
point. His reading of the Vanzetti letter, following a
solemn appeal for tolerance at the end, is a profoundly
moving performance. It gives genuine significance to
this film."

Bosley Crowther, *The New York Times*

"It's funny all the way through. With Henry Fonda
playing the professor brilliantly and Olivia de Havilland
contributing a radiant portrayal of his wife, the movie
has a solid foundation of human drama. When their
lives are turned topsy-turvy in the midst of a big football rally, every situation takes on a keen edge of satire
and humor. . . . Henry Fonda is a good screen actor.
He's much more than that in *The Male Animal*. His
portrayal of the poky teacher who suddenly gets up on
his hind legs is magnificent. Without ever caricaturing
the role, he makes it tremendously amusing, as well as
sympathetic. I'd call it his best film performance. The
drunk scene is terrific. The romantic moments are genuinely touching. And the big climax, thanks to his quiet
sincerity, comes off with a bang."

Howard Barnes, *Liberty*

Henry Fonda and Gene Tierney

Rings on Her Fingers

20th Century-Fox. 1942. Directed by Rouben Mamoulian. Produced by Milton Sperling. Screen play by Ken Englund from a story by Robert Pirosh and Joseph Schrank.

HENRY FONDA played *John Wheeler* in a cast that also included: Gene Tierney, Laird Cregar, John Shepperd,

Spring Byington, Marjorie Gateson, George Lessey, Clive Morgan, Frank Orth, Iris Adrian, Thurston Hall, Clara Blandick, Charles Wilson, Edgar Morgan, George Lloyd, Sarah Edwards, Gwendolyn Logan, Evelyn Mulhall, Kathryn Sheldon.

THE PICTURE: 20th Century-Fox had little imagi-

Hemry Stephenson, Gene Tierney, Henry Fonda, Spring Byington, and Laird Cregar

Henry Fonda and extras

nation about the way they cast Fonda while he was under contract. He had scored strongly (away from the studio) as a naïve young man, the target of swindlers, with the scheming "girl in the case" turning straight when she finds it's true love. 20th-Fox used the same theme with Gene Tierney in the "Stanwyck role," other good actors like Laird Cregar and Spring Byington, and one of the best, Rouben Mamoulian, to direct. Fonda was likeable, of course, and the picture passably amusing but trivial and reminiscent of its betters. *Rings on Her Fingers* was no *Lady Eve*.

THE CRITICS
"This offering dresses up an old screen yarn with new faces. It does have some incisive and amusing acting by Henry Fonda, Laird Cregar and, of all people, Gene Tierney. The Tierney performance is probably the most distinctive thing about this none-too-distinctive show, for the much-publicized young actress finally gives some justification of the promise which rocketed her to stardom. She is still no star but she does a bit of acting for a change.... Meanwhile, Fonda contributes an uneven but occasionally inspired performance as the gold-brick buying hero. His system of beating a roulette game, when the croupiers have been instructed to let him win, constitute a hilarious interlude. His wooing of Miss Tierney is restrained and effective.... It is the acting which makes *Rings on Her Fingers* worth seeing."
Howard Barnes, *New York Herald Tribune*

Director Rouben Mamoulian guides Henry Fonda, Gene Tierney, and dance extras

The Magnificent Dope

20th Century-Fox. 1942. Directed by Walter Lang. Produced by William Perlberg. Screen play by George Seaton, based on original story by Joseph Schrank.

HENRY FONDA played *Tad Page* in a cast that also included: Lynn Bari, Don Ameche, Edward Everett Horton, George Barbier, Frank Orth, Roseanne Murray, Kitty McHugh, Marietta Canty, Hobart Cavanaugh,

Hal K. Dawson, Josephine Whittell, Arthur Loft, Chick Chandler, Paul Stanton, Claire Du Brey, William Davidson, Harry Hayden, Pierre Watkin.

THE PICTURE: Now with Gary Cooper as Mr. Deeds going to town and Jimmy Stewart as Mr. Smith going to Washington, what more apt, according to the copy-cat minds of the movie moguls, than Henry Fonda

Henry Fonda and Don Ameche

Henry Fonda and Lynn Bari

as Mr. Page going to New York? They resisted the temptation to title it that but its antecedents were unquestionable. Here Fonda was a yokel, brought to New York by Success School operator Don Ameche, as the result of a publicity stunt to find the most complete failure in the country. Of course, Wiseguy Ameche and his Jean Arthur-ish sidekick, Lynn Bari, try to use the "dope" and, of course, the latter winds up by converting them all to his school of happy laziness. Such a role was easy as pie for Fonda. But the screen play grabbed at all the clichés and Walter Lang was no Frank Capra. *The Magnificent Dope* would have been no great shakes even if it arrived before Messrs. Deeds and Smith showed up. This many years later, it was unforgiveable.

THE CRITICS

"With Henry Fonda giving one of his best drawling performances in the title role, it has all sorts of comic inflections while the dope is showing up the city slickers. The trouble is that the dope doesn't stick to his guns in the script and his final victory over go-getters and sophistication is tepid. Since the romantic underlining is definitely muddled, the show offers diminishing returns in the way of entertainment. Fonda does the major job

in leavening *The Magnificent Dope*. He succeeds in holding a sure line between a two-faced characterization. Either as hayseed or go-getter, he captures whatever amusement resides in the narrative. Don Ameche is merely Don Ameche; Lynn Bari is tolerable as the heroine and Edward Everett Horton tries hard, but not too successfully, to sneak in some random clowning."

Howard Barnes, *New York Herald Tribune*

"Perhaps this story of the external yokel and the manner in which he confounds the big town careerists is not the most crackling satire of the season, but with Henry Fonda as the loose-jawed hayseed and Don Ameche as a brassy "con" man, the film does hold a barrelful of chuckles. It has a point of view; it pokes fun at all those energetic get-ahead-at-any-cost maxims that found their purest expression in *Poor Richard's Almanac* and have been the foundation of big business, high blood pressure and heart disease ever since.... As the Green Mountain Jeeter Lester who says: 'I haven't any respect for a man who was born lazy; it took me a long time to get where I am,' Mr. Fonda gives a joyous portrait of rural inertia."

T. S., *The New York Times*

Tales of Manhattan

20th Century-Fox. 1942. Directed by Julien Duvivier. Produced by Boris Morros and S. P. Eagle. Original stories and screen play by Ben Hecht, Ferenc Molnar, Donald Ogden Stewart, Samuel Hoffenstein, Alan Campbell, Ladislaus Fodor, L. Vadnai, L. Gorog. Lamar Trotti, Henry Blankfort.

HENRY FONDA played *George* in a cast that also included: Charles Boyer, Rita Hayworth, Ginger Rogers, Charles Laughton, Edward G. Robinson, Paul Robeson, Ethel Waters, Eddie (Rochester) Anderson, Thomas Mitchell, Eugene Pallette, Cesar Romero, Gail Patrick, Roland Young, Marion Martin, Elsa Lanchester, Victor

Henry Fonda, Ginger Rogers, and Cesar Romero

Tales of Manhattan *stars* (*Henry Fonda, Charles Boyer, Rita Hayworth, Charles Laughton, Edward G. Robinson*) *leave their handprints at Grauman's Chinese Theatre, as Sid Grauman looks on.*

Francen, George Sanders, James Gleason, Harry Davenport, James Rennie, J. Carrol Naish, Frank Orth, Christian Rub, Sig Arno, Harry Hayden, Morris Ankrum, Don Douglas, Mae Marsh, Clarence Muse, George Reed, Cordell Hickman, Paul Renay, Barbara Lynn, Adeline DeWalt Reynolds, Helene Reynolds, Hall Johnson Choir.

THE PICTURE: *Tales of Manhattan* was one of those trick pictures—irresistible in prospect to stargazers, something considerably less than that in the viewing. This had the extremely slim premise of the adventures of a suit of tails as it is passed from hand to hand. The stories tied together by this device and written by ten authors—some of the stature of Hecht, Molnar, Donald Ogden Stewart, Lamar Trotti—were about as substantial as those *Liberty* short-shorts of the thirties and even more contrived. Fonda shared an episode with Ginger Rogers and Cesar Romero, but there were honors to none of the stars trapped in their trite roles.

THE CRITICS

Tales of Manhattan is one of those rare films—a tricky departure from the norm, which, in spite of its five-ring-circus nature, achieves an impressive effect. . . . The big surprise is that the actors never dwarf the little fables they play and that the whole film never exposes the fragile framework on which it is built. . . . Ginger Rogers and Henry Fonda are very amusing in the romance-switching episode. . . . Julien Duvivier has directed the film with surprising evenness and has matched the moods and tempos of the various episodes with delicacy. Much of the credit for this picture must go to him, and a good bit more must go to Boris Morros and S. P. Eagle, who persuaded Twentieth Century-Fox to make it. The venture was obviously risky, but the result is sufficient compensation."

Bosley Crowther, *The New York Times*

Howard Barnes, in the *New York Herald Tribune,* said the film "has very little motion picture distinction" but allowed that Fonda has "some bright moments in the farcical section."

Henry Fonda and Lucille Ball

The Big Street

RKO-Radio. 1942. Directed by Irving Reis. Produced by Damon Runyon. Screen play by Leonard Spigelgass from the story, "The Little Pinks," by Damon Runyon.

HENRY FONDA played *The Little Pinks* in a cast that also included: Lucille Ball, Barton MacLane, Eugene Pallette, Agnes Moorehead, Sam Levene, Ray Collins, Marion Martin, William Orr, George Cleveland, Vera Gordon, Louise Beavers, Millard Mitchell, Juan Varro, Harry Shannon.

Director Irving Reis rehearses Lucille Ball and Henry Fonda

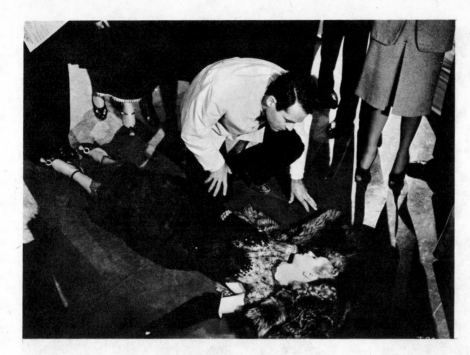

Henry Fonda and Lucille Ball

THE PICTURE: It pretty well depended on your feelings about the Broadway fables of Damon Runyon how you felt about *The Big Street*. Did you swing with his individual characters or were they perhaps a little overcute and sentimentalized for your tastes? This was Runyon's own production of one of his own stories, coming long enough after *Lady For a Day* and *Little Miss Marker* that it had very little novelty and well before *Guys and Dolls* made it all in the mode again.

In 1942, *The Big Street* seemed dated and just this side of mawkish. Yet, seen again many years later, it becomes an extraordinarily touching little fairy tale.

This was due primarily to the fact that Fonda was so believable in what might have been the most unbelievable of roles. He was The Little Pinks, a Mindy's busboy and the most self-sacrificing of human innocents—a regular doormat for the bitchy night-club babe whom he adores. When she is incurably crippled after being

Damon Runyon, author of The Big Street, *and its star, Henry Fonda*

Lucille Ball, and Henry Fonda in the moving climactic scene.

knocked down by a gang mogul, she loses everything except her nasty disposition and her firm belief that she just has to hit Miami to have the millionaires fighting over her again. So The Little Pinks hitch-hikes with her, pushing her most of the way in her wheelchair. And, of course, it doesn't work even when Pinks enlists the aid of his buddies to shanghai top socialites to a party in her honor. And it's there that Pinks becomes the Prince, dancing with his Lady, whose feet, of course, never touch the floor. And she expires in his arms—doesn't it all sound horrible? But actually it was curiously moving.

Fonda played this most naive of all movie heroes with absolute conviction. Lucille Ball didn't attempt to soften her disagreeable character and gave her finest movie performance. Eugene Pallette, Sam Levene, Ray Collins, Agnes Moorehead were among the quainter types encountered.

It was a thoroughly appealing picture.

THE CRITICS

"Out of his galaxy of guys and dolls, Damon Runyon, making his bow as a film producer with *The Big Street,* has provided a smartly paced and colorful comedy drama. The picture is basically a love story of no great weight, but the author, as Broadway's accredited bard, is a man who can 'make with the dialogue' as his heroine pithily puts it. That is the tale's chief attribute.... Henry Fonda, as Little Pinks makes an acutely sympathetic hero opposite Miss Ball's able portrayal of the singer."

A. Weiler, *The New York Times*

"The part of the bashful, simple busboy, Little Pinks, was made to order for Henry Fonda. He plays the role for all it's worth and only a Runyon could possibly invent such a naive individual."

E. G., *New York Herald Tribune*

The Immortal Sergeant

20th Century-Fox. 1943. Directed by John Stahl. Produced by Lamar Trotti. Screen play by Lamar Trotti, based on a novel by John Brophy.

HENRY FONDA played *Cpl. Colin Spence* in a cast that also included: Maureen O'Hara, Thomas Mitchell, Allyn Joslyn, Reginald Gardiner, Melville Cooper, Bramwell Fletcher, Morton Lowry, Donald Stuart, Jean Prescott, Heather Wilde, Bob Mascagno, Italia De Nubila.

THE PICTURE: Fonda's last picture before entering the service was *The Immortal Sergeant*. (*The Ox-Bow Incident*, released later, was made before this one.)

Melville Cooper, Henry Fonda, and Allyn Joslyn

By the time of the release of *The Immortal Sergeant*, Fonda was already in the uniform of a Naval officer. It was a good, straightforward account of warfare in the Libyan desert and the emergence of a retiring young corporal as a military leader. It was better than most being made at the time but far from one of the war classics which stay in the memory.

THE CRITICS

"Immortal Sergeant has been directed by John Stahl with more emphasis on the exciting details of desert fighting than on the psychological metamorphosis of a young man under the guidance of a tough sergeant. . . . The novel's author was more concerned with a young man's development from a shy, retiring fellow into an aggressive soldier. On the other hand, Twentieth Century-Fox is more interested in offering fireworks. But they are substantial and entertaining fireworks. . . . The cast has been chosen with care. Henry Fonda has a tailored role in Corporal Spence, a timid newspaper man and novelist. He plays it poker-faced and, surprisingly enough, effectively. Thomas Mitchell is persuasive as a tough old soldier. Maureen O'Hara's duties are chiefly to act as foil for the unhappy corporal."

Joseph Pihodna, *New York Herald Tribune*

Henry Fonda

Maureen O'Hara and Henry Fonda

The Ox-Bow Incident

20th Century-Fox. 1943. Directed by William A. Wellman. Produced and screen play by Lamar Trotti. Based on a novel by Walter Van Tilburg Clark.

HENRY FONDA played *Gil Carter* in a cast that also included: Dana Andrews, Mary Beth Hughes, Anthony Quinn, William Eythe, Henry Morgan, Jane Darwell, Matt Briggs, Harry Davenport, Frank Conroy, Marc Lawrence, Paul Hurst, Victor Kilian, Chris-Pin Martin, Ted North, George Meeker, Almira Sessions, Margaret Hamilton, Dick Rich, Francis Ford, Stanley Andrews, Billy Benedict, Rondo Hatton, Paul Burns, Leigh Whipper, George Chandler, George Lloyd.

THE PICTURE: Nobody had any faith in *The Ox-Bow Incident* except star Henry Fonda and director William Wellman. These two browbeat Darryl F. Zanuck into making it despite the grim, uncompromising story which Zanuck felt—rightly as it turned out an original release—would be sure and sudden death at the box office. But Fonda agreed to do *The Magnificent Dope* and Wellman to direct *Thunder Birds* if they could have their chance at "Ox-Bow." They had it and, despite almost unanimously brilliant reviews, the picture was not popular with the war-year audiences, who were

much more used to the kind of movie in which Betty Grable takes off her glasses and turns groovy. *The Ox-Bow Incident* has had a long life, though. It eventually made its money back—even turned a profit—and is now generally regarded as a classic of the West. It is one of the most frequently shown films on TV and is one of the two favorite Fonda films with film societies and college groups. (*Twelve Angry Men* is the other.) In the mid-sixties, it was released for the first time in Germany and caused something of a sensation, both with critics and the box office.

Here Fonda was the star but only by right of his stature. If ever there was a perfect example of ensemble acting—no performance played to outshine the others—it was *The Ox-Bow Incident*. (*Twelve Angry Men* is another in which Fonda subordinated his own star personality to become a member of an ideal actors' ensemble.)

Here Fonda, far from the standard Wayne brand of Western hero, rides into town, reckless and raunchy, with a scruffy sidekick. They are primarily observers, rather than participants, in the events that follow. A rancher is reported killed by cattle rustlers and a lynch mob is formed. The culprits are found and, although they protest their innocence and although a few men try to dissuade the leaders, they are the victims of the mob fury and passion fanned into flame particularly by the sadistic Army officer who is their leader. After the men are hanged, it is learned that they are innocent of the murder and, in fact, that there has been no murder.

Fonda's finest moment was reminiscent of so many of his fine moments (the reading of the words written for Grampa Joad's grave, the reading of the Vanzetti letter, the numbed recounting of battle horror in *Drums Along the Mohawk*, etc.). Here, to a barroom, full of members of the mob, now sobered by the news that it had all been a mistake, he read a letter from one of the executed men to his wife.

Dana Andrews has probably never been more effective as the bewildered, accused man. But then the entire cast was extraordinary, with particular note to Frank Conroy, Anthony Quinn, Henry Morgan, William Eythe, and Paul Hurst. Wellman's direction was starkly uncompromising.

THE CRITICS

"An ugly study in mob violence, unrelieved by any human grace save the futile reproach of a minority and some mild post-lynching remorse, is contained in *The Ox-Bow Incident* which was delivered to the screen in as brazen a gesture as any studio has ever indulged. For it is hard to imagine a picture with less promise commercially. In a little over an hour, it exhibits most of the baser shortcoming of men—cruelty, blood-lust,

Anthony Quinn, Francis Ford, Dana Andrews, Henry Fonda, Frank Conroy, and Jane Darwell

ruffianism, pusillanimity and sordid pride. It shows a tragic violation of justice with little backlash to sweeten the bitter draught. And it puts a popular actor, Henry Fonda, in a very dubious light. But it also points a

The innocent men are captured by a lynch **mob***.*

Harry Davenport, Matt Briggs, Henry Fonda, Henry Morgan, and Ted North

moral, bluntly and unremittingly, to show the horror of mob rule. And it has the virtue of uncompromising truth. . . . William Wellman has directed with a realism that is as sharp and cold as a knife, with a script by Lamar Trotti which is beautifully brief with situations and words. And an all-round excellent cast has played the film brilliantly. The manner in which Mr. Wellman has studied his characters is a lesson in close-up art. And the terror which he has packed into that night "trial" with the ruthless lynchers glowering around a mountain fire while the doomed men face their fate in pitiful misery, is drama at its cruel and cynical best. A heart-wringing performance by Dana Andrews as the stunned and helpless leader of the doomed trio does much to make the picture a profoundly distressing tragedy, while Frank Conroy's performance of the demagogue (all rigged out in a Confederate officer's uniform) imparts to it a perceptive significance which is good to keep in mind. Mr. Fonda is cryptic and bitter as one of the stauncher hold-outs for justice, while Harry Davenport and Leigh Whipper are more affecting emotionally as champions of the right. Mary Beth Hughes has been pulled in for a brief, ironic scene with Mr. Fonda which gives a justification for his mood. And the rest of the cast can take bows for small but impressive roles. *The Ox-Bow Incident* is not a picture which will brighten or cheer your day. But it is one which, for sheer, stark drama, is hard to beat."

Bosley Crowther, *The New York Times*

"In *The Ox-Bow Incident,* which is not a horse opera, a dreadful side of human beings is portrayed in a magnificent film. It marks a break in Hollywood's ugly movie career because the people behind it—William Wellman, Lamar Trotti, Walter Van Tilburg Clark—director, producer and writer—and Henry Fonda, Frank Conroy and Henry Morgan, the players, had their say without losing a scene, a character or a line of dialogue to the Hays Office, the studio or the box office. As the work of unhampered artists, it is for the audience a thrilling experience. . . . The movie is an examination of an incident—the lynching of three men at The Ox-bow, Nevada, in 1885. Aside from its extraordinary indictment of lynching, it shows the failure of liberal men, inspired by justice, when they are opposed by irrational and powerful men of anger. . . . But its soundest, most original declaration is its realistic, pedestrian view of violence, that there is nothing unusual about it in our society, that the men who participated in it did not regard it as violence. The main reason offered by the movie for the success of the lynching is that the majority of the people were either irresponsible, ignor-

Victor Kilian, Marc Lawrence, Rondo Hatton, Henry Fonda, and Henry Morgan

ant or moronic, the lynching a form of self-esteem, and a natural product of such characters as the film had already built. There was no hysteria. The introduction to this situation is an example of perfection in movie techniques of camera work and acting. Free for once to play into the character without being pushed around by unlikelihoods, Henry Fonda is magnificent in his projection of an unremarkable, bored, sexually frustrated cowboy, who has been on the range too long, analyzing a nude painting over the saloon mirror, getting drunk fast and beating someone half to death just out of meanness. Alongside, his buddy, Henry Morgan, creates an insensitive, moronic cowboy by a masterpiece of restrained playing. The camera pace is slow, monosyllabic and stolid, it drills persistently into the scene, seeing the event as less important than the behavior of the people making it. Its violence is blunt and dreadful,

its details beautiful to watch. More than anything I would like to emphasize the psychological tension built out of visual movement, which is the movies' own baby. It is overpowering in such scenes as that of the Negro preacher walking toward the hostile crowd, the pace so felt that the air into which the man walks seems to be pressing him back. I tell you this is a movie. . . . It is an American legend that Hollywood cannot produce a serious work of art because of censorship, the role of the movies as the entertainer of the masses and the synthetic, mechanical quality of the medium, which esthetes say makes it incapable of personal expression. For the good of everyone, that legend can now be called extinct. *The Ox-Bow Incident* is a significant moment in our culture. Cheer for it and hope it will not stand alone."

Manny Farber, *The New Republic*

Henry Fonda as Wyatt Earp

My Darling Clementine

20th Century-Fox. 1946. Directed by John Ford. Produced by Samuel G. Engel. Screen play by Engel and Winston Miller, based on a story by Sam Hellman, from a book by Stuart N. Lake.

HENRY FONDA played *Wyatt Earp* in a cast that also included: Linda Darnell, Victor Mature, Walter Brennan, Tim Holt, Cathy Downs, Ward Bond, Alan Mowbray, John Ireland, Jane Darwell, Roy Roberts, Grant Withers, J. Farrell MacDonald, Russel Simpson, Don Garner, Francis Ford, Ben Hall, Arthur Walsh.

THE PICTURE: Out of the Navy came Henry Fonda

and into another Western drama, almost as distinguished as his last pre-service film to hit theatres, *The Ox-Bow Incident*. And *My Darling Clementine* had a much greater popular appeal than the earlier, first-unappreciated classic. Of course, this was a reunion with John Ford, also freshly returned from the wars, and it was the first for director and star together in an area in which both excel—the Western.

This was the story of Wyatt Earp, the marshal of Tombstone, who, with his brothers and the wild and reckless Doc Holliday, who becomes his friend, track down the killer Clantons. This is certainly shopworn now—how many Wyatt Earp movies and television films

Victor Mature, as Doc Holliday, is "prepared" by volunteer nurses Cathy Downs and Henry Fonda

have you seen since 1946? But, even then, it was far from a departure in Western drama. Think of the Wyatt Earps you have seen: Randolph Scott, Errol Flynn, Burt Lancaster, Hugh O'Brian, James Garner, just for starters. And the basic story line went back to William S. Hart.

But certainly Fonda's was the definitive characterization. Certainly Ford's picture was supreme when compared even to *Gunfight at the OK Corral,* the best of the others. Seen at the 1968 Lincoln Center Film Festival Western Retrospective, *My Darling Clementine* had not dated an iota. Yet *Hour of the Gun,* following the same story line, was already old-hat by the time it was released twenty years later.

In addition to Fonda's performance—the epitome of "cool"—*My Darling Clementine* gave Victor Mature something more than a "beautiful hunk of man" role, had Walter Brennan playing just this side of low comedy but far enough this side to present a portrayal of repellent evil, gave us a couple of photogenic leading ladies in Linda Darnell and Cathy Downs, and supplied one of those superior Ford supporting casts—Ward Bond, Tim Holt, John Ireland, Alan Mowbray, Jane Darwell and others.

THE CRITICS
"The eminent director John Ford is a man who has a

Henry Fonda, Jane Darwell, and Roy Roberts

way with a Western like nobody in the picture trade. Seven years ago his classic *Stagecoach* snuggled very close to fine art in this genre. And now, by George, he's almost matched it with *My Darling Clementine.* . . . Every scene, every shot is the product of a keen and sensitive eye—an eye which has deep comprehension of the beauty of rugged people and a rugged world. . . . And the humans whom Mr. Ford imagines are not the ordinary stereotypes of films, no matter how hackneyed and conventional the things they are supposed to do. Henry Fonda, for instance, plays a Wyatt Earp such as we've never seen before—a leathery, laconic young cowpoke who truly suggests a moral aim. Through his quiet yet persuasive self-confidence—his delicious intonation of short words—he shows us an elemental character who is as real as the dirt on which he walks. . . . The gentlemen are perfect. Their humors are earthy. Their activities are taut. The mortality rate is simply terrific. And the picture goes off with several bangs."

Bosley Crowther, *The New York Times*

"Henry Fonda gives an easy and likeable portrayal of Wyatt Earp, a homespun Westerner who can outshoot anyone but who also has a soft-spoken respect for the law. Victor Mature is also good in a restrained characterization. The deliberation in Ford's direction allows time for these two roles to become slightly more human than mere Western symbols. . . . Last, but not least, in *My Darling Clementine,* there is the panorama of the Western plains, which has been spread out before the camera with considerable visual appeal. Horse chases, gunfire and galloping stagecoach teams are as much a part of this action as of the most trivial border thriller; but besides staging these with as much excitement as possible, Ford has also recorded clouds at twilight, the

Henry Fonda confronts Victor Mature (J. Farrell MacDonald is bartender)

dust raised across the prairie by drumming hooves and the slant of the shadows on a Tombstone street in early morning. Such directorial 'extras' as these make *My Darling Clementine* a smooth and superior motion picture, wild and woolly Western though it certainly is."

Otis L. Guernsey, Jr., *New York Herald Tribune*

"Having assembled all the elements of a conventional Western in *My Darling Clementine,* John Ford as director proceeds to make an excellent film out of his material, using the formula technique to say something about pioneer days in Arizona. What he has done bespeaks his artistry, his humor, and his understanding of human nature. . . . Wyatt Earp, portrayed by Henry Fonda, is a superb interpretation—shy, slow-moving, easy-going, imperturbable, and likeable. The marshal getting a haircut, dancing a two-step, and walking a lady to church is as funny as though he were in a comedy, yet Mr. Fonda's characterization of a down-to-earth Westerner, free as air, is so persuasive that his Wyatt Earp becomes one of the great 'Western' heroes."

Christian Science Monitor

Henry Fonda as Wyatt Earp

Walter Brennan and Henry Fonda

The Long Night

RKO-Radio. 1947. Directed by Anatole Litvak. Produced by Robert and Raymond Hakim. Screen play by John Wexley, based on a story by Jacques Viot.

HENRY FONDA played *Joe* in a cast that also included: Barbara Bel Geddes, Vincent Price, Ann Dvorak, Howard Freeman, Moroni Olsen, Elisha Cook, Jr., Queenie Smith, David Clarke, Charles McGraw, Patty King, Robert A. Davis.

THE PICTURE: The postwar demand was not for moody melodrama, so *The Long Night* had pretty tough sledding at the box office. There were critical shots, too, at an over-talkative script and at compromises

Henry Fonda and Vincent Price

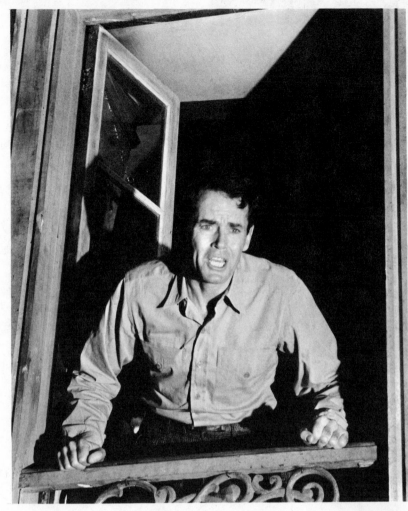

Henry Fonda

which had weakened this remake of a Jean Gabin
drama which, as *Daybreak,* had played in the United
States in 1940. This was the first film for Barbara Bel
Geddes, whose extremely individual stage personality
never registered nearly as effectively in celluloid. And
Vincent Price's sleazy seducer lacked any reality at all,
being much closer in performance to those elegant,
sinister gentlemen he was to play so well in a series of
horror movies.

Even so, Henry Fonda was remarkably sympathetic
and sensitive as a murderer, barricaded in his tenement
room against police and remembering through the long
night of the title the events that had brought him here.
Set in a Pennsylvania mill town, the film-flashed back
to follow the love story of Fonda and Bel Geddes, his
discovery that she is involved in a sordid liaison with
an older man—a small-time entertainer—and the even-
tual confrontation of the two men, with murder as the
result. Ann Dvorak gave an effective performance as

Henry Fonda

Ann Dvorak and Henry Fonda

the magician's assistant with an unrequited yen for Fonda. While *The Long Night* was far from a success, it had some extraordinarily affecting moments.

THE CRITICS

"In short, Mr. Litvak's production is an obvious theatrical fake, exposed by its own pretensions and an over-talked John Wexley script. And a lay-out of flashy performances do not match the French originals. Henry Fonda, while moody and pathetic as the holed-up fugitive, is not the wrath-tortured killer that Mr. Gabin was in the role."

Bosley Crowther, *The New York Times*

"If atmosphere and mood could alone sustain a motion picture, this latest melodrama would rank among the most effective of the year. With Henry Fonda as a killer besieged by the dowdy steel-town rooming house. *The Long Night* flashes back and forward between the past

Henry Fonda

Henry Fonda and Barbara Bel Geddes

and present to recount the steps leading up to an impulsive murder. A triangular love story and a rather confused development are never quite as absorbing as the manner of their telling supposes them to be, but Anatole Litvak's staging gives the piece a colorful personality which compensates for whatever defects it may have.... Fonda's natural performance helps to give the tale a feeling of sincerity, even in the somewhat theatrical love affair which motivates the story.... Whatever its faults, *The Long Night* has the rare quality of style, which makes it well worth watching.

Otis L. Guernsey, Jr., *New York Herald Tribune*

"Fonda has the ability to reverse the coin of the character he is most generally identified with, to show the other side, and underside, of that type. In a remarkable, albeit flawed, little melodrama, *The Long Night,* he enacted with stunning perceptiveness a quite ordinary man who goes berserk when his sweetheart is lured away by a carnival magician."

Nathan Cohen, *Toronto Star*

Ann Dvorak and Henry Fonda

Henry Fonda

The Fugitive

Argosy-RKO Radio. 1947. Directed by John Ford. Produced by Merian C. Cooper, John Ford. Screen play by Dudley Nichols, based on a novel by Graham Greene.

HENRY FONDA played a *Fugitive* in a cast that also included: Dolores Del Rio, Pedro Armendariz, J. Carrol Naish, Leo Carillo, Ward Bond, Robert Armstrong, John Qualen, Fortunio Bonanova, Cris-Pin Martin, Miguel Inclan, Fernando Fernandez.

THE PICTURE: Graham Greene's novel, *The Labyrinthine Ways,* (also known as *The Power and the Glory*), formed the basis for a John Ford picture which the director considers one of his few personal favorites. Closer in style to his *The Informer* than to any of his other films, in this one Ford concentrated on an escaping man—a runaway priest in an anti-clerical country—and on the events and people involved in his flight.

Greene's slovenly "whiskey priest," living with a woman, was tidied up for the screen play by Dudley Nichols, which made him neither an adulterer nor an alcoholic. Even, so, as played with intensity by Fonda, his agonized flight was arresting. It was one of Ford's most artistic (some critics scoffed at it as "arty") films with notable characterizations by a distinguished cast and with striking photography by Gabriel Figueroa.

THE CRITICS
"Out of the flood of pictures which opened on Broadway yesterday emerges in monolithic beauty John Ford's *The Fugitive*. For here, in this strange and haunting picture, imaged a terrifying struggle between strength and weakness in a man's soul, a thundering modern parable on the indestructibility of faith, a tense and significant conflict between freedom and brute authority. It is difficult to fashion in a few lines an indication of the nature of this film because of its violent eccen-

tricities and its crashing overtones. But it is enough to say that Mr. Ford has accomplished in it a true companion piece to *The Informer,* which he directed some years back. . . . Taking place in a fictitious Latin-American land which has been appropriately pictured by filming in Mexico, Mr. Ford has made *The Fugitive,* a symphony of light and shade, of deafening din and silence, of sweeping movement and repose. And by this magnificent ordering of a strange, dizzying atmosphere, he has brewed a storm of implications of man's perils and fears in a world gone mad. . . . The performances are all of them excellent, from the anguished straining of Henry Fonda as the priest to Ward Bond's stony arrogance as an American gangster on the lam. Dolores Del Rio is a warm glow of devotion as an Indian Magdalene and Pedro Armendariz burns with scorching passion as a chief of military police. The musical score by Richard Hageman is a tintinabulation of eloquent sounds. Let us thank Mr. Ford for giving us one of the best films of the year."

Bosley Crowther, *The New York Times*

Henry Fonda, J. Carrol Naish (kneeling), and Pedro Armendariz

Dolores Del Rio and Henry Fonda

Henry Fonda and Ward Bond

Wire to Henry Fonda from Merian Cooper, producer of The Fugitive: WE RAN THE COMPLETE PICTURE OF THE FUGITIVE FOR THE FIRST TIME TONIGHT PERIOD I THINK YOUR PERFORMANCE ONE OF THE TRULY GREAT ONES IN ENTIRE HISTORY OF MOTION PICTURES PERIOD DRIVING BACK FROM STUDIO JACK FORD SAID TO ME THAT HE BELIEVED YOUR WORK THE BEST OF ANYONE HE HAD DIRECTED IN HIS CAREER PERIOD THE PICTURE ITSELF IS UNIQUE AND IN MY OPINION IS FORD'S TOP DIRECTION PERIOD I KNOW THE EXPRESSION FILM CLASSIC IS ABUSED AND OVERUSED NEVERTHELESS I THINK JACK HAS AGAIN MADE A TRULY CLASSICAL PICTURE PERIOD I WANT TO THANK YOU FOR YOUR SUPERB PORTRAYAL PERIOD REGARDS.

COOP

"Along with *The Informer,* this is Ford's most consciously artistic movie, a personal and visually intoxicating story of a priest in a police state, considerably altering the Graham Greene novel on which it is based. Fonda is particularly expressive in the title role."

Peter Bogdanovich,
New Yorker Theatre
Fonda Festival Program Notes

Henry Fonda as The Priest, with extras

Daisy Kenyon

20th Century-Fox. 1947. Directed and produced by Otto Preminger. Screen play by David Hertz, based on a novel by Elizabeth Janeway.

HENRY FONDA played *Peter* in a cast that also included: Joan Crawford, Dana Andrews, Ruth Warrick, Martha Stewart, Peggy Ann Garner, Connie Marshall, Nicholas Joy, Art Baker, Robert Karnes, John Davidson, Vic-

toria Horne, Charles Meredith, Roy Roberts, Griff Barnett, Tito Vuolo.

THE PICTURE: With one last picture owed on his detested 20th Century-Fox contract, Fonda settled by accepting the kind of role he hadn't played since the thirties days of *That Certain Woman* and *I Met My Love Again*. Here again he was the nice young man

Dana Andrews and Henry Fonda

Henry Fonda and Joan Crawford

her meeting and marriage to the solid and substantial Fonda, her embroilment in a divorce case and her final choice between her men. It was all lots of fun for the ladies with Daisy's problems played out against a variety of smart New York settings. And, for Fonda, it stood for the end of a restricting contract.

THE CRITICS

"*Daisy Kenyon* is 'back street' drama with added complications, but it is somewhat more mature and compelling than the usual run of pictures of this sort. That is, it should be hastily added, up to a point and then the story goes completely to pot. The weakness here is the scenario, for after David Hertz builds up his problem he obviously doesn't know how to resolve it, at least, not with any noticeable ingenuity. Miss Crawford is, of course, an old hand at being an emotionally confused and frustrated woman and she plays the role with easy competence. Henry Fonda, too, is likable but somewhat more sympathetic and passive than a husband in such circumstances has any right to be. As the philandering father, Dana Andrews gives a performance that is full of vitality and technical grace, but it lacks authority. Mr. Andrews, somehow, just doesn't appear to be the type. As the producer-director of *Daisy Kenyon,* Otto Preminger keeps the film going at a nice clip and this helps greatly to gloss over the threadbare portions of the narrative, which would be a lot more obvious in the hands of less attractive players."

T. M. P., *The New York Times*

who sits and waits while one of those slick magazine females goes through all kinds of amorous complications before finally realizing that true love and happiness are waiting for her right there at home in the person of Mr. Fonda. Daisy Kenyon was Joan Crawford and we followed her affair with married Dana Andrews,

Henry Fonda, Joan Crawford, Ruth Warrick, Peggy Ann Garner, Walter Winchell, and Dana Andrews

Henry Fonda, James Stewart, and Dorothy Ford

A Miracle Can Happen

United Artists. 1948. Produced by Benedict Bogeaus, Burgess Meredith. Directed by King Vidor, Leslie Fenton. Uncredited directors of Fonda-Stewart sequence were George Stevens, John Huston. Screen play by Laurence Stallings, Lou Beslow, based on original story by Arch Oboler. Original material for Fonda-Stewart sequence by John O'Hara.

HENRY FONDA played *Lank* in a cast that also included: (in this sequence) James Stewart, Harry James, Eduardo Ciannelli, Dorothy Ford; (in other portions of film) Burgess Meredith, Paulette Goddard, Fred Mac-Murray, Hugh Herbert, Dorothy Lamour, Victor Moore, Eilene Janssen, William Demarest, Charles D. Brown, Betty Caldwell, David Whorf, Frank Moran, Tom Fadden, Paul Hurst.

THE PICTURE: *A Miracle Can Happen*—its title was changed to *On Our Merry Way* after its initial release—was one of those hodge-podges in which rickety short stories are tied together to provide an excuse for using a gaggle of stars. The device in this case was the question of an inquiring reporter, "How has a child changed your life?" It was hopelessly hokey and submerged the talents involved.

The one exception was the sequence in which Fonda and his old friend James Stewart—here teamed for the first time—played two footloose jazz musicians mixed up with a shapely "baby" in a bathing suit. Their performances were sharply observed and only slightly caricatured and their material was a healthy cut above that of the rest of the picture, since it was written especially for them by John O'Hara. Fonda and Stewart, given their choice of writer and director, also picked John Huston for the latter assignment. But Huston had completed only one segment of their section when work had to stop because of previous Fonda commitments. When he returned, Huston was no longer available. Their choice to direct the body of the section was George Stevens, who brought all of his slapstick comedy training to the hilarities of the particular spot. At their request, neither Stevens nor Huston received screen credit but they should have taken it—their part of the picture was a bright oasis in a dreary desert.

THE CRITICS
"The pleasure of the actors seems to be a great deal

James Stewart, Burgess Meredith,
and Henry Fonda

more satisfying than that which the audience can expect, allowing for one burlesque episode in which James Stewart and Henry Fonda appear. Playing a couple of beat-up bandsmen who get themselves into a hilarious mess with a supposedly 'fixed' music contest, Mr. Stewart and Mr. Fonda whip a purely ridiculous script into an act of low comedy mugging that is a good bit of slapstick fun."

Bosley Crowther, *The New York Times*

"In this, their only film together, the two old friends romp through an extremely silly but also quite funny vignette about two luckless jazz musicians."

Peter Bogdanovich,
New Yorker Fonda Festival Program Notes

"Fonda enlivened the otherwise dispensable *On Our Merry Way* with a side-splitting impersonation of a jazz trumpeter on a rocking rowboat, and don't ask me why or how he got there, blowing himself into a volcanic eruption of *mal-de-mer*."

Andrew Sarris, *The Village Voice*

James Stewart and Henry Fonda

*George O'Brien and Ward Bond
with the dying Henry Fonda*

Fort Apache

Argosy-RKO Radio. 1948. Directed by John Ford. Produced by Ford and Merian C. Cooper. Screen play by Frank S. Nugent, suggested by the story "Massacre" by James Warner Bellah.

HENRY FONDA played *Col. Owen Thursday* in a cast that also included: John Wayne, Shirley Temple, Pedro Armendariz, Ward Bond, George O'Brien, John Agar, Victor McLaglen, Anna Lee, Irene Rich, Miguel Inclan, Jack Pennick, Grant Withers, Dick Foran, Guy Kibbee.

THE PICTURE: Henry Fonda as a ramrod martinet, inflexible and all Army. It was an unlikely a piece of casting as you'd be apt to imagine, and Fonda fans hated it. But he played the role with chilly authority and made you forget that he had ever portrayed such winsome fellows as Chad Hanna and young Abe Lincoln. It was an uncompromising characterization with no attempt to turn the colonel into one of those lovable, if misguided, types.

Here, Fonda, as Col. Owen Thursday, had to deal with such problems as a rebellious daughter and some sloppy, undisciplined troops before getting involved with the warring Apaches. John Wayne, Ward Bond, Pedro Armendariz, Victor McLaglen were more in the style of the usual John Ford drinking and brawling military types. Here was also Shirley Temple in one of her first adult roles, romancing with John Agar, her real-life husband at the time. And the supporting cast was loaded with the kind of once-names—Irene Rich, George O'Brien, Anna Lee, Grant Withers, Dick Foran, Guy Kibbee—that Ford so often gives another chance.

This was Fonda's last film before returning to the stage for *Mister Roberts,* and by the time his cold-hearted military man was seen on the screen, he was already warming the hearts of Broadway audiences with his portrayal of the most beloved officer of them all.

THE CRITICS
"Apparent in this picture, for those who care to look, is a new and maturing viewpoint upon one aspect of the American Indian wars. For here it is not the 'heathen Indian' who is the 'heavy' of the piece but a hard-bitten Army colonel, blind through ignorance and

*Henry Fonda with John Wayne,
George O'Brien, and Ward Bond*

a passion for revenge. . . . For the standard movie audience *Fort Apache* will chiefly provide a handsome and thrilling outdoor drama of 'war' on the American frontier—a salty and sizzling visualization of regimental life at a desert fort, of strong masculine personality and of racing battles beneath the withering sun. For, of course, Mr. Ford is a genius at directing this sort of thing and Frank S. Nugent has ably supplied him with a tangy and workable script. . . . Mr. Ford never disappoints us. Every episode, every detail of drama and personality is crisply and tautly realized. . . . Performing this dandy panorama of frontier cavalry life is a cast which, in every aspect, is nigh impeccable. Henry Fonda is withering as the colonel, fiercely stubborn and stiff with gallantry, and John Wayne is powerful as his captain, forthrightly and exquisitely brave. . . . In his rich blend of personality, of the gorgeously picturesque outdoor Western scenery, of folk music and intrinsic sounds, plus his new comprehension of frontier history, Mr. Ford here again fires keen hope that he will soon turn his unsurpassed talents to a great and sweeping drama of the west."

Bosley Crowther, *The New York Times*

Henry Fonda and Irene Rich lead the Grand March (Shirley Temple, Ward Bond, George O'Brien, Anna Lee, Victor McLaglen, Dick Foran, Mae Marsh, and Jack Pennick, among others).

Henry Fonda and Shirley Temple

"When Ford is dealing with fighting men, horses and vivid scenic pageantry, the film has pulse and dramatic power. Unfortunately he has lingered too long over a conventional narrative. . . . As usual Ford has assembled knowing character actors to carry the main line of the story. Although a star, Henry Fonda uses his rich acting background to make the ambitious Colonel Thursday a striking figure, as he apologizes to his officers before Chief Cochise and his warriors wipe them out. John Wayne is excellent as a captain who escapes the slaughter and protects his superior's name for the sake of the service and Pedro Armendariz, Ward Bond, Victor McLaglen, Irene Rich and Anna Lee never miss a trick. *Fort Apache* is a visually absorbing celebration of violent deeds. It is not one of John Ford's better achievements."

Howard Barnes, *New York Herald Tribune*

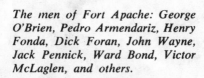

The men of Fort Apache: George O'Brien, Pedro Armendariz, Henry Fonda, Dick Foran, John Wayne, Jack Pennick, Ward Bond, Victor McLaglen, and others.

Jigsaw

United Artists. 1949. Directed by Fletcher Markle. Produced by Edward J. and Harry Lee Danziger. Screen play by Fletcher Markle and Vincent O'Connor from a story by John Roeburt.

HENRY FONDA played an unbilled bit in a cast which included: Franchot Tone, Jean Wallace, Myron McCormick, Marc Lawrence, Winifred Lenihan, Betty Harper, Hedley Rainnie, Walter Vaughn, George Breen, Robert Gist, Hester Sondergaard, Luella Gear, Alexander Campbell, Robert Noe, Alexander Lockwood, Ken Smith, Alan Macateer.

THE PICTURE: While Fonda was playing in *Mister Roberts,* he and other stars took bit parts in a film made in New York as a favor to its star, their friend, Franchot Tone.

THE CRITICS

Bosley Crowther, in *The New York Times,* disliked the film and added, "An irresistible temptation to get a few recognizable stars to play bit roles in the picture was accepted unfortunately. John Garfield is seen as a loafer, Henry Fonda as a waiter in a club, Burgess Meredith as a bartender, Marsha Hunt a secretary, Marlene Dietrich as a patron, and such. This tom-foolery doesn't help the picture. It gives the whole thing a faintly prankish look."

Fonda in a guest appearance with Betty Harper and Franchot Tone

Fonda and the Captain's palm tree

Mister Roberts

Warner Bros. 1955. Directed by John Ford and Mervyn LeRoy. Produced by Leland Hayward. Screen play by Frank Nugent and Joshua Logan, based on the play by Thomas Heggen and Joshua Logan.

HENRY FONDA played *Lt. Douglas Roberts* in a cast that also included: James Cagney, William Powell, Jack Lemmon, Betsy Palmer, Ward Bond, Phil Carey, Nick Adams, Harry Carey, Jr., Pat Wayne, Ken Curtis, Frank Aletter, Fritz Ford, Buck Kartalian, William Henry, Stubby Kruger, Harry Tenbrook, Perry Lopez, Robert Roark, Tiger Andrews, Jim Moloney, Denny Niles, Francis Conner, Shug Fisher, Danny Borzage, Jim Murphy, Kathleen O'Malley, Maura Murphy, Mimi Doyle, Jeanne Murray, Lonnie Pierce.

THE PICTURE: In the seven years since he had last been seen on screen, Henry Fonda had never been idle. First there was his long-run in one of the most popular plays ever brought to Broadway, *Mister Roberts*. Then he had two more solid and distinguished Broadway characterizations—in *Point of No Return* and in *The Caine Mutiny Court Martial*.

But by the time *Mister Roberts* was ready for transfer to the screen, its producer, Leland Hayward, was talking in terms of such hot box-office names as Marlon Brando or William Holden for the film title role. Fonda,

he had decided, had been too long away from films—he was a stage star now.

To the everlasting credit of director John Ford, he would have none of it. If Henry Fonda did not recreate his role on the screen, he made it plain, they would have to do without John Ford, as well.

It would be pleasant to report that Fonda and Ford, reunited, made the picture they wanted to make and that everyone lived happily ever after. Sadly, it did not work out that way. From the beginning of the filming, the once good friends were at serious odds over the making of the picture. Fonda, after being so long a part of it, regarded the original play almost as sacred. He resented what he felt were Ford's attempts to overplay laugh scenes and to turn the crew of the *Reluctant* into a brawling, low-comedy group. The antagonism between star and director finally exploded, it is said, into an actual fistfight.

Shortly after this, Ford left the film because of illness and Mervyn LeRoy took over. It was an unhappy ending to the association of two great talents who had done such memorable work together. Fonda and Ford still speak of each other with affection and respect, but there has been no reconciliation.

Perhaps *Mister Roberts* purists did feel that, in the screen version, the sentiment was spread on a little too thickly and that the comedy may have been a little

William Powell, Henry Fonda, and Jack Lemmon

overboard. *Mister Roberts,* on the screen, used six girls where one had done nicely on the stage, and its drunken leave sequence comes perilously close to slapstick. But the reservations about the film were shared by only a few—audiences all over the world adored it. James Cagney as the Captain, Jack Lemmon as Ensign Pulver, and William Powell as Doc, were all quite right and Fonda, in spite of his personal unhappiness about the picture, was once again ideal.

THE CRITICS

"It's hard to believe that *Mister Roberts* is a work of fiction, that Roberts is only a character invented by Thomas Heggen. By now he seems like a real person—someone we know quite well. It's also easy to think of the *Reluctant* as a real ship and to feel that we know its curious inmates—the peevish captain, the gentle Doc, the lecherous Pulver and the whole crew of sex-starved sailors. Perhaps this is why *Mister Roberts* is a modern classic. Two people in particular have put together this vivid image. One is Joshua Logan, who collaborated with Heggen on the play and directed it with a subtle mixture of gusto and tenderness. The other is Henry Fonda, who seems not to be acting Mister Roberts but

Roberts makes a deal with the Captain (James Cagney)

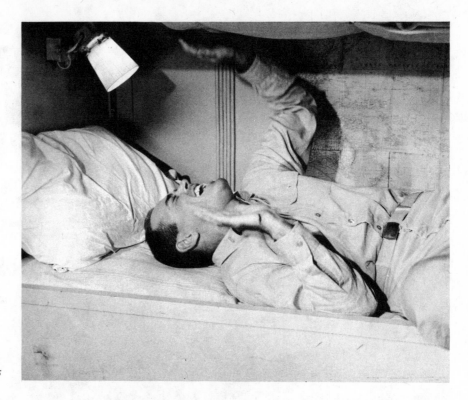

Henry Fonda as Mister Roberts

to be Mister Roberts. Actor and character have long since blended into one. Both are back on the job in the movie. Fonda is giving the same magnificent performance and Logan collaborated with Frank Nugent on a screen play that retains all of the values of the original. It is enormously funny; it is sensitive, and it is very moving. It shifts magically from rowdy humor to deep emotion, and back. . . . It's hard to say whether the men who made the movie gave it this extra depth, or whether we bring our own emotion to this story every time we meet it. It doesn't matter. The main thing is that it doesn't disappoint those of us who have prized the play. That's a high tribute to its producer, Leland Hayward, to directors John Ford and Mervyn LeRoy, and to the many fine actors."

William K. Zinsser, New York Herald Tribune

Between scenes James Cagney entertains William Powell, Henry Fonda, Ward Bond, and Jack Lemmon

— 153 —

Fonda and the binoculars

"Fonda is perfect as Roberts. He has all the qualities of quiet leadership that make the men revere him; he has the maturity to win the friendship of the older Doc, and his passive resistance to red tape and hokum is the most nettling thing the Captain has ever known. His humor is subtle, especially when he needles the indolent Pulver, and his earnest wish to catch up with the war gives his character great depth. Fonda creates this complex man with deceptive ease. . . . Since Henry Fonda already has earned his stripes as Mr. Roberts on stage, it should be noted that he does not simply give the role a professional reading. It now appears as though he *is* Mr. Roberts. It evolves as a beautifully lean and sensitive characterization, full of dignity and power."

Bosley Crowther, *The New York Times*

"*Mister Roberts* has had a lot of people working on it during its long trip from Thomas Heggen's popular book to Heggen's and Logan's hit Broadway play and on to Nugent's and Logan's screen play. Leland Hayward stayed with it as producer all the way and Henry has made a full-scale career out of the title role, but many others have entered the act without changing it noticeably. . . . Fonda doesn't create Roberts; he is the man. . . . On one occasion the movie broadens its scope to include the slapstick of a motorcycle roaring off the end of a pier into the water. Even this is acceptable within the broad, sardonic confines of this rear-end view of a war effort."

Archer Winsten, *New York Post*

War and Peace

Paramount. 1956. Directed by King Vidor. Produced by Dino DeLaurentiis. A Ponti-DeLaurentiis Production. Screen play by Bridget Boland, King Vidor, Robert Westerby, Mario Camerini, Ennio De Concini, Ivo Perilli, based on the novel by Leo Tolstoy.

HENRY FONDA played *Pierre* in a cast that also included: Audrey Hepburn, Mel Ferrer, Vittorio Gassman, John Mills, Herbert Lom, Oscar Homolka, Anita Ekberg, Helmut Dantine, Barry Jones, Anna Maria Ferrero, Milly Vitale, Jeremy Brett, May Britt, Lea Seidl, Sean Barrett, Tullio Carminati, Wilfred Lawson.

THE PICTURE: "I knew I was physically all wrong for Pierre," says Henry Fonda. "But I decided that, with the right kind of spectacles, some strategically placed padding and my hair combed forward, I could pass. Then it seems that they didn't want a Pierre who looked like Pierre. One who looked like Rock Hudson is closer to what they had in mind. They went into nervous shock when they saw my original makeup. The padding went immediately—over my anguished protests. And, from that point on, it was a constant struggle between the producer and me as to whether or not I'd wear the spectacles. I won about half the time—usually when he was nowhere near the set." Fonda may have been unhappy that his Pierre could not more closely resemble the characterization he had planned. But *Time,* for instance, said of him that he "sometimes gives the impression of being the only man in the huge cast who has read the book."

In spite of *Time,* however, Audrey Hepburn was quite a lovely Natasha and the others in a fine cast were, for the most part, effective. Certainly this version, at three-hours-and-a-half, may not have had the fullness of the marathon Russian production that was to come

Henry Fonda, May Britt,
Audrey Hepburn, and Barry Jones

Henry Fonda as Pierre

a decade later but it also avoided the long, dragging sequences that were part of the later picture. In an opulent physical production, moments stand out in the memory—a duel in a white winter morning . . . a whirling ballroom scene . . . and, more particularly, the stunning sequences of battle and of Napoleon's retreat from Moscow. The production cost a reported $6,000,000 and looked it. King Vidor's handling, particularly of the spectacular scenes, was impressive.

THE CRITICS

"*War and Peace* is a superb film, well worth waiting

for. . . . This is a story of such vast scale that it is constantly fascinating. In broad outline it is like a Homeric epic. It tells of entire nations convulsed by war. . . . Audrey Hepburn, as Natasha, has the irresistible radiance of youth. She is very beautiful and she has a shining exuberance. . . . At the end there is a maturity about her, a compassion, that is very touching. And yet she has not lost the gaiety that was so captivating when she was young and life was a game. This is a rare and subtle feat of acting. A fleeting look in her eyes can express all the pain of growing up. Certainly it is the best feminine performance of the year. . . . Pierre is

Fonda and John Mills

Mel Ferrer and Henry Fonda

played by Henry Fonda. It is a wonderfully gentle performance. He is certain of nothing. He always asks questions. He wants to know 'what happiness is, what value there is in suffering, why 'men go to war' and all the other answers. He goes about his search with a clumsiness that would be comic if it were not so desperately earnest. Once he blunders into a pistol duel and, in the bleak light of a winter sunrise, accidentally wins it. He straggles like a sleepwalker around the battlefields of Borodino, wearing a gray top hat and carrying a yellow flower, to see what war is. Finally, when he trudges as a prisoner with Napoleon's troops on their endless retreat, he achieves the deeper intuition and strength that he has sought at such length and hardship. Fonda builds his role with eloquent restraint. . . . Of course, all of Tolstoy's *War and Peace* is not here. Many characters have been omitted and many have been pared to one dimension. But the essential story remains, and it makes a brilliant movie."

William K. Zinsser, *New York Herald Tribune*

"This tireless and changeless progression through the episodes of Tolstoy's cluttered tale make for an oddly mechanical and emotionally sterile air. The characters

Henry Fonda and Audrey Hepburn (He hated it when they made him step out of Pierre's character to be handsome like this)

seem second-rate people, hackneyed and without much depth. You view them with an objective interest as they do their parade across the screen, giving off little more personal vibrance than the nameless soldiers in the massive scenes of war. . . . Alas the human stories that Tolstoy told so significantly in the book are sketchy and inconsequential, despite the time devoted to them. Naturally Pierre and Natasha emerge as the focal characters but neither is intense or meaningful. Pierre, as played by Mr. Fonda is an amiable, plodding, thoughtful man whose proclaimed intellectual curiosity is uncertainly satisfied. And Natasha, played by Miss Hepburn, is a charming girlish sort whose amorous infatuations with Prince Andrey and the leering Anatole are represented without warmth."

Bosley Crowther, *The New York Times*

"Of the films three stars, only Audrey Hepburn, with her precocious child's head set upon a swanlike neck, looks the part. She is perfectly the Natasha described by Tolstoy. In her playing, Audrey catches the gamine qualities of Natasha and her softness. What is lacking is the steely courage that would let Natasha brand her flesh with a red-hot iron to prove her love. Instead of a total commitment to life, there is more often a quiet acceptance of fate. Mel Ferrer's Prince Andrey has a certain sullen grandeur, but his diction is often unclear, and he is more wooden than reserved, more testy than proud. Henry Fonda's leanness at first seems all wrong for the massive, moon-faced, soul-tortured Pierre. But Fonda builds beautifully into his part, using a physical clumsiness as a counterpoise to his soaring spirit, making his rages seem the more terrible since they flash out from passivity. As he struggles for the answers to the great questions (Why does a man live? Why does he kill? Who owns his loyalty?), Fonda acts to the very limit of his considerable powers, and sometimes gives the impression of being the only man in the huge cast who has read the book."

Time

Henry Fonda and Vera Miles

The Wrong Man

Warner Bros. 1957. Directed by Alfred Hitchcock. Screen play by Maxwell Anderson and Angus MacPhail, from a story by Anderson.

HENRY FONDA played *Manny Balestrero* in a cast that also included: Vera Miles, Anthony Quayle, Harold J. Stone, Charles Cooper, John Heldabrand, Esther Minciotti, Doreen Lang, Laurinda Barrett, Norma Connolly, Nehemiah Persoff, Lola D'Annunzio, Kippy Campbell, Robert Essen, Richard Robbins, Dayton Lummis, Frances Reid, Peggy Webber.

THE PICTURE: *The Wrong Man* was quite an unexpected film from Alfred Hitchcock. Here were no chases through the Statue of Liberty . . . no fights to the death on a runaway carousel . . . no cliffhanging from the nose of a Mount Rushmore president . . . no heart-in-the-mouth anticipation of a cymbal being struck.

For this was not a film of suspense in the usual Hitchcock style. Rather it was stark, unadorned, almost documentary in its treatment of the true story of Manny

Balestrero, the Stork Club musician, wrongly identified as the perpetrator of a series of armed robberies. The film followed his arrest, showed how evidence piled up against this innocent man and detailed the personal tragedies that resulted before he is finally proven innocent when the real thief is caught.

Fonda had played innocent victims of the law before, in pictures like *Let Us Live* and *You Only Live Once,* and played them with bitterness and passion. Here, though, Hitchcock seemed to want him to play as if dazed and uncomprehending. It was effective in its way but, without strong reaction, it seriously cut into the drama inherent in the situation. So *The Wrong Man* became a constantly engrossing study but seldom a very affecting one.

THE CRITICS
"The theory that truth can be more striking than fiction is not too forcibly supported by the saga of *The Wrong Man*. Although he is recounting in almost every clinical detail a startling near-miscarriage of justice, Alfred

Henry Fonda

Sherman Billingsley and Henry
Fonda in Stork Club sequences

Fonda and bit players

after his exoneration, that his wife has been sent to a mental home, ideally revealed this quality in him."

Nathan Cohen, *Toronto Star*

"Henry Fonda was perfect, very natural and just as authentic as any man on the street."

François Truffaut interviewing Alfred Hitchcock from *Hitchcock/Truffaut*, published by Simon and Schuster

"Fonda is magnificent as the Stork Club musician who is arrested for a robbery he did not commit in this brilliant Alfred Hitchcock nightmare—a far more effective vision of a Kafkaesque world than Welles' *The Trial* because it is founded entirely in reality (it is a true story shot entirely on actual locations). Vera Miles is superb as the wife who cracks under the strain. A key Hitchcock, among his most personal and serious works, and one of Fonda's finest performances."

Peter Bogdanovich, New Yorker Theatre Fonda Festival Program Notes

Hitchcock has fashioned a somber case history that merely points a finger of accusation. His principals are sincere and they enact a series of events that actually are part of New York's annals of crime but they rarely stir the emotions or make a viewer's spine tingle. Frighteningly authentic, the story generates only a modicum of drama. . . . In re-enacting the role of the real Manny Balestrero, Henry Fonda gives a disquietingly even portrayal. Only on rare occasions does he depart from a slightly stooped, trancelike attitude as he is arrested, interrogated, finger-printed, booked, jailed and bailed out. However, Vera Miles as his wife whose mind snaps under this sudden shock, does convey a poignantly pitiful sense of fear of the appalling situation into which they have been cast. . . . Mr. Hitchcock has done a fine and lucid job with the facts in *The Wrong Man* but they have been made more important than the hearts and dramas of the people they affect."

A. H. Weiler, *The New York Times*

"Fonda was just as credible in Alfred Hitchcock's *The Wrong Man,* a gritty, unappreciated film based on the true story of a New York jazz musician wrongfully sent to jail. Fonda has a subtle capacity for conveying mute, below the surface, suffering. His reaction to the news,

Nehemiah Persoff, Henry Fonda and Vera Miles

Anthony Perkins and Henry Fonda

The Tin Star

Paramount. 1957. Directed by Anthony Mann. Produced by William Perlberg and George Seaton. Screen play by Dudley Nichols. Based on a story by Barney Slater and Joel Kane.

HENRY FONDA played *Morg Hickman* in a cast that also included: Anthony Perkins, Betsy Palmer, Michel Ray, Neville Brand, John McIntire, Mary Webster, Peter Baldwin, Richard Shannon, Lee Van Cleef, James Bell, Howard Petrie, Russell Simpson, Hal K. Dawson, Jack Kenney, Mickey Finn.

THE PICTURE: *The Tin Star* was a very unpretentious Western. It was also a very good one. With elements of both *Shane* and *High Noon,* it may have been reminiscent of them at times, but Dudley Nichols' screen play was literate and engrossing. Fonda was a loner—a bounty hunter who had once been a sheriff but who had given up the badge in disgust because of the shabby way he had been treated by the townspeople in time of crisis. Anthony Perkins is the sheriff—and a more inept man of the law would be hard to find. The veteran undertakes the education of the youngster. The interplay between the two men and their growing relationship gave the picture stature above the ordinary movie of its type.

THE CRITICS

"That type, the reluctant sheriff, which showed up so bravely in *High Noon* and has since been a chronically recurrent neo-hero in Western films, is with us again in *The Tin Star*. This time he is played by Henry Fonda, and he is just about the most reluctant yet. . . . He doesn't lack courage, that's for certain. His lonesome bounty-hunter in this film, which has been written by the veteran Dudley Nichols, is one of the calmest bravest pokes you ever saw. There may be some low-grade skepticism among the citizens of the ratty Western town, into which he rides saturninely, at the beginning, packing a bad-man's corpse. But there can't be much doubt among the audience. All you have to do is look at his eyes. Mr. Fonda has the steadiest pair of optics of anyone in the trade. He can gaze at somebody for five minutes without the flutter of an eyelash or a nerve. And though the townsfolk may think he is looking at the vision of a $500 bounty claim, anybody who knows Mr. Fonda (and Western movies) can sense he's looking that way because he's brave. . . . This may be a fairly routine story, but it makes for a pretty good show. It is played in that lean, laconic fashion fancied in Western films, and it has plenty of dusty action in it, but you can always see what's going on. Mr. Perkins is a bit too much of a hayseed, but John McIntire is fine

Michel Ray, Henry Fonda, and Betsy Palmer

as the old doc and Neville Brand is real ornery as the bully. Mr. Fonda? What a question! Just look at his eyes!"

Bosley Crowther, *The New York Times*

"There are certain classic ways of beginning a Western and *The Tin Star* is as classic as you can get. Henry Fonda, a lone stranger, comes ridin' slowly into one of those picturesque old towns, past the bank and the hotel, the saloon and the jail, and all the folks turn out to watch. Their curiosity seems justified as a dead man is draped over Fonda's pack horse. . . . These conversations (between Fonda and Perkins) are the heart of the movie, which deals more with character than gunplay, and Dudley Nichols' script has intuition and humor. This is lucky, for the plot of *The Tin Star* is a stereotype at every turn. . . . The two stars bring unusual depth to their roles. Fonda is sincere and appealing. Behind his dirty, unshaven face when he comes to town—and no Western hero can look quite as seedy as Fonda—there obviously lurks a kind and lonely man. As he instructs the boy it is clear that he knows not only his guns but human nature. Perkins is also attractive in his hesitant, self-conscious way, eager as a puppy to be a firm marshal, and almost as inept."

William K. Zinsser, *New York Herald Tribune*

"Once its premise is established, *The Tin Star* is mighty satisfactory frontier drama. Anthony Perkins helps Henry Fonda make it so; the two performances are simpatico, with Perkins looking to the veteran Fonda for leadership. And Fonda gives, but comes out star anyway with his quiet, sure, graceful underplaying."

Irene Thirer, *New York Post*

Anthony Perkins and Henry Fonda

12 Angry Men

United Artists. 1957. Directed by Sidney Lumet. Produced by Henry Fonda and Reginald Rose. Story and screen play by Reginald Rose.

HENRY FONDA played *Juror No. 8* in a cast that also included: Lee J. Cobb, Ed Begley, E. G. Marshall, Jack Warden, Martin Balsam, John Fiedler, Jack Klugman,

Edward Binns, Joseph Sweeney, George Voscovec, Robert Webber, Rudy Bond, James A. Kelly, Bill Nelson, John Savoca.

THE PICTURE: Of all of his films, Henry Fonda takes special pride in *12 Angry Men*. He admired Reginald Rose's original television play and, when he could

Lee J. Cobb and Henry Fonda

The jurors (clockwise from Martin Balsam, standing): John Fiedler, Lee J. Cobb, E. G. Marshall, Jack Klugman, Edward Binns, Jack Warden, Henry Fonda, Joseph Sweeney, Ed Begley, George Voscovec, and Robert Webber.

find no studio interest in a film version, he decided to produce it himself, with Rose as his partner. They selected Sidney Lumet, already a television and theatre director of distinction but without any feature movie credit, to direct and hand-picked a cast of the best New York actors. It was filmed in only twenty days in New York for the unbelievably low budget of $340,000.

12 Angry Men went on to win awards all over the world. It never received anything less than the most laudatory reviews. It is one of the most in-demand of all pictures for showings in schools, colleges and special groups. Its frequent airings on television bring good ratings. Yet this honored picture barely brought back its money, and Fonda, as its producer, has never received a cent of profits or of his deferred salary.

If *12 Angry Men* had been booked into small art theatres, as such a picture would be today, it could undoubtedly have run for months on the strength of its reviews. But, treated as just another commercial release and booked into conventional large movie houses, it never had a chance to find its audiences and closed quickly for lack of them. Rose's play and script was confined to one jury room where twelve men are deciding the fate of a boy who is accused of killing his father. One of them has doubts. Little by little, his calm logic sways others and, in this battle of minds, unexpected motivations and twists of character are revealed. Although Fonda dominated the proceedings as the one reasonable man, it was another instance of his submerging himself as a star to become one of an extra-

Henry Fonda

Eleven jurors face down the last holdout: Warden, Binns, Marshall, Fiedler, Fonda, Begley, Webber, Klugman, Voscovec, Balsam, and Sweeney.

Henry Fonda, producer-star of Twelve Angry Men, *and its director, making his screen debut, Sidney Lumet*

ordinary ensemble of artists. There is no point in singling out other major performances. Just read the cast list. Each actor listed was as good as it is possible for an actor to be. But then the same would apply to every talent involved in the making of this landmark motion picture.

THE CRITICS

"Reginald Rose's excellent film elaboration of his fine television play of 1954, is a penetrating, sensitive and sometimes shocking dissection of the hearts and minds of men who obviously are something less than gods. It makes for taut, absorbing and compelling drama that reaches far beyond the close confines of its jury room setting. Credit the power of this lucid study to the fact that the attributes, failings, passions and prejudices of these talesmen is as striking and important as the awesome truth that they hold a boy's life in their hands. Director Sidney Lumet, who is making his debut in the movie medium and Boris Kaufman, an Academy Award-winning camera man, made expert use of a superb cast, which is ingeniously photographed in what normally would have been static situations. Above all, they have made full use of the trenchant words and ideas of the author to plumb the characters of their principals. . . . Henry Fonda gives his most forceful portrayal in years as the open-minded juror. In being strik-

ingly emotional he is both natural and effective. . . . Messrs. Rose, Lumet, Fonda, *et al.* have kept the fair sex out of their jury room. Although it may seem ungallant, these *12 Angry Men* are all right without distaff glamour. Their dramas are powerful and provocative enough to keep a viewer spellbound."

A. H. Weiler, *The New York Times*

"Henry Fonda has a most reassuring face. Something about the set of the jaw, the leanness of the cheeks, the moodiness of the eyes, inspires respect and confidence. The parts he has played have made him close to an American symbol of the unbiased, uncorrupted man and he is just about perfect for the role of Juror #8 in Reginald Rose's *12 Angry Men.*"

Hollis Alpert, *Saturday Review*

"The other night I saw a private showing of Henry Fonda in *12 Angry Men.* He is magnificent, but the whole cast is made up of excellent actors. As a character study, this is a fascinating movie, but more than that, it points up the fact which too many of us have not taken seriously, of what it means to serve on a jury when a man's life is at stake. In addition, it makes vivid what 'reasonable doubt' means when a murder trial jury makes up its mind on circumstantial evidence."

Eleanor Roosevelt, "My Day"

Henry Fonda, Susan Strasberg, Joan Greenwood, and Christopher Plummer

Stage Struck

RKO-Buena Vista. Directed by Sidney Lumet. Produced by Stuart Millar. Screen play by Ruth and Augustus Goetz, based on the play *Morning Glory* by Zoë Akins.

HENRY FONDA played *Lewis Easton,* in a cast that also included: Susan Strasberg, Joan Greenwood, Christopher Plummer, Herbert Marshall, Sally Gracie, Patricia Englund, Dan Ocko, Jack Weston, Harold Grau, Pat Harrington, Frank Campanella, John Fiedler, Nina Hansen.

THE PICTURE: Primarily out of affection for Sidney Lumet, Henry Fonda agreed to play second fiddle to Susan Strasberg, essaying her first movie starring role after having created something of a Broadway sensation in *The Diary of Anne Frank.*

Stage Struck had other lures for him—the opportunity to film in New York, which he prefers, and a role in which he could play a suave, well-dressed man of the world, a character who had something in common with the off-screen Fonda.

But too many backstage stories about too many young actors seeking Broadway fame had come along since the 1933 *Morning Glory* for this 1958 remake to

Susan Strasberg, Herbert Marshall, and Henry Fonda

Henry Fonda and Susan Strasberg

graphed in vivid and lovely color nearly every nook and cranny connected with the theatre—from poetry-filled Greenwich Village bistros to swank penthouses, from rehearsal calls on bare stages to glamorous, tense first nights, from the fascinating mechanics of backstage operations to the hysteria indigenous to producers' offices and dressing rooms. . . . Director Sidney Lumet, who won his professional spurs with éclat with *12 Angry Men* is no flash in the pan. In shooting the film here in its entirety, he and his cinematographers have captured the singular beauties of a veritable Bagdad-on-the-Hudson. . . . The dialogue of Ruth and Augustus Goetz has caught the character of theatre people. . . . Susan Strasberg is competent as the determined Eva Lovelace. She is petite and fragile and sometimes expressive but strangely pallid in a role that would seem to call for fire, not mere smoldering. . . . Henry Fonda is largely a placid type as the producer who discovers his heart can be reached by love as well as the theatre."

A. H. Weiler, *The New York Times*

"The Goetz' screen play is literate and often penetrating, but it is mortally deficient on real humor. The direction is sometimes attractive, particularly in the opening sequences. . . . But it plays slow and loose when it allows such scenes as Miss Strasberg's recitation of the entire balcony scene . . . Fonda plays with customary quiet authority and disarming command."

Powe, *Variety*

be more than trite. And Miss Strasberg, normally a capable and appealing young actress, was out of her depth, unable to dispel memories of Katharine Hepburn's strongly individual performance in the original.

Stuart Millar selected interesting people for his cast—Joan Greenwood, in her American film debut; Christopher Plummer, in his first picture; Herbert Marshall, returning to the screen. But their roles were conventional and, outside of some exciting Lumet use of New York backgrounds and some brittle theatre talk, there was little of film value in *Stage Struck*.

THE CRITICS

"The moviemakers who here have restaged with reverence Zoë Akins' play and film *Morning Glory* have not come up with a solution to an enigma or a work that is strikingly inspirational. They obviously are devoted people, whose emotions, unfortunately, rarely move a viewer. Perhaps Miss Akins' story has been told too often. The fact is that the bare bones of the plot do not constitute a great revelation in a sophisticated age. The director, scenarists and cast, however, are serious about their assignments. They have searched out and photo-

Susan Strasberg and Henry Fonda

Warlock

20th Century-Fox. 1959. Produced and directed by Edward Dmytryk. Screen play by Robert Alan Aurthur, based on the novel by Oakley Hall.

HENRY FONDA played *Clay Blaisdell* in a cast that also included: Richard Widmark, Anthony Quinn, Dorothy Malone, Dolores Michaels, Wallace Ford, Tom Drake, Richard Arlen, DeForrest Kelley, Regis Toomey, Vaughn Taylor, Don Beddoe, Whit Bissell, J. Anthony

Hughes, Donald Barry, Frank Gorshin, Ian MacDonald, Stan Kamber, Paul Comi, L. Q. Jones, Micky Simpson, Robert Osterloh, James Philbrook, David Garcia, Robert Adler, Joel Ashley, Joe Turkel, Saul Gorse, Bartlett Robinson, Ann Doran.

THE PICTURE: A curiously underrated Western movie, full of dark psychological twists but with the elements of the best Westerns, was *Warlock*. Here

Fonda in a shootout—Anthony Quinn is the gun at the left

Dorothy Malone, Anthony Quinn, and Henry Fonda

Fonda again played an ideal Western hero—a cool, nerveless marshal and the "fastest gun in the West." But there was also Anthony Quinn, curiously cast as his hanger-on, who adores him and lives in the reflection of his glory. Richard Widmark had the third, and much more conventional, lead. Conventional, too, were the roles of the women as played by Dorothy Malone and Dolores Michaels. But, particularly in the strange relationship of the Fonda-Quinn characters, with its hints of latent homosexuality, *Warlock* was something more than just a conventional Western thriller.

THE CRITICS

"It is beginning to look as if a Western can't amount to very much these days unless it's in CinemaScope and color, runs for at least two hours, mixes three or four plots and subplots, and has as many stars. That's how it is with *Warlock*. What's more, it's pretty exciting, once it gets all the plots staked out and its several important characters distributed to their proper sides. For the major conflicts, while not unusual, are fundamental and raw, and a first-rate cast plays them to the limit under Edward Dmytryk's practiced hand.... Hand it

Henry Fonda, Dolores Michaels, and Richard Widmark

Quick-draw Henry Fonda

to Mr. Aurthur and to Mr. Dmytryk. They have put the whole picture together in a straight, precise layout of plots and accumulating action that hold interest up to the big scenes. Then when the shooting commences and climax follows climax—bang, bang, bang—and strong men fight with their emotions, it is good, solid, gripping Western fare. Mr. Fonda, as usual, is excellent—melancholy, laconic and assured—and Mr. Widmark is properly nervous but full of sincerity and spunk. Mr. Quinn lays it on a little heavy in a slightly pathetic role, but he adds his measure of drama to the final rock-bottom goings-on. . . . Incidentally, that title refers to the name of the town where it all takes place, and has nothing to do with male witches, unless there's still a further subplot that we missed."

Bosley Crowther, *The New York Times*

"Big Western. . . . Many of the familiar elements of the western story, the frontier town cowed by unruly elements, the imported lawman with a killer's reputation, the citizens who finally assert themselves to gain control of their community, these are all part of *Warlock*. But

the 20th-Fox presentation is an effort to take such a theme, familiar in its basic outline and carry it beyond the ordinary conclusion and behind the usual facade. . . . The plot, dealing as it does, with very complicated people, is involved, but not puzzling. Aurthur's characters and their dialogue are fresh and picturesque . . . Fonda is particularly fine. It may not be a romantic conception, but Fonda gives his role great validity. It embodies the qualities of mock-chivalric disillusion that characterized some of these members of the 19th Century 'lost generation,' rootless and eventually aimless as the frontier outgrew them. Quinn's brooding performance is menacing and purposely perplexing, given considerable breadth by this actor's native intelligence."

Powe, *Variety*

"His cultured, alienated law officer and killer, with a homoerotic relationship with Anthony Quinn in *Warlock,* a Western of real depth and sophistication, had a steel-like base and bristled with kinetic energy and vivid emotional force."

Nathan Cohen, *Toronto Star*

The Man Who Understood Women

20th Century-Fox. 1959. Directed, produced and written by Nunnally Johnson. From the novel *Colors of the Day,* by Romain Gary.

HENRY FONDA played *Willie Bauche* in a cast that included Leslie Caron, Cesare Danova, Myron McCormick, Marcel Dalio, Conrad Nagel, Edwin Jerome, Bern Hoffman, Harry Elerbe, Frank Cady, Ben Astar.

THE PICTURE: An odd piece of casting put Fonda into the role of a Hollywood "wonder boy"—somewhat of a cross between Orson Welles, Erich von Stroheim and Charles Chaplin—in Nunnally Johnson's *The Man Who Understood Women*. Although the role was unexpected, the Fonda performance was interesting and the picture was fascinating, filled with touches of sly parody, up to a point. Then it degenerated into outlandish, confused melodrama and lost any point of view. Leslie Caron was a lovely Trilby to the Svengali of Mr. Fonda —or, in Hollywood terms, the Dietrich or Hayworth to his Von Sternberg or Welles.

THE CRITICS
"For the first half hour, *The Man Who Understood Women* looks as if it might pan out into a clever and hilarious spoof about Hollywood. The pace is fast, the lines are funny and the overtones of romance promising. What happens after that is something of a mystery. As if Nunnally Johnson couldn't make up his mind in which direction to proceed, the film fusses and fumes, roams between long and dull stretches and then back to exquisitely acted and staged sophistication and humor. . . . The sudden lapses from high comedy to deep drama are confusing and disturbing. One never knows whether Johnson means it or he doesn't. . . . The Fonda character, a key part, is both diffuse and obvious. This isn't Fonda's fault—in fact, he turns in a thoroughly enjoyable performance that mingles aspects of comedy and tragedy—but must be blamed on the script which lets the picture down. . . . Miss Caron is delightful, though her constant changes of mood—as directed—are hard to take. . . . Johnson's direction has a great flair, particularly in the farcical and satirical scenes and he has a way of pulling delightfully impish surprises on the audience. Some of the dialogue lines are very funny, which makes it the more surprising that other passages of the film are so tedious."

Hift, *Variety*

"Johnson is indubitably one of the most talented men

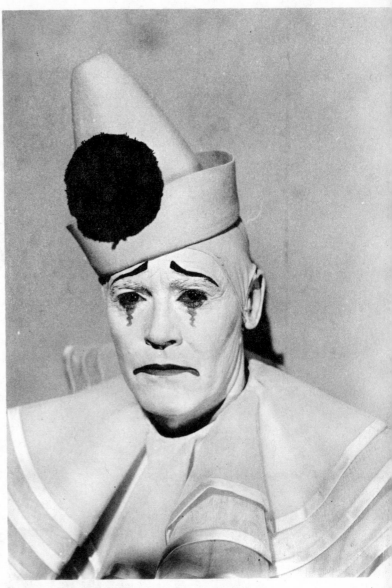

The Henry Fonda character went in for flamboyant impersonations

in Hollywood. . . . In *The Man Who Understood Women* he seems to want to be confidential—about film-makers in and out of Hollywood. I wish I had seen the first rough cut of this picture, for I suspect subsequent editing caused many good things to be left on the cutting room floor. As now being shown, *The Man Who Understood Women* seems to have had its heart cut out. What remains is curious, and below the surface, quite surprising. Some of it is not always coherent and one vital plot-point is never explicated. . . . Fonda does well in his none-too-consistent role, especially in the early, and best, sequences, in which he mocks the Hollywood rat race he has become part of. When he says of himself, only half-truthfully, 'beneath this gaudy haberdashery beats the heart of a simple Methodist,' one

— 173 —

Leslie Caron and Henry Fonda

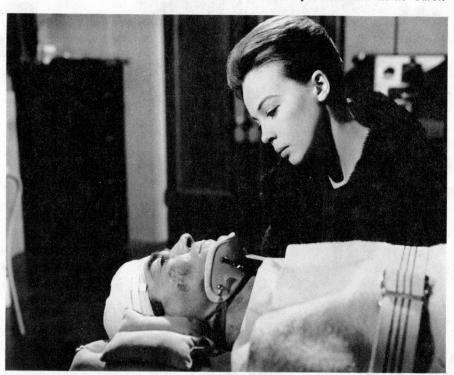

Fonda, the Oscars, and Myron McCormick

hears, or thinks he hears, Nunnally Johnson speaking of himself."

Henry Hart, *Films in Review*

"In a sneak preview of this film at a Manhattan movie theatre, a woman in the roped-off guest section raised her voice in the dark to cry, 'Good heavens, how could Hank have accepted such a role?' There on the screen, prancing awkwardly in mandarin robes, flamenco suits, a clown costume, a silly goatee, was Henry Fonda in the role of Willie Bauche, Hollywood producer-director-writer-actor and the most elaborate phony since the big

bad wolf. Another question is in order. How could a smoothly expert screenwriter like Nunnally Johnson (*The Desert Fox, Three Faces of Eve*) have wrung so much carbonated pap out of a skillfully written Romain Gary novel? . . . The film alternates between unsuccessful farce and success-formula soap opera, but it never quite lives up to its pressagentry as *'twists of tender pathos sublimated by laughter, before the pathos can descend to bathos.' The Man Who Understood Women* is bathos cubed."

Time

Jane Fonda and Anthony Perkins

Tall Story

Warner Bros. 1960. Produced and directed by Joshua Logan. Screen play by J. J. Epstein, based on the play by Howard Lindsay and Russel Crouse and the novel *The Homecoming Game,* by Howard Nemerov.

JANE FONDA played *June Ryder* in a cast that also included: Anthony Perkins, Ray Walston, Marc Connelly, Anne Jackson, Murray Hamilton, Bob Wright, Bart Burns, Karl Lukas, Elizabeth Patterson, Tom Laughlin, Barbara Darrow, Van Williams, Phil Phillips, Ruthie Robinson, Rick Allen.

THE PICTURE: It was just a lark when Jane Fonda joined her father and Dorothy McGuire in an Omaha Community Theatre production of *The Country Girl* and, again, when she played the ingenue role in a Cape Cod production of *The Male Animal,* which also starred her father. She had made it very clear that she had no thought of becoming an actress. But she met the Strasbergs, became exposed to Actors Studio, and her ideas changed.

It was her father's early associate and her own god-father, Joshua Logan, who introduced her as, successively, a stage and screen actress. Neither the play *There Was a Little Girl* nor the movie *Tall Story* found much favor with critics. But Jane Fonda won universal plaudits—not just as the pretty daughter of a distinguished actor, but as a more-than-promising young actress and very much a star in her own right.

Tall Story was a tired little movie about college basketball and gambling and it had been a tired little play before that. No matter. It has its place in the histories as the movie which introduced Jane Fonda and that is reason enough for it to be remembered.

THE CRITICS

"If a tall ear of comedy corn called *Tall Story* barely held up on Broadway, the movie camera really shucks it down to size. . . . With a trim enough little cast, the moviemakers could easily have shifted gears and served

Anthony Perkins, Jane Fonda, Barbara Darrow, and Tom Laughlin

some simple, good-natured fun. Instead we get a frantic attempt at sophistication and a steady barrage of jazzy wisecracks (most of them pretty stale) about campus sex and the business of education.... Though we barely see inside a classroom, at least Faculty Row comes to life at cocktail time, in a steady flow of martinis.... On the court, the gangly Mr. Perkins jounces around convincingly enough. Near Miss Fonda, he generally gapes and freezes, and who can blame him? The pretty newcomer shows charm and promise in her film debut. If Miss Fonda seems to be looking a bit askance, now and then, who can blame her?"

Howard Thompson, *The New York Times*

"Nothing could possibly save the picture, not even the painfully personable Perkins doing his famous awkward act, not even a second-generation Fonda with a smile like her father's and legs like a chorus girl. The lines ('Beget—isn't that a sweet word for it?') are stupefyingly cute, the sight gags frantically unfunny, the climax about as exciting as a soggy sweat sock."

Time

"The picture wouldn't be reviewed in these pages but for the fact that Henry Fonda's daughter, Jane, makes her screen debut in it. She is a good looking lass and she can act.... There are a few moments in this picture, when, in Miss Fonda's eyes, it is possible to see the lineaments of her father. Such moments are rare on the screen and rare in film history."

Ellen Fitzpatrick, *Films in Review*

Anthony Perkins, Marc Connelly, and Jane Fonda

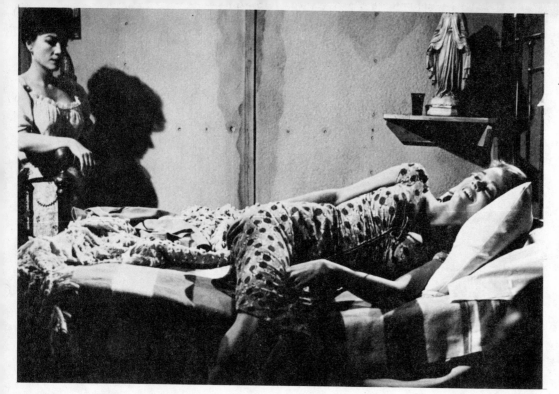

Walk on the Wild Side

Columbia. 1962. Directed by Edward Dmytryk. Produced by Charles K. Feldman. Screen play by John Fante and Edmund Morris, based on the novel by Nelson Algren.

JANE FONDA played *Kitty Twist* in a cast that also included: Laurence Harvey, Capucine, Anne Baxter, Barbara Stanwyck, Joanna Moore, Richard Rust, Karl Swenson, Donald Barry, Juanita Moore, John Anderson, Ken Lynch, Todd Armstrong, Lillian Bronson, Adrienne Marden, Sherry O'Neil, John Bryant, Kathryn Card, Paul Maxey, Virginia Holden, Barbara Hines, Elaine Martone, Pat Tiernan, Florence Wyatt.

THE PICTURE: Again, in another critically-chastised picture, Jane Fonda came off with a few personal laurels. But *Walk on the Wild Side,* related almost not at all to the Nelson Algren novel on which it was "based," was lurid, unbelievable melodrama, filled with lurid, unbelievable characters. In the story of a Texan looking for his lost love and finding her the most popular girl in a bordello, and the beloved of its Lesbian madam, Jane Fonda came off rather better in a peripheral role than did Laurence Harvey, Capucine, Barbara Stanwyck and Anne Baxter as sides of shifting triangles. But the alley cat who prowled through the Saul Bass credits came off best of all.

THE CRITICS

"That cornball from cheap romantic fiction, the prostitute with a heart of gold, staggers through *Walk on the Wild Side* and she has no more substantiality in this instance than she had in the works of the old dime novelists. . . . Everything in this sluggish picture, which Charles K. Feldman has produced from a novel by Nelson Algren (which it doesn't resemble in the least) smacks of sentimentality and social naivete. It is incredible that anything as foolish would be made in this day and age. And the suggestions in advertisements and awesome press releases that there is something 'adult' about it, that it is a little too strong for the kids, are sheer, unadulterated eyewash. It's as naughty as a cornsilk cigarette. There is ever so slight a suggestion that the prostitute is admired by the madam of the bordello. But that this is any more than the admiration of an employer for a highly productive employee is a thing that only the most susceptible to press-agentry might suspect. . . . As the heroine, the tall, thin actress who calls herself Capucine is as crystalline and icy as her elegant mononym. Laurence Harvey is barely one-dimensional and Barbara Stanwyck is like something out of mothballs. Jane Fonda is elaborately saucy and shrill (a poor exposure for a highly touted talent) and Anne Baxter is wasted in a weak role. Edward Dmytryk's direction makes you wonder whether he read

Jane Fonda and Laurence Harvey

Anne Baxter, Jane Fonda, and Laurence Harvey

the script before he started shooting. If he did, he should have yelled."

Bosley Crowther, *The New York Times*

"An excess of violence, bathos and melodramatic cliches. . . . The movie has oversimplified and overstated Algren's novel. The characters seem pretentious, overdone, leading one to take them too seriously on the one hand and not seriously enough on the other. The compassion, the sense of personal waste that could make the film unusual and penetrating instead of usual and paltry, is crowded out by the constant underlining, the strain for violent emphasis, the insistence on vulgarity

rather than precise definition. . . . It is not the actor who is at fault here. Laurence Harvey plays the Texan with more authenticity than one might expect. Capucine, in addition to her natural elegance, here uncovers an infinite capacity for langorous intensity. Jane Fonda is a bouncy, wiggly, bratty little thief and prostitute, seems more like a Nelson Algren character than anyone else in the picture."

Paul V. Beckley, *New York Herald Tribune*

"Jane Fonda cops the show, audiences will say, with her hoydenish behavior."

Gene, *Variety*

Ken Lynch, Jane Fonda, Capucine, Laurence Harvey, and Barbara Stanwyck

Henry Fonda and Don Murray

Advise and Consent

Columbia. 1962. Produced and directed by Otto Preminger. Screen play by Wendell Mayes, based on the novel by Allen Drury.

HENRY FONDA played *Robert Leffingwell* in a cast that also included: Charles Laughton, Don Murray, Walter Pidgeon, Peter Lawford, Gene Tierney, Fronchot Tone, Lew Ayres, Burgess Meredith, Eddie Hodges, Paul Ford, George Grizzard, Inga Swenson, Paul McGrath, Will Geer, Edward Andrews, Betty White, Malcolm Atterbury, J. Edward McKinley, William Quinn, Tiki Santos, Raoul DeLeon, Tom Helmore, Hilary Eaves, Rene Paul, Michele Montau, Raj Mallick, Russ Brown, Paul Stevens, Janet Jane Carty, Chet Stratton, Larry Tucker, John Granger, Sid Gould, Bettie Johnson, Cay Forester, William H. Y. Knighton, Jr., Henry Fountain Ashurst, Hon. Guy M. Gillette.

THE PICTURE: Although Henry Fonda was top-billed in Otto Preminger's *Advise and Consent,* his role was shadowy and his character, a controversial nominee for Secretary of State, seemed abruptly dropped by the script. Actually, in attempting to crowd in as much as possible from Allen Drury's best-selling political novel—and adding a bit to boot—Preminger introduced us to a good dozen major characters and a number of minor ones but gave few of them any real definition. Even so, it was an interesting enough glimpse at political machinations and Washington intrigue and there were some impressive performances, particularly by Charles Laughton, George Grizzard, Don Murray and Burgess Meredith. Fonda had great stature and dignity, of course, and that is what was called for in his role. But it cannot be listed among his stronger film assignments.

THE CRITICS
"*Advise and Consent,* as a novel, play and film, has applied to Washington politics the popular American notion that every public event contains an inside story wildly signaling to be let out. An event treated in this way tends to become polarized either as an exposé, which is a form of ethical idealism, or as gossip and innuendo, which are the scuttlebutt of sensationalism. Neither has much to do with the basic reality of U.S. politics, which is a blended genius for compromising and bargaining. Part of the appeal of Allen Drury's best-selling Pulitzer Prize-winning novel was that it was a tantalizing 'Who's Who of Washington,' a hit-and-run foray among the political movers and shapers of the '40's and early '50's. In Otto Preminger's film, the identity tags

Franchot Tone and Henry Fonda

*Burgess Meredith, Paul Stevens,
and Henry Fonda*

are so blurred as to be almost unintelligible, and the milieu is forced to become the meaning. . . . Compared with the props, the people and situations are strangely unreal, all but bogus. In Preminger's handling, the idealism (the future good of the country) and the sensationalism (the homosexual past of a Senator) split the picture in two, and both stories are melodramatically told not in trenchant filmed images but in thousands and thousands of words. . . . The blandly inconclusive ending is typical of the film. Since none of the characters are properly developed, the actors wrench the roles about to suit their own personalities. Charles Laughton retains his rating as a prime ham's ham. A jowly, jiggling panorama of obesity, Laughton's Seab Cooley drips rhetoric like a honeyed asp. No proof is offered that Leffingwell is fit or unfit to be Secretary of State, but the grieving spaniel eyes of Henry Fonda transmit their customary message: simpleness is next to godliness. Franchot Tone, gasping for life from the first reel, has no more authority than a beached flounder. But George Grizzard's bristly, non-clubbish troublemaker is splendid—and a welcome distraction from all the pious filibustering pother about 'this great body.' "

Time

The Longest Day

20th Century-Fox. 1962. Produced by Darryl F. Zanuck. Directed by Andrew Marton, Ken Annakin, Bernhard Wicki. Associate producer and co-ordinator of battle episodes: Elmo Williams. Screen play by Cornelius Ryan, based on his book. Additional material by Romain Gary, James Jones, David Pursall, Jack Seddon.

HENRY FONDA played *General Roosevelt* in a cast that also included: John Wayne, Robert Mitchum, Robert Ryan, Rod Steiger, Robert Wagner, Richard Beymer, Mel Ferrer, Jeffrey Hunter, Paul Anka, Sal Mineo, Roddy McDowall, Stuart Whitman, Eddie Albert, Edmond O'Brien, Fabian, Red Buttons, Tom Tyron, Alexander Knox, Tommy Sands, Ray Danton, Henry Grace, Mark Damon, Steve Forrest, John Crawford, Ron Randell, Nicholas Stuart, Richard Burton, Kenneth More, Peter Lawford, Richard Todd, Leo Genn, Jack Gregson, Sean Connery, Jack Hedley, Michael Medwin, Norman Rossington, John Robinson, Patrick Barr, Donald Houston, Trevor Reid, Irina Demich, Bourvil, Jean-Louis Barrault, Christian Marquand, Arletty, Madeleine Renaud, Georges Riviere, Georges Wilson, Jean Servais, Fernand Ledoux, Curt Jurgens, Werner Hinz, Paul Hartmann, Peter Van Eyck, Gerd Froebe, Hans Christian Bloech, Wolfgang Preiss, Heinz Reincke, Richard Munch, Ernst Schroeder.

THE PICTURE: Reportedly the most expensive black-and-white movie ever made (over $10,000,000),

The Longest Day was also a giant at the box office. Darryl F. Zanuck produced it independently and is said to have directed most of the interiors of the British and American sequences. An exceptionally strong cast played cameo roles and some of them stood out in spite of the brevity of their roles—Fonda being one and Richard Burton, Robert Mitchum, Jeffrey Hunter, Red Buttons, among others. But all roles were well cast and played. And the picture was one of the most impressive, and seemingly most authentic, documentations of war ever put on film.

THE CRITICS

"All of the massive organization of the Normandy invasion, all the hardship and bloodiness of it, all the courage and sacrifice involved, are strongly and stalwartly suggested in the mighty mosaic of episodes and battle-action details that are packed into this film. . . . No character stands out particularly as more heroic or significant than anyone else. Dozens of actors are convincing (and identifiable) in roles that call for infrequent appearances or only single shots in the film. Intelligently, the picture has been photographed in black-and-white to give a virtual newsreel authenticity to the vivid, realistic battle scenes. . . . The total effect of the picture is that of a huge documentary report, adorned and colored by personal details that are thrilling, amusing, ironic, sad."

Bosley Crowther, *The New York Times*

The Chapman Report

Warner Bros. 1962. A Darryl F. Zanuck production, produced by Richard D. Zanuck. Directed by George Cukor. Screen play by Wyatt Cooper and Don M. Mankiewicz. Adaptation by Grant Stuart and Gene Allen, based on the novel by Irving Wallace.

JANE FONDA played *Kathleen Barclay* in a cast which also included: Efrem Zimbalist, Jr., Shelley Winters, Claire Bloom, Glynis Johns, Ray Danton, Ty Hardin, Andrew Duggan, John Dehner, Harold J. Stone, Corey Allen, Jennifer Howard, Cloris Leachman, Chad Everett, Henry Daniell, Hope Cameron, Roy Roberts, Evan Thompson, John Baer, Jack Cassidy.

THE PICTURE: There was quite a little to-do about the propriety of putting Irving Wallace's best-selling

Claire Bloom, Glynis Johns, Jane Fonda, and Shelley Winters

novel on the screen. Dealing with a Kinseyish team in Los Angeles conducting a survey on the sex habits of American women and with some of their subjects, it was considered rather racy fare for the Hollywood of 1962. (How tame would even the subject matter seem on the screen not more than four years later!)

But even then the picture seemed fairly placid, and the problems of the ladies involved, which ranged from nymphomania to frigidity, were presented without startling innovation. All four of the female stars—Miss Fonda, Shelley Winters, Claire Bloom and Glynis Johns —are expert actresses and George Cukor is an old hand at putting "women's pictures" on the screen. But the filmed result hardly justified the controversy.

THE CRITICS

"A new talent is rising—Jane Fonda. Her light is hardly under a bushel, but as far as adequate appreciation is concerned, she might as well be another Sandra Dee. I have now seen Miss Fonda in three films. In all of them she gives performances that are not only fundamentally different from one another but are conceived without acting cliché and executed with skill. Through them all can be heard, figuratively, the hum of that magnetism without which acting intelligence and technique are admirable but uncompelling. . . . In *The Chapman Report,* which (to put it in a phrase) is not up to the level of the novel, she plays a frigid young middleclass widow. The girl's pathological fear of sex, exacerbated by her hunger for love, is expressed in neurotic outbursts that cut to the emotional quick, with a truth too good for the material. . . . It would be unfair to Miss Fonda and the reader to skimp her sex appeal. Not conventionally pretty, she has the kind of blunt startling features and generous mouth that can be charged with passion, or the cartoon of passion as she chooses. Her slim, tall figure has thoroughbred gawky grace. Her voice is attractive and versatile; her ear for inflections is secure. What lies ahead of this gifted and appealing young actress? With good parts in good plays and films, she could develop into a first-rate artist. Meanwhile, it would be a pity if her gifts were not fully appreciated in these lesser, though large, roles."

Stanley Kauffmann, *The New Republic*

"Nothing to report. . . . In the end, kindly Dr. Chapman explains that figures show that most U.S. wives are actually awfully good sorts, and the latest local sampling should not be taken too seriously. Neither should *The Chapman Report.*"

Time

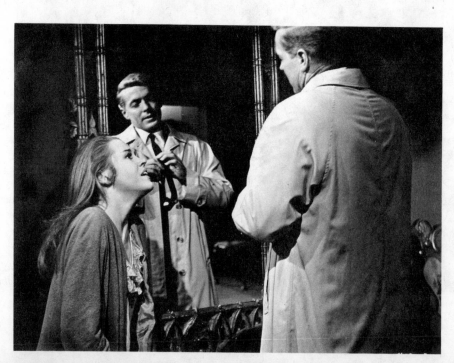

Jane Fonda and John Baer

Anthony Franciosa and Jane Fonda

Period of Adjustment

MGM. 1962. Directed by George Roy Hill. Produced by Lawrence Weingarten. Screen play by Isobel Lennart based on the play by Tennessee Williams.

JANE FONDA played *Isabel Haverstick* in a cast that also included: Tony Franciosa, Jim Hutton, Lois Nettleton, John McGiver, Mabel Albertson, Jack Albertson.

THE PICTURE: Nobody would include *Period of Adjustment* among the major Tennessee Williams plays. But had it been written by another playwright, it is doubtful that it would have been kissed off by the critics and public as it was in its 1961 Broadway run. Brought to the screen a year later, it remained a perceptive and intelligent comedy, given additional wit by Isobel Lennart's screenplay.

The plot line detailed the "period of adjustment" in the marriages of two couples—a nervous pair of honeymooners and a longer-married twosome on the verge of breaking up. Tony Franciosa, heretofore a rather intense type, showed warmth and comic flair as the veteran, Lois Nettleton was appealing as his wife and John McGiver amusingly blustering as her father. Jane Fonda and Jim Hutton played the honeymooners—he quite likeable, and Miss Fonda bewitching in a role that gave her a little more chance to sparkle than had her other dreary dramas of the year. George Roy Hill, who also directed the original play, made an impressive debut as a movie director.

THE CRITICS
"A tart little motion picture. . . . Since this is the kind of study in human relations they know how to make in Hollywood, it is put on and played in proper fashion:

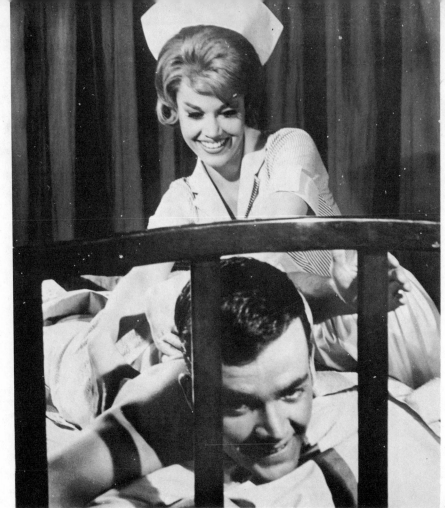

Jane Fonda

much better, we would say, than it was on the Broadway stage. Jane Fonda is appropriately shallow and jittery. Her vague emotions and wispy feelings seem no deeper than her goose-pimples which are revealed in some strangely familiar acting. Could it be the late Marilyn Monroe that Miss Fonda seems to resemble? She surely won't mind our saying so. Jim Hutton is apt as her husband, gangling and comical, obviously removed from boyhood by only two or three feet of added height. Tony Franciosa (it used to be Anthony) toils through the role of the six-year husband with charm and authority. A new girl, Lois Nettleton, is sweet as his slightly vapid wife and John McGiver is beautifully crude and snarly as her meanly possessive dad. Isobel Lennart's screen play adds a few mild embellishments and George Roy Hill has directed in a nice, clear, uncomplicated way. The humor and pathos of 'adjusting' by clumsy young people is fairly put. The only questions are whether it's worth their efforts and whether it's worth your money to watch them fight."

Bosley Crowther, *The New York Times*

"In Tennessee Williams' comedy, *Period of Adjustment*, which is amusing enough, Jane Fonda plays a nervous Southern bride, anxious in more than one sense. Her

Jane Fonda

comic touch is as sure as her serious one. Besides the gift of timing, she has what lies below all comedy: confidence in one's perception of the humorous—where it begins and, especially, where it ends. Her performance is full of delights, like the moment when the desolate bride telephones her father long-distance and her tears flood out as she manages to gasp: 'Precious Daddy!' "

Stanley Kauffmann, *The New Republic*

"In 1960, with the sly delight of a cannibal devouring a cookie, Shock Merchant Tennessee Williams shocked everyone by writing a play about normal people. Well, almost normal. . . . As a marriage counselor, Williams is somewhat less than convincing, but as a carpenter of situation comedy, he knows his trade—and so does Director George Roy Hill. Furthermore, the film is favored with the fine young foolishness of Jim Hutton and Jane Fonda, and with one brutal bit of Williamsy whimsey, interpolated by Scenarist Isobel Lennart, that catches in a phrase the horror of filial relations in a Spock-marked generation. Only once in the entire film does the father speak in a soothing, amiable tone of voice to his son. "Hello, son," he says. The little boy flinches, glances about guiltily, and then in querulous confusion replies: 'I'm not biting my nails.' "

Time

Jim Hutton and Jane Fonda

How the West Was Won

MGM-Cinerama. 1963. Directed by Henry Hathaway, John Ford, George Marshall. Produced by Bernard Smith. Screen play by James R. Webb, based on the *Life* Magazine series.

HENRY FONDA played *Jethro Stuart* in a cast which also included: Spencer Tracy, Carroll Baker, Lee J. Cobb, Carolyn Jones, Karl Malden, Gregory Peck, George Peppard, Robert Preston, Debbie Reynolds, James Stewart, Eli Wallach, John Wayne, Richard Widmark, Brigid Bazlen, Walter Brennan, David Brian, Andy Devine, Raymond Massey, Agnes Moorehead, Harry Morgan, Thelma Ritter, Mickey Shaughnessy, Russ Tamblyn, Tudor Owens, Barry Harvey, Jamie Ross, Kimm Charney, Brian Russell, Claude Johnson, Jerry Holmes, Rudolph Acosta.

THE PICTURE: Cinerama had been the "ooh-ahh!" medium of movies which overpowered you with its bigness and gave the audience the feeling that it was actually on a wild rollercoaster ride or hedge-hopping in a plane. For these kinds of tricks, Cinerama had stuck to documentaries and travelogues, where the seams that joined the three simultaneous pictures that made up the big screen, and the difference in shading between them, would not be so obvious.

Finally, though, the time came to try a "story" picture in the medium—the technical problems having been toned down, if not vanquished. As the kickoff picture in Cinerama, they presented, *The Wonderful World of the Brothers Grimm,* a children's picture with plenty of fantasy. And shortly afterward came the big one. *How the West Was Won* was loaded with runaway trains, buffalo stampedes, peril on the churning river rapids and as many other excitements as could be crowded into near three hours of film. To put this all on screen, they enlisted the services of three old-hand directors—Henry Hathaway, John Ford and George Marshall—and a couple of dozen top and second-flight stars.

But, of course, there had to be a story, and there was the rub. The screenplay was a compendium of just about every cliché known to the history of Western movies and, although it was fun to see all those stars get into all that action on that big, big screen, the picture wound up as pretty old sombrero.

Characters played by Debbie Reynolds and George

Peppard carried through the entire picture, with most of the other stars limited to spots in specific sequences. Henry Fonda, with flowing hair and mustaches and looking something like an early hippie, was virtually unrecognizable as a grizzled buffalo hunter—that is, until he walked. Nobody's else has Fonda's graceful lope. Some of his role was cut—he figured in the romance of Peppard with Hope Lange, who played a saloon girl who was the daughter of the Fonda character. This episode and Miss Lange's entire role were eliminated from the finished picture. Stars like Robert Preston, Gregory Peck, James Stewart, John Wayne, Richard Widmark and a number of others had similar short but meaty roles. And the picture lined them up at the box office.

THE CRITICS

"Cinerama has always been big, but now it's bigger, not that it is any broader or any higher, but that the movie *How the West Was Won* has given it dramatic dimensions that it never had.... *How the West Was Won* is for everybody, not only a tribute to the American past, but to American movie-making."

Paul V. Beckley, *New York Herald Tribune*

"Everything is a dutiful duplication of something you have already seen in one to a thousand Western movies in the last sixty years. . . . In short, what's been done is to stitch together a mammoth patchwork of Western fiction clichés. With little or no imagination and, indeed, with no pictorial style, they have fashioned a lot of random episodes, horribly written, into a mat of outdoor vignettes that tell you nothing of history. . . . All in

Henry Fonda

all, an excellent opportunity to do a real historical drama of the West was wasted in this Hollywoodsy 'epic.' It should be called *How the West Was Done—to Death.*"

Bosley Crowther, *The New York Times*

Fonda and Indians

Henry Fonda

Spencer's Mountain

Warner Bros. 1963. Produced, directed and written by Delmer Daves. Based on the novel by Earl Hamner, Jr.

HENRY FONDA played *Clay Spencer* in a cast that also included: Maureen O'Hara, James MacArthur, Donald Crisp, Wally Cox, Mimsy Farmer, Virginia Gregg, Lillian Bronson, Whit Bissell, Hayden Rorke, Kathy Bennett, Dub Taylor, Hope Summers, Ken Mayer, Bronwyn Fitzsimmons, Barbara McNair, Buzz Henry, Larry Mann, Jim O'Hara, Victor French, Michael Greene, Med Florey, Ray Savage, Mike Henry, Veronica Cartwright, Susan Young, Michele Daves, Michael Young, Rocky Young, Gary Young, Ricky Young, Kym Karrath.

THE PICTURE: When Henry Fonda signed with a new agency, after the dissolution of his long-time representatives, M.C.A., he agreed to follow their advice about the number of pictures he would do in relation to the number of plays, which he prefers. He immediately insisted on going through with a commitment to star in

A Gift of Time, a play in which he believed, even though his agency, quite correctly as it turned out, forecast that audiences would not want to see a play about a man dying of cancer.

When the play closed, the agency insisted that Fonda sign for the movie, *Spencer's Mountain,* even though he protested vehemently and insisted that "the script is old-fashioned corn—it will set movies back twenty-five years." But he consented to honor his agreement.

While working on the picture, which he continued to loathe, he picked up a New York paper in his agent's office and commented on an item. "I see that young Albee has a play opening in New York tonight. What a great talent! I loved those short plays of his."

"Oh, Albee," commented the agent. "He wanted you to do this play but we turned it down."

FONDA: "But why do you turn down plays for me without even letting me know? You know, I'm always looking for a good one."

James MacArthur, Henry Fonda, and Maureen O'Hara

AGENT: "We felt you should do this picture. And this play won't run—there's nothing to it except a husband and wife fighting with each other."

The play, of course, was *Who's Afraid of Virginia Woolf?* Fonda was hardly mollified when the reviews came out and even less happy when friends like Jimmy Stewart, Joshua Logan and his daughter, Jane, returned from New York, excited about the play and stating that they thought of Fonda all the time they were watching it.

Albee, told of the incident, commented, "I had sent the play right to Fonda—it's the first time I really had a star in mind—and I was so hurt when it was sent back without a word from him."

As soon as he finished the hated *Spencer's Mountain,* Fonda returned to New York and went the first night to the theatre. "I sat there, sliding further and further down in my seat. I think I would have given up any role I've ever played—Tom Joad or Mister Roberts, any of them—to have had a chance at that part. And I couldn't even say, 'This should have been my part!' because, up on that stage, Arthur Hill was giving an absolutely perfect performance."

Henry Fonda and Maureen O'Hara

(When "Virginia Woolf" was to be filmed, there was talk of Fonda's playing George opposite Bette Davis, with Fred Zinnemann directing. When Zinnemann backed out and Elizabeth Taylor was set, there was talk of Fonda again. He is a particular favorite actor of both Miss Taylor and of director Mike Nichols. But Richard Burton was persuaded to take the screen role and that was the last of Henry Fonda and *Who's Afraid of Virginia Woolf?*)

About *Spencer's Mountain*—it was just as successful at the box office as the agents predicted it would be. And, as a picture, it justified all of Fonda's worst fears.

THE CRITICS

"As pointless a package of piety and prurience as has been concocted in quite a while, and everybody connected with its creation and exhibition ought to be strung up—or just made to sit through it with their eyes open. . . . The leitmotif for the film is set early on when the folks gather round to watch a bull and a heifer mate and when Paw Henry Fonda, an inveterate non-churchgoer makes friends with the new minister. And from that point on, the folks seem to spend most of their time either prayin' or playin' around with propagation in view. . . . Despite some pretty natty kitchen equipment, a sitting room right out of *Better Homes and Gardens,* and Paw's never lacking for whiskey or poker money, the Spencers seem to operate on the economic as well as cultural level of Tobacco Road folk.

There's just one crisis after another in their various attempts to raise money but Maw manages through it all to retain her Charles of the Ritz-Bergdorf Country Casual outward appearance, despite a couple of tearful outbursts. Anger is fired by the realization that this movie is being offered as 'wholesome' entertainment, as embodying the American dream, let alone presenting a lovable group of real, folksy Americans. And oh, how very American it is! America the beautiful—a Negro girl sings, every verse of it, in fact, at the tiny outdoor high school ceremony—even though we can only conclude that she parachuted down for it; there's not another Negro face or family in the community. You can trust writer Delmar Daves to reach for every possible means of maintaining the tasteless patronizing tone he has set himself. The novel on which this effusion is based was set in the Blue Ridge Mountains, but Mr. Daves moved the whole thing to Wyoming. Picture-postcard scenery notwithstanding, Wyoming ought to sue."

Judith Crist, *New York Herald Tribune*

"With less ingratiating and expert performers than Fonda and Miss O'Hara as the central characters the chances are Daves might have found himself in trouble. Fonda, in particular, can take what easily could have been an ordinary hayseed and invest such a role with depth, purposefulness and dignity."

Pryr, *Variety*

Peter Finch and Jane Fonda

In the Cool of the Day

MGM. 1963. Directed by Robert Stevens. Produced by John Houseman. Screenplay by Meade Roberts, based on the novel by Susan Ertz.

JANE FONDA played *Christine Bonner* in a cast that also included: Peter Finch, Angela Lansbury, Arthur Hill,

Constance Cummings, Alexander Knox, Nigel Davenport, John Le Mesurier, Alec McCowen, Valerie Taylor, Andreas Markos.

THE PICTURE: Nobody came off with honors in *In the Cool of the Day,* a heavy romantic soap opera,

Peter Finch and Jane Fonda

set in Greece. Jane Fonda, now safely established, may shudder a little when the picture occasionally shows up on television but, otherwise, it is as forgotten as is *The Fun Couple,* a three-performance Broadway disaster in which she was also involved around that time.

THE CRITICS

"If such matters were legally actionable, Jane Fonda would have grounds for suit against the director Robert Stevens, the screenwriter Meade Roberts, the cinematographer Peter Newbrook, and the wardrobe designer Orry-Kelly, each of whom has put her at a disadvantage in her new film, *In the Cool of the Day.* Originally, I suppose, it was Miss Fonda's fault for having accepted her role in this John Houseman production. Houseman's name is practically synonymous with compromised quality; a producer whose ambitious conscience does not let him rest until, in his commercial pictures, he has tampered with something or someone serious. But, once she took the assignment in this glutinous tale, Miss Fonda was then consistently handicapped by all the gentlemen named. One sees her struggling intelligently to give life to the lumber, and one also sees her consistently defeated. None of these matters handicaps Peter Finch, her lover, who is safely asleep throughout."

Stanley Kauffmann, *The New Republic*

Jane Fonda and Peter Finch

Angela Lansbury, Jane Fonda, and Peter Finch

Peter Fonda and Sandra Dee

Tammy and the Doctor

Universal. 1963. Directed by Harry Keller. Produced by Ross Hunter. Screenplay by Oscar Brodney, based on characters created by Sid Ricketts Sumner.

PETER FONDA played *Dr. Mark Cheswick* in a cast that also included: Sandra Dee, MacDonald Carey, Beulah Bondi, Margaret Lindsay, Reginald Owen, Alice Pearce, Adam West, Joan Marshall, Stanley Clements, Doodles Weaver, Mitzie Hoag, Alex Gerry, Robert Foulk, Jill Jackson, Forrest Lewis, Sondra Rodgers, Charles Seel, Susie Kaye, Paul Nesbitt.

THE PICTURE: Now a third Fonda came to the screen. Young Peter, fresh from good notices in his Broadway stage debut, started his movie career as a routine young leading man for Tammy. By that time, even the tots were pretty tired of Tammy. Beulah Bondi, the perceptive, brilliant character actress, who had appeared with Henry Fonda when Dad was not much older than Peter, was in this one, too—wasted unhappily. But she reported that she felt Peter had much of the same appeal and sensitivity as his young father had twenty-five years before.

THE CRITICS
"Peter Fonda, sprig of Henry, who resembles a cross between his dad and Fred Astaire, makes his screen bow. It's an unfortunately inane role for a debut."
                                                            Tube, *Variety*

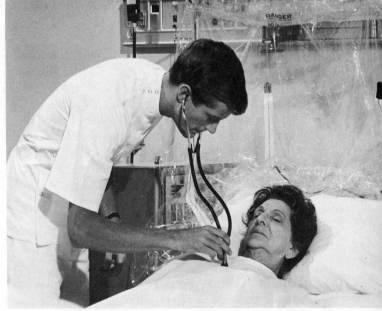

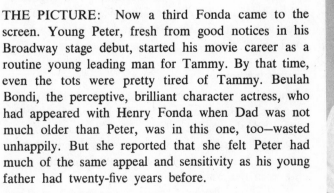

Peter Fonda and Beulah Bondi

George Hamilton and Peter Fonda

The Victors

Columbia. 1963. Produced, directed, written by Carl Foreman. Based on the book *The Human Kind* by Alexander Baron.

PETER FONDA played *Weaver* in a cast that also included: George Hamilton, George Peppard, Vince Edwards, Albert Finney, Eli Wallach, Melina Mercouri, Jeanne Moreau, Maurice Ronet, Romy Schneider, Rosanna Schiaffino, Elke Sommer, Michael Callan, Peter Vaughan, Jim Mitchum, Tutte Lemkow, Malya Nappi, Patrick Jordan, John Rogers, Joel Flateau, Milo Sperberg, Alf Kjellin, James Chase, Mervyn Johns, Bee Duffle, Alan Barnes, George Mikell, George Roubicek, Albert Lieven, Marianne Deming, Senta Berger, Riggs O'Hara, Robert Nichols, Colin Maitland, Larry Caringhi, Tony Wallace, Charles De Temple, Tom Busby, Graydon Gould, Ian Hughes, Vanda Godsell.

THE PICTURE: Peter Fonda played a small role, but one that made an impression, in a big (three-hour)

picture in which a great many "names" played small roles, many without leaving any impression at all. This was Carl Foreman's attempt at a definitive picture about the horrors of war and its aftermath. Although individual episodes had impact, the picture was too scattered in its various stories and punched home its points too hard to score as strongly as intended.

THE CRITICS
"What's wrong with most of the picture is that it is specious, sentimental and false to the norm of soldier nature and the realities of war. Mr. Foreman's direction is generally artless, highly romanticized, and there is really not one good performance—one strong characterization—in the whole film."

Bosley Crowther, *The New York Times*

"Peter Fonda is a standout as the exasperatingly juvenile newcomer to the squad."

Land, *Variety*

Sunday in New York

MGM-7 Arts. 1964. Directed by Peter Tewksbury. Produced by Everett Freeman. Screen play by Norman Krasna, based on his play.

JANE FONDA played *Eileen Tyler* in a cast that also included: Cliff Robertson, Rod Taylor, Robert Culp, Jo Morrow, Jim Backus, Peter Nero.

THE PICTURE: One of those brisk, inconsequential little Broadway sex comedies made one of those brisk, inconsequential little movie sex comedies—freer in its treatment than similar comedies of a few years earlier (*The Moon Is Blue* was chastised and censored for using the word "virgin") but cut out of the same cloth. This was hardly something for anybody's memory book but it was fun, and director Peter Tewksbury used Manhattan well enough to give it a nice New Yorky flavor. And the cast—Cliff Robertson, Robert Culp, Rod Taylor, and, particularly, a delectable Miss Fonda—fitted pleasantly.

THE CRITICS
"Another brightly salacious Hollywood comedy about the way of a man with a maid who just may.... As usual, winking wickedness turns out to be merely eye-

wash, but the plot—more to be pitied than censored—gets a buoyant lift from Stars Jane Fonda, Cliff Robertson and Rod Taylor. All three of them abandon themselves to the film version of Norman Krasna's trite Broadway farce, with disarming faith, as though one

Rod Taylor, Jane Fonda, and Robert Culp

Jane Fonda and Rod Taylor

more glossy, glittering package of pseudo-sex might save the world. . . . 'Sunday' scores on style. Director Peter Tewksbury has caught Manhattan in a mood of after-the-rain freshness—and the gags are all neatly paced and frequently funny. Even the obligatory we-were-just-drying-off-in-bathrobes scene squeaks by—probably because Jane, in a plain blue wrapper, looks so honey-hued and healthy that her most smoldering invitation somehow suggests that all she really has in mind is tennis."

Time

"Jane Fonda's last film, *In the Cool of the Day,* was an insurmountable disaster, but it does not disprove her emotional powers in *The Chapman Report* or her comic powers in *Period of Adjustment* and this film. Miss Fonda has wit, even when Krasna doesn't. It is in the immediacy of her voice, her readings of lines, her sharp sense of timing. The combination of her slightly coltish movements and her unpretty but attractive face gives her a quality that cuts agreeably across the soft grain of most young actresses. Her presence has the instant incisiveness and interest that are usually summed up in the term 'personality.' This last is certainly not identical with talent; Alec Guinness has large talent, little personality. Miss Fonda has considerable of both. It is still worth wondering—up to now, anyway—what will become of her."

Stanley Kauffmann, *The New Republic*

Jo Morrow, Cliff Robertson, and Jane Fonda

Henry Fonda, Margaret Leighton, and Cliff Robertson

The Best Man

United Artists. 1964. Directed by Franklin Schaffner. Produced by Stuart Millar and Lawrence Turman. Screenplay by Gore Vidal, based on his play.

HENRY FONDA played *William Russell* in a cast that also included: Cliff Robertson, Edie Adams, Margaret Leighton, Shelley Berman, Lee Tracy, Ann Sothern, Gene Raymond, Kevin McCarthy, Mahalia Jackson, Howard K. Smith, John Henry Faulk, Richard Arlen, Penny Singleton, George Kurgo, George Furth, Anne Newman, Mary Lawrence, H. E. West, Michael Mac-Donald, William R. Ebersol, Natalie Masters, Blossom Rock, Bill Stout, Tyler McVey, Sherwood Keith.

THE PICTURE: Henry Fonda went back into politics on the screen to become a presidential candidate in the witty and perceptive film version of Gore Vidal's very successful Broadway play, *The Best Man*. Here Fonda played a former Secretary of State, a man of intellect and principles. The obvious and frequent comparison to Adlai Stevenson seemed more than coincidental. Parallels between real-life counterparts of the political figures played by Cliff Robertson and Lee Tracy were noted, too. Both actors, incidentally—Mr. Tracy repeating his enormous stage success as the ex-president in the same role on screen and Mr. Robertson unexpectedly but very effectively cast as the principal

antagonist to the Fonda character. With Fonda's brilliant characterization and good acting in lesser roles, it made for an almost impeccable cast. (Only Shelly Berman's too-broad playing struck a jarring note.)

With just about everything going for it, *The Best Man* failed to make a sizeable dent in the box office. And finally, it seems, the point had been proved—nothing interests the vast majority of the American movie going public less than a study of the American political scene.

THE CRITICS
"*The Best Man* has come to the screen, considerably improved in the process of transition. The original casting imbalances which reduced Melvyn Douglas and Frank Lovejoy to mere antagonists in the presence of Lee Tracy's protagonist has been righted somewhat by the substitution of Henry Fonda and Cliff Robertson in the Stevenson-Nixon roles. Fonda and Robertson not only act more subtly than Douglas and Lovejoy, they are richer in those iconographical associations which enable movies to excel in that realm which the late Robert Warshow designated as intermediate excellence. Over the years, Fonda has become entrenched as Hollywood's populist of the left virtually in opposition to James Stewart's populist of the ruggedly individualistic right. Against Fonda's classic awkwardness, Robertson's

Henry Fonda and Lee Tracy

to the screen with dexterity. Franklin Schaffner has directed it with good visual and rhythmic sense and achieved the effect of our being seated on the bow of a figurative ship, observant and calm, as waves of bustling people part on either side of us. The dialogue is bright, the cast—with one dreadful exception (Shelley Berman)—is at the least, good. The tone is more frisky and venturesome than one expects in an American political film. Segregationists, the DAR, anti-intellectualism, as well as the machinations of machine politics, are nicely stung. . . . Henry Fonda could play Russell in his sleep but has refused to do so; it is an alert, humorous, rueful performance."

Stanley Kauffmann, *The New Republic*

Margaret Leighton, Henry Fonda, and Ann Sothern

compressed grace makes its own comment on the modern politician losing in passion what he gains in poise. In fact, Robertson can serve double duty in 1964 as an approximation of both Dick Nixon and Bobby Kennedy, on record as two of Gore Vidal's lesser enthusiasms. To round out the analogies, Fonda portrayed young Abe Lincoln more than a quarter of a century ago, and Robertson young Jack Kennedy less than a year ago."

Andrew Sarris, *The Village Voice*

"Gore Vidal has adapted his comedy, *The Best Man*,

Kevin McCarthy, Cliff Robertson, Gene Raymond, Henry Fonda, and Margaret Leighton

Fail Safe

Columbia. 1964. Directed by Sidney Lumet. Produced by Max E. Youngstein. Screenplay by Walter Bernstein, based on the novel by Eugene Burdick and Harvey Wheeler.

HENRY FONDA played *The President* in a cast that also included: Dan O'Herlihy, Walter Matthau, Frank Overson, Edward Binns, Fritz Weaver, Larry Hagman, William Hansen, Russell Hardie, Russell Collins, Sorrell Booke, Nancy Berg, John Connell, Frank Simpson, Hildy Parks, Janet Ward, Dom DeLouise, Dana Elcar, Stuart Germain, Louise Larabee, Frieda Altman.

THE PICTURE: When the novel *Fail-Safe* was published, the excitement was immediate. But frenzied bidding for the movie rights ceased abruptly when the word got around that the administration frowned on the idea that the book should be made into a movie. (Henry Fonda claims he knows from first-hand authority that the administration had no such feelings about it.)

Not frightened off were independent producers Max E. Youngstein and Sidney Lumet, but when they had acquired the film rights, they faced an unexpected situa-

tion—a suit for plagiarism against the book's authors by Stanley Kubrick then ready to film a picture based on an earlier, little-known novel, Peter George's *Red Alert*. The suit was settled when Columbia, set to release both pictures, agreed that Kubrick's film would have the first release.

This was a giant blow to *Fail Safe* (the picture's title dispensed with the hyphen of the novel). For *Fail Safe* was a study in shattering suspense on the startling theme of an accidental world holocaust. The Kubrick film—the matchless *Dr. Strangelove*—dealt with the same theme but in hilarious, devastatingly satiric terms. With the initial impact lost, *Fail Safe,* while still highly effective, became somewhat anticlimactic.

Fonda, who had portrayed a hopeful presidential candidate just a few months earlier and a controversial Secretary of State two years before that, was the President of the United States this time in a role that confined him to a small room, a telephone glued to his ear. Lumet is gifted in developing drama in confined quarters and, with Fonda's persuasive performance, made these sequences which could have been static into the most highly-charged moments of the movie.

Henry Fonda as the President

THE CRITICS

"Henry Fonda, who plays the President in *Fail Safe,* admitted recently to *Newsweek's* Movies editor that it would have been impossible for him to do the role, to talk on the hot line with the Premier of the U.S.S.R., if he had seen Peter Sellers in *Dr. Strangelove.* The mundane absurdity of Muffley's wry, dry, 'I'm just as sorry as you are, Dmitri,' was a supreme statement about the incommensurability of any human reaction to the end of the world. And it was an honorable admission for Fonda to make. Henry Fonda, without any question, is the best thing in *Fail Safe.* Everybody else is hopeless or helpless. There is nothing in the script, and there was nothing in the novel, to hint to anyone how to behave, how to think, how to be. Fonda plays himself—as an old-time star always does anyway—and gets away with it. Between him and the Albert Brenner sets with electronic maps on which drama and chase and life and death are reduced to little blips, there is a kind of surface tension to the film."

Newsweek

"Henry Fonda, whether he is a Secretary of State, which he has been twice, or a President, as he is here, makes sane government seem possible and makes credible the melodramatic telephone conversations with the Russian premier."

Stanley Kauffmann, *The New Republic*

Henry Fonda and Larry Hagman

"In scene after scene, *Fail Safe* plays like a humdrum remake of Kubrick's picture. In both films the U.S. President (Henry Fonda, a presidential candidate in *The Best Man,* was evidently elected before the release of *Fail Safe*) hops to the hot line and tries to persuade the Soviet Premier that the assault is unintentional. Their first two conversations are harrowing. Walled up in a white cell somewhere under Washington, President Fonda speaks steadily and carefully in a voice that is intense but curiously flat, as though every word were crushed by a burden of significance too great to bear. And as the voice drones on and on, pleading and reasoning and pleading the figure of the actor slowly swells and charges with tension and importance, the presence of the man becomes the person of mankind and his voice the voice of the species pleading for its life. The whole of history seems consummated in an instant; Armageddon rages in a telephone booth."

Time

Henry Fonda

Lilith

Columbia. 1964. Directed, produced and screen play by Robert Rossen. Based on the novel by J. R. Salamanca.

PETER FONDA played *Stephen Evshevsky* in a cast that also included: Warren Beatty, Jean Seberg, Kim Hunter, Anne Meachum, James Patterson, Jessica Walter, Gene Hackman, Robert Reilly, Rene Auberjenois, Lucy Smith, Maurice Brenner, Jeanne Barr, Richard Higgs, Elizabeth Bader, Alice Spivak, Walter Arnold, Kathleen Phelan, Cecilia Ray, Gunnar Peters, L. Jerome Offutt, W. Jerome Offutt, Robert Jolivette, Jason Jolivette, Jeno Mate, Dina Paisner, Pawnee Sills, Donn Donnellan, Ron Cunningham, Katherine Gregg, Edith Fellows, Page Jones, Olympia Dukakis, Mildred Smith, Wendell

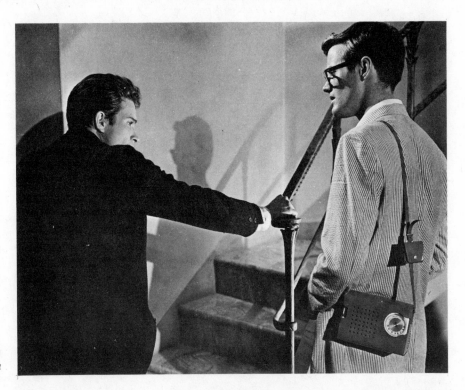

Warren Beatty and Peter Fonda

Phillips, Jr., Tony Gray, Harvey Jason, Gordon Phillips.

THE PICTURE: Robert Rossen, notable for his direction of such hard-hitting dramas as *All the King's Men* and *The Hustler,* moved in another direction with his last film, *Lilith.* This was a study of mental aberration, symbolic and poetic in its approach as opposed to the more straightforward treatment given a similar subject in *David and Lisa,* released a few months earlier.

It was not a happy picture in production—Rossen was already ill (he died before being able to make another film) and there was considerable dissension on the set. It was originally selected as the American entry in the Venice Film Festival but then rejected by festival officials with unflattering comments.

The reviews were almost uniformly scathingly negative—most critics actually so angry that they ignored really striking moments in the confused whole. Peter Fonda had felt so strongly about the potentials of the sensitive young mental patient, whose suicide triggers the final descent into madness of the girl he has loved, that he personally pleaded for the role. But the character was not developed with sufficient clarity and the picture was not a success for Fonda either. Interestingly enough, a small but vocal group of film buffs and critics, particularly in Europe, have made *Lilith* a "cult" picture and over the years it has acquired a reputation in some circles as Rossen's neglected masterpiece.

THE CRITICS
"It's a muddle of Americana and schizophrenia, sex and sophistry, with a ludicrously lubricious plot and

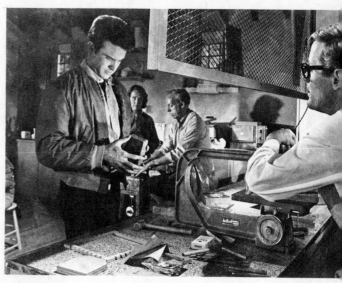

Warren Beatty and Peter Fonda (Kim Hunter in background)

enough fuzzy-wuzzy incoherent camera work to turn it into an unwilling parody on 'art' or 'festival' films at their worst . . . Peter Fonda provokes our interest from time to time."

Judith Crist, *New York Herald Tribune*

"There is an honest striving for freshness, originality and quality that makes even a relative failure, like *Lilith,* worthy of attention if not unqualified admiration. Clearly the failure of *Lilith* is less in intent than in execution."

Arthur Knight, *Saturday Review*

Peter Fonda, Jean Seberg, and Warren Beatty

Sharon Hugueny and Peter Fonda

The Young Lovers

MGM. 1964. Directed and produced by Samuel Goldwyn, Jr. Screen play by George Garrett. Based on the novel by Julian Halevy.

PETER FONDA played *Eddie Slocum* in a cast that also included: Sharon Hugueny, Nick Adams, Deborah Wal-

ley, Beatrice Straight, Malachi Throne, Kent Smith, Joseph Campanella, Jennifer Billingsley, Nancy Rennick.

THE PICTURE: Two distinguished second generation names, Peter Fonda and Samuel Goldwyn, Jr., were the chief reasons for interest in *The Young Lovers*.

Sharon Hugueny and Peter Fonda

Sharon Hugueny and Peter Fonda

Long before he became a "Wild Angel" or "Easy Rider," Peter Fonda shared a motorbike with Sharon Hugueny

The story—about two college students who fall in love, run into problems when she becomes pregnant, separate when she considers but rejects an abortion—was hardly particularly daring. But, to the credit of all concerned, they avoided both extremes, soap opera sentimentalism and over-sensationalizing. The result was mildly touching but without any great insight into the problems of today's youth.

THE CRITICS

"The Young Lovers has a lot of things going for it even though it's an uneven production with awkward spots and slow build-up. While the story is no longer the shocker it would have been a generation ago, the talk is frank and the switch to problems of the unwed father, rather than to mother, will stir more than usual interest and controversy . . . Peter Fonda's overall portrayal fits the character and he delivers key bits of dialogue well."

Hogg, *Variety*

Jane Fonda and Alain Delon

Alain Delon and Jane Fonda

Joy House

MGM. 1964. Directed by Rene Clement. Produced by Jacques Bar. Screen play by Rene Clement, Pascal Jardin, Charles Williams, based on the novel by Day Keene.

JANE FONDA played *Melinda* in a cast that also included: Alain Delon, Lola Albright, Carl Studer, Sorrell Booke, Andre Oumansky, Arthur Howard, Nick Del Negro, Jacques Bezard, Berett Arcaya.

THE PICTURE: You can understand why Jane Fonda agreed to do *Joy House*. Alain Delon is an attractive leading man, Rene Clement has done interesting pictures, and Jane does have an affinity for France. But here, in this strange, murky melodrama, she was given a role inappropriate for her youth, beauty and general grooviness. It probably wouldn't have worked for Jeanne Moreau—it was just all wrong for Jane.

THE CRITICS
"The question of Jane Fonda's development as into an extraordinarily good actress, which I still think quite possible, is beclouded by her poor choice of vehicles. Her latest film is an absurd suspense picture called *Joy House,* in which Lola Albright and that talented character actor, Sorrell Booke, are also mired. No summary of the silly plot is needed."
Stanley Kauffmann, *The New Republic*

"Miss Fonda has some mysterious hold over Miss Albright. It's not all Miss Fonda has—or at least so she attempts to indicate by alternately impersonating the Madwoman of Chaillot, Baby Doll and her father Henry; she's a sick kid, this one."
Judith Crist, *New York Herald Tribune*

Lola Albright, Alain Delon, and Jane Fonda

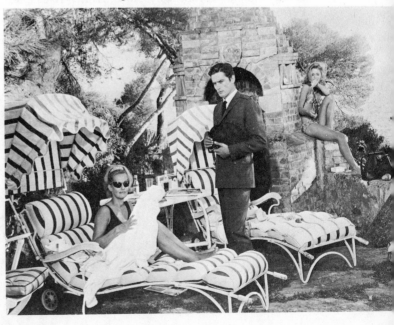

Sex and the Single Girl

Warner Bros. 1964. Directed by Richard Quine. Produced by William T. Orr. Screen play by Joseph Heller and David R. Schwartz, from a story by Joseph Hoffman, based on the book by Helen Gurley Brown.

HENRY FONDA played *Frank* in a cast that also included: Natalie Wood, Tony Curtis, Lauren Bacall, Mel Ferrer, Fran Jeffries, Leslie Parrish, Edward Everett Horton, Larry Storch, Stubby Kaye, Howard St. John, Otto Kruger, Max Showalter, William Lanteau, Helen Kleeb, Curly Klein, Count Basie Orchestra.

THE PICTURE: Henry Fonda kept saying no to the producers of *Sex and the Single Girl* and they kept enticing him with such blandishments as Lauren Bacall to play opposite, the necessity of his doing a comedy at

Henry Fonda

this stage, and lots of lovely money. The final irresistible lure was that the screen play was to be written by Joseph Heller, author of *Catch-22*, a book that Fonda adored. (*Catch-22*, incidentally, made quite a point of the fact that one of its principal characters, Major Major, looked exactly like Henry Fonda.)

Only the title of Helen Gurley Brown's best-selling-non-novel was used. The story made up for the movie was a dreadfully coy and flimsy thing, in spite of—we fervently believe not because of—Heller's writing participation. Fonda and Miss Bacall were wasted in the kind of roles which, in an earlier era of movies, would be more congenially cast with the likes of Edgar Kennedy and Dot Farley.

THE CRITICS

"This is the kind of Technicolor film in which Tony Curtis, Henry Fonda and Mel Ferrer all have navy blue hair and only Mr. Curtis' peculiar dialect distinguishes him from the other two actors whose mutual embarrassment at the proceedings in which they are involved turns them into identical twins . . . *Sex and the Single Girl* is enough to put one off sex, single girls and movies for the season."

Judith Crist, *New York Herald Tribune*

"Off to a brisk start, the picture is steadily suggestive. And while Miss Wood is extremely wide-eyed and jittery throughout and Mr. Curtis tends toward cuteness, their scenes hit only one dull, sour snag, in a fumbling near-seduction. It's the old timers—Miss Bacall, Mr. Fonda and Mr. Ferrer—who really count, as

Henry Fonda and Lauren Bacall

they suavely steal the show. . . . As for Miss Wood and Mr. Curtis, at least they deserve each other. But Mr. Ferrer, surprisingly deft as a casual psychiatrist, and Mr. Fonda and Miss Bacall as Mr. Curtis' scrappy neighbors, supply the real spice and fun, especially Miss Bacall who has the wittiest lines and all but pierces the picture with her buzzsaw growl. *Sex and the Single Girl?* Fooey. Three cheers for the old folks at home."

Howard Thompson, *The New York Times*

Lauren Bacall and Henry Fonda

Henry Fonda and Glenn Ford between scenes

The Rounders

MGM. 1965. Dircted by Burt Kennedy. Produced by Richard E. Lyons. Screen play by Burt Kennedy, based on a novel by Max Evans.

HENRY FONDA played *Howdy Lewis* in a cast that also included: Glenn Ford, Sue Ann Langdon, Hope Holiday, Chill Wills, Edgar Buchanan, Kathleen Freeman, Joan Freeman, Denver Pyle, Barton MacLane, Doodles Weaver, Allegra Varron.

THE PICTURE: Everybody loved *The Rounders* except its studio. One after another, delighted reviews heralded it as bright, original and entertaining. But they were too late to save the film from its own distributors. Apparently on the theory that nobody would want to see a picture about two middle-aged cowpokes, in which the "romantic interest" was a sorry looking, stubbornly unbroken roan, the studio booked it into neighborhood theatres on the second half of a double bill with a dreadful "B" picture, called *Get Yourself a College Girl*. By the time the news about the reviews got out, the picture had run its week, almost unnoticed, and had disappeared.

THE CRITICS
"*The Rounders* is a complete delight, from start to finish. If audiences don't take to this, it's their mistake and their loss. The MGM presentation is a wacky comedy, with sex and action, and, only incidentally, is a contemporary Western. It is not a Western, that is to say, but a comedy. Burt Kennedy's direction and screenplay are at the basis of its success, but a great deal of credit must go, too, to two nonpareil stars, Henry Fonda and Glenn Ford. . . . It is, of course, Ford and Fonda who give the heart and the mind to the picture. . . . Burt Kennedy just guides them, with lines, camera work and pointing a finger here and there, to let them be as good as they can be. Which is very good indeed. Watching two veterans work together, as F&F do here, should be required watching for young actors. They can't swipe the basic ingredients, but they might get some pointers on the recipe."

James Powers, *Hollywood Reporter*

"Those two seasoned old-timers, Henry Fonda and Glenn Ford, may not be pink-cheeked collegians but they certainly mopped the squealing young folks off the

Henry Fonda

Henry Fonda

Henry Fonda, Hope Holiday, Sue Ann Langdon, and Glenn Ford

screen yesterday. [The picture was reviewed as part of a double bill with *Get Yourself a College Girl*.] The picture is one of those low-budget Westerns, with plenty on the ball, but it doesn't quite hit the target as a sleeper. Even so, in the perfectly meshed characterizations and trouping of the stars, it has two of the most likable Western heroes in many moons—a couple of aging, rather seedy and none-too-bright bronco busters. ...*The Rounders* is a good, small Western—far from perfect but beautifully personified by two wise, winning veterans."

Howard Thompson, *The New York Times*

"Beguiling, easy-to-take spoof Western omelet, which is seasoned to a delightful turn by some wild, free-wheeling performances. ... We hope they have a sequel or two up their buckskin sleeves—with Ford and Fonda, of course, who are plumb perfect."

Bob Salmaggi, *New York Herald Tribune*

"I believe that Burt Kennedy deserves some recognition for his careful craftsmanship in an area where it doesn't seem to matter commercially. After all, it must be depressing to make a picture with Henry Fonda and Glenn Ford and have it wind up on the bottom half of a double bill with a stupid juke box movie like *Get Yourself a College Girl*, starring such luminaries as Mary Ellen Mobley and Nancy Sinatra. Aside from the aesthetic reversal of the billing, the juvenile antics of 'College Girl' keep away a large portion of the audience which might enjoy *The Rounders*, and more's the pity. Not that *The Rounders* is any earth-shaking revelation of the Real West. Fonda and Ford, its two amiable cowpokes, drawl their way through their off-beat characterizations with just a dash of cynical realism to lend flavor to the corny, old-fashioned but still sure-fire sentimentality of two men's attachment to the most ornery horse in creation. Of the two practiced pros, Ford gets the part and the lines, but Fonda still hits the ball farther when he connects. ... *The Rounders* is remarkably free of malice and meanness and there are moments when Burt Kennedy manages an evocative chord of nostalgia for the easy-going virility of bygone movies."

Andrew Sarris, *The Village Voice*

The Fondas and the Fords: Henry and Glenn with sons, both named Peter

Roger Vadim, directing his wife, Jane Fonda, shows Jean-Claude Brialy how to carry her

Circle of Love

Continental-Walter Reade/Sterling Inc. 1965. Directed by Roger Vadim. Produced by Robert and Raymond Hakim. Screen play by Jean Anouilh, based on the play, *La Ronde (Reigen)*, by Arthur Schnitzler.

JANE FONDA played *The Married Woman* in a cast that also included: Marie Dubois, Claude Giraud, Anna Karina, Valerie Lagrange, Jean-Claude Brialy, Maurice Ronet, Catherine Spaak, Bernard Noel, Francine Berge, Jean Sorel.

THE PICTURE: When a picture has attained the status of a minor movie classic and has been available all through the fifties, it would seem that the mid-sixties would be too early for a remake. The original *La Ronde* was just too fresh in the mind of cinema

Jane Fonda

The controversial Circle of Love
Broadway billboard

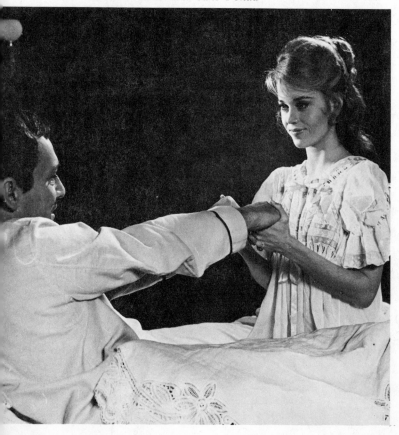

Maurice Ronet and Jane Fonda

buffs for its remake, *Circle of Love,* to come off with any distinction. And only Jane Fonda had enough star power to compete with any of the members of the dazzling star cast of the earlier film—Gerard Philipe, Simone Signoret, Danielle Darrieux, Jean-Louis Barrault, Simone Simon, etc.

So, in the final analysis, the most attention won by *Circle of Love* was Miss Fonda's angry threat to sue if a giant unauthorized nude billboard on Broadway was not covered up. The picture was directed by the dashing and controversial young Roger Vadim. Before too long Miss Jane Fonda would be Mme. Roger Vadim.

THE CRITICS
"The dubbed *Circle of Love* is a dull, pointless, ineptly acted vulgarization of a distinguished play, with nothing to recommend it beyond some attractive color photography by Henri Decae. . . . The only tolerable voice in the collection belongs to Jane Fonda, who uses her own—though it has no relationship to her lip movements, since she played the part in French. Wildly miscast, as the discreet and timid matron, the part Miss Darrieux made hers for life, the improving Miss Fonda plays against type. With some comic skill, she creates a perverse imp who speaks modestly while her gestures and expressions pointedly belie her words. In the film's most diverting episode, Miss Fonda cavorts in bed with Jean-Claude Brialy."

Eugene Archer, *The New York Times*

Henry Fonda

In Harm's Way

Paramount. 1965. Produced and directed by Otto Preminger. Screen play by Wendell Mayes, based on the novel by James Bassett.

HENRY FONDA played *CINCPAC II Admiral* in a cast that also included: John Wayne, Kirk Douglas, Patricia Neal, Tom Tryon, Paula Prentiss, Brandon DeWilde, Jill Haworth, Dana Andrews, Stanley Holloway, Burgess Meredith, Franchot Tone, Patrick O'Neal, Carroll O'Connor, Slim Pickins, James Mitchum, George Ken-

John Wayne, Burgess Meredith, and Henry Fonda

Henry Fonda

nedy, Bruce Cabot, Barbara Bouchet, Tod Andrews, Larry Hagman, Stewart Moss, Richard LaPore, Chet Stratton, Soo Young, Dort Clark, Phil Mattingly.

THE PICTURE: As a favor to its producer-director, Otto Preminger, and for other considerations—such as a vacation in Hawaii—Henry Fonda played the cameo role of an admiral in Preminger's star-and-cliché studded drama, *In Harm's Way*. Playing a very minor role, Fonda was the one actor to come off with any distinction in at least one notice, that of *The New York Times*.

THE CRITICS
"Slick and shallow . . . a straight, cliché-crowded melodrama. . . . The only character who finally emerges with any firmness and credibility is the admiral in command of the Pacific theatre, who is played by Henry Fonda. At least, Mr. Fonda makes this admiral a firm, crisp, decisive type. He seems more interested in naval operations than in promoting a personality. This is refreshing and convincing in a film that is virtually awash with flimsy and flamboyant fellows with all the tricks of the trade of Hollywood."

Bosley Crowther, *The New York Times*

"Henry Fonda, as the four-star boss of this Navy show, moves in and out of the story, hitting the mark every time."

Pry, *Variety*

Cat Ballou

Columbia. 1965. Directed by Elliot Silverstein. Produced by Harold Hecht. Screenplay by Walter Newman and Frank R. Pierson, based on the novel by Roy Chanslor.

JANE FONDA played *Cat Ballou* in a cast that also included: Lee Marvin, Michael Callan, Dwayne Hick-man, Nat King Cole, Stubby Kaye, Tom Nardini, John Marley, Reginald Denny, Jay C. Flippen, Arthur Hun-nicutt, Bruce Cabot, Burt Austin, Paul Gilbert.

THE PICTURE: *Cat Ballou* might have been most notable for the giant boost it gave to the career of Lee Marvin—but it was a bullseye for Jane Fonda, too. Here

The villainous Lee Marvin lays hands on Jane Fonda

Jane Fonda and the good Lee Marvin (second from right) with Dwayne Hickman, Michael Callan, and Tom Nardini

we had all the conventions of Western melodrama but in the form of a wild spoof that completely demolished every last cliché.

Lee Marvin, hitherto a good reliable secondary screen villain, kicked over all the traces in a dual role. He was the most sinister badman of them all—an outlaw with a silver nose (his own having been bitten off in a fight.) And, even better, he was the boozy Kid Shelleen —the hollow shell of a once-terrorizing gunfighter. He won an Academy Award and top stardom for the performance. But Jane Fonda, as the very model of a demure Old West heroine—except that her sweet schoolmarm turns out to be as handy with her guns as any Tom Mix of movie history, was a complete and absolute joy as well.

Cat Ballou was a big and deserved hit, both with critics and with the public.

THE CRITICS

"As honest-to-gosh Westerns go, *Cat Ballou* is disgraceful. As a shibboleth-shattering spoof, it dumps all the heroic traditions of horse opera into a gag bag, shakes thoroughly, and pulls out one of the year's jolliest surprises. What's good about the comedy is nigh irresistible. What's best about it is probably Lee Marvin. Dressed in snaky black, with a silver schnozz tied on where his nose used to be before 'it was bit off in a fight,' Marvin

soberly parodies several hundred Western badmen of yore, then surpasses himself as the dime-novel hero, Kid Shelleen. A 'good' killer, the Kid arrives in town unable to live up or even stand up to his legend. His eyes are bloodshot from poring over whisky labels. On ceremonial occasions he wears a corset. When he is primed with rotgut, his fast draw is apt to pull his pants off.... Director Elliot Silverstein, freshly sprung from television, sows this wild-oater with all manner of trickery, and most of it works.... In a performance that nails down her reputation as a girl worth singing about, Actress Fonda does every preposterous thing demanded of her with a giddy sincerity that is at once beguiling, poignant and hilarious. Wearing widow's weeds over her six-guns, she romps through one of the zaniest train robberies ever filmed, a throwback to Pearl White's perilous heyday. Putting the final touches on a virginal white frock to wear at her own hanging, she somehow suggests that Alice in Wonderland has fallen among blackguards and rather enjoys it. Happily, *Cat Ballou* makes the enjoyment epidemic."

Time

"It is a carefree and clever throwing together of three or four solid Western stereotypes in a farcical frolic that follows—and travesties—the ballad form of Western story-telling made popular in *High Noon*. . . . The

Jane Fonda as Cat Ballou

heroine—the Cat Ballou—of Jane Fonda, is a big-eyed, big-hearted grown-up child, a veritable Little Mary Sunshine, who takes to gunning and robbing a train with the gee-whiz excitement of a youngster confronted with a huge banana split."

Bosley Crowther, *The New York Times*

"Well, let's get those old superlatives out again, this time for a small package of enormous delight labeled *Cat Ballou,* a Western to end all Westerns (or at least our ever looking at another with a straight face) and a comedy that epitomizes the sheer fun of movie-making and movie-watching. . . . Jane Fonda is marvelous as the wide-eyed Cat, exuding sweet feminine sex appeal every sway of the way. . . . This *Cat Ballou* is just a honey."

Judith Crist, *New York Herald Tribune*

Marvin, Fonda, Callan, Hickman, and Nardini

Henry Fonda (Robert Ryan in center background)

Battle of the Bulge

Warners-Cinerama, 1965. Directed by Ken Annakin. Produced by Milton Sperling and Philip Yordan. Screen play by Yordan, Sperling, John Nelson.

HENRY FONDA played *Lt. Col. Kiley* in a cast that also included: Robert Shaw, Robert Ryan, Dana Andrews, George Montgomery, Ty Hardin, Pier Angeli, Barbara Werle, Charles Bronson, Werner Peters, Hans Christian Blech, James MacArthur, Telly Savalas.

THE PICTURE: *The Battle of the Bulge* was just about as big and spectacular in Cinerama as any war picture ever made. It was also a bonanza at the box office. Critically, though, it was chastised for its inaccuracies, its phony "movie" touches and the character stereotypes. Henry Fonda was heroic in a role which had little believability and none of the rest of the excellent cast, headed by Robert Ryan and Robert Shaw,

could make anything more than cardboard soldiers out of their parts. But audiences loved it.

THE CRITICS
"What is offensive about this picture—and offensive is the word—is the evident distortion of the material and of history to suit the giant Cinerama screen. It is the crude alteration of conditions and tactics during the German breakthrough to provide the wide-screen cameras with mammoth spectacles. . . . It is offensive to see heavy artillery being brought to the front aboard a train that races wildly along a single, down-grade mountain track, twisting and jerking around the curves in the fashion of that famous Cinerama roller-coaster ride. And it is a cruel deception to describe the climax of the Battle of the Bulge as a ranging of German tanks against Americans across a broad plain in the manner of a Western movie cavalry-and-Indian change. Mr.

Henry Fonda and Robert Ryan

Henry Fonda and Charles Bronson

Fonda, Mr. Ryan and Mr. Andrews play their American officers well enough...*Battle of the Bulge* may please the youngsters who go for loud and flame-filled spectacles, but it will be a likely irritation to those who have some sober, rueful sense of World War II, and also a respectful regard for the memory of the men who fought and died in the real 'bulge.' "

Bosley Crowther, *The New York Times*

"Fonda is excellent in his warm, restrained underplay-

ing which takes the edge off what otherwise could have become unbelievable derringdo."

Murf, *Variety*

"The genius of Messrs. Fonda and Shaw is evidenced by their ability to play along with their roles, Mr. Fonda serving, however, to underline by his relaxed manner the stiff banalities around him."

Judith Crist, *New York Herald Tribune*

James MacArthur and Henry Fonda

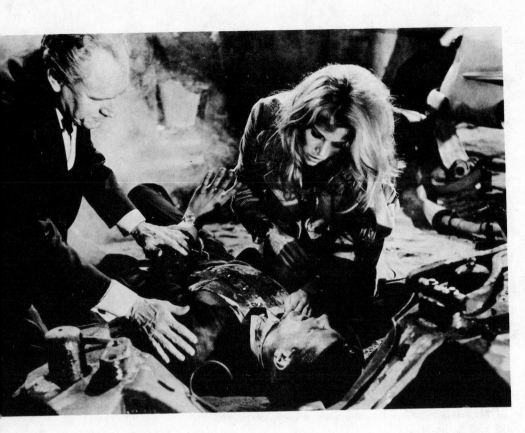

E. G. Marshall, James Fox, and Jane Fonda

The Chase

Columbia. 1966. Directed by Arthur Penn. Produced by Sam Spiegel. Screen play by Lillian Hellman, based on the novel and plays by Horton Foote.

JANE FONDA played *Anne Reeves* in a cast that also included Marlon Brando, Robert Redford, E. G. Marshall, Angie Dickinson, Janice Rule, Miriam Hopkins, Martha Hyer, Richard Bradford, Robert Duvall, James Fox, Diana Hyland, Henry Hull, Jocelyn Brando, Katherine Walsh, Lori Martin, Marc Seaton, Paul Williams, Clifton James, Malcolm Atterbury, Nydia Westman, Joel Flueleen, Steve Ihnat, Maurice Manson, Bruce Cabot, Steve Whittaker, Pamela Curran, Ken Renard.

THE PICTURE: Certainly Sam Spiegel is not one for stinting, and he gave *The Chase* everything in the way of production values that anyone could ask. The cast was loaded with good names. Lillian Hellman wrote the screen play and Arthur Penn directed. But all of these impressive elements added up to a less than ex-

citing whole. *The Chase* was a major movie disappointment.

At the root of it all was the story, and whether this is the fault of the distinguished Lillian Hellman or of the capable Horton Foote can be decided only by those who know Foote's original stories and short-run play. But Miss Hellman's screen play did little enough to make anything real out of the conglomeration of hysterical situations.

You've seen that small town in movies and television as long as there have been movies—and it's the same set of characters in Mr. Foote's Texas whom you have met in Kings Row and Peyton Place and on a Violent Saturday and in many, too many, other movie towns. It was another step in the sad descent of Marlon Brando and the script offered little worth the playing for Jane Fonda, Robert Redford, Janice Rule, James Fox and Angie Dickinson. In the large supporting cast, three screen newcomers—Steve Ihnat, Robert Duvall and Richard Bradford—showed up well, but such a usually reliable veteran as Miriam Hopkins was almost embarrassingly shrill and strident. A lot was expected of *The Chase*. Its failure was unexpected and regretted.

THE CRITICS

"*The Chase* is a shockworn message film, smoothly overacted and topheavy with subtle bigotry, expertly exploiting the violence, intolerance and mean provincialism that it is supposed to be preaching against. With Star Marlon Brando as the chief jeerleader, the movie smugly points an accusing finger at all the wrong, wrong deeds done by precisely the right people. . . . It has very few dull moments, nor does it lack the courage to cash in on its convictions, most of which are half-truths deftly rigged to attract liberal non-thinkers. Miss Hellman seldom lets a scene end without tacking on her comment; except for a handful of courageous, long-suffering Negroes and Sheriff Brando, no Texan escapes being singed by a Statement. Brando ably plays the stereotyped champion of human rights that he seems compelled to endorse in film after film, changing only his dialect. Jane Fonda conquers a casting error as Bubber's faithless wife, making trollopy white trash seem altogether first class."

Time

Jane Fonda and James Fox

"*The Chase* is a contrivance from beginning to end—a successful contrivance, I am quick to report, a series of shameless clichés and stereotypes bailed up with such skill that you roll along with them to a smashing conclusion. And hate yourself for having been hooked a half hour later. . . . We've seen it all over and over—and yet we're stuck to it, at first in fascination over all the incoherencies and ellipses and suggestions and irrelevant details. Then we go along in expectation of the big switch: for certainly Miss Hellman and director Arthur Penn must have *something* new to say to us. And finally, about halfway through, the slow walk has become a trot that has turned into a gallop, and we are being hurtled almost helplessly, to the smashing finale. There were no revelations, no twists along the old familiar mob-psychology, gun-morality paths, not until the final twist, the one startling turnabout by the voiceless bystander, the only familiarity bemused us. . . . The big-name performers offer professionalism, some with their accustomed polish, some in a manner befitting the stereotypes they are called upon to be."

Judith Crist, *New York Herald Tribune*

Between scenes with Jane Fonda and director Arthur Penn

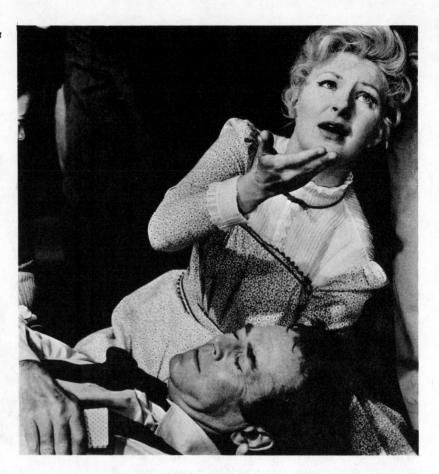

A Big Hand for the Little Lady

Warners. 1966. Produced and directed by Fielder Cook. Screen play by Sidney Carroll, based on his TV play, "Big Deal in Laredo."

HENRY FONDA played *Meredith* in a cast that also included: Joanne Woodward, Jason Robards, Paul Ford, Charles Bickford, Burgess Meredith, Kevin McCarthy, Robert Middleton, John Qualen, James Kenny, Allen Collins, Jim Boles, Gerald Michenaud, Virginia Gregg, Chester Conklin, Ned Glass, Mae Clarke, James Griffith, Noah Keen, Milton Selzer, Louise Glenn, William Court.

THE PICTURE: *A Big Hand for the Little Lady* was the rather coy and misleading (don't you think of Texas Guinan and her girls?) title for the movie version of an excellent television play, Sidney Carroll's *Big Deal in Laredo*. Here was a Western in which all of the action was confined to a poker game in a saloon back room and in which the suspense had nothing to do with whether the bad man would come gunning but depended on the next card to be turned up.

That this slim plot managed to retain tension throughout the entire film was due to shrewd direction, a crackling screen play and the performances of some of the best actors in movies—most notably Henry Fonda, Joanne Woodward, Jason Robards, Kevin McCarthy, Paul Ford, Burgess Meredith and Charles Bickford. Perhaps the final big twist at the end of the film was a letdown—entertaining in itself, it should have been cut off as soon as the point was made. Instead it was milked vigorously as if the writer and director did not want to let go of the joke. But this was a minor quibble in what was an almost completely satisfying entertainment.

THE CRITICS
"While Joanne is away, Fonda is lured into the game, taking $1000 or one quarter of their life's savings to enter. His performance at this point is a thing of absolute beauty, perhaps the best he's ever done."

Archer Winsten, *New York Post*

"And Henry Fonda's characterization of the shamblin', gamblin' man is a joy, a deeply comic portrayal of the

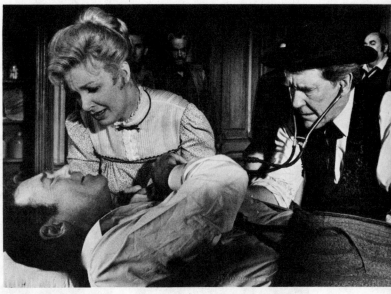

Jason Robards, Henry Fonda, Gerald Michenaud, Charles Bickford, and John Qualen

Henry Fonda, Joanne Woodward, and Burgess Meredith

self-abasement and whining desperation of a man caught up in an ignominious passion. In this, his 60th movie, he transcends his customary image without sacrificing that graceful ease that is his hallmark. 'Little Lady' may be low, even unsophisticated, comedy but it does make you laugh, and it is never afflicted with the silliness of desperation. That puts it way ahead of those failed attempts at high style that currently glut the comic market; low style realized is infinitely more satisfying than sophisticated aspirations embarrassingly unattained. All concerned with 'Little Lady' deserve a big hand."

Richard Schickel, *Life*

"*A Big Hand for the Little Lady* is a Western, although it spends most of its brief screen time in the back room of a saloon rather than out on the lone prairie. Sidney Carroll's bright script peoples that room with funny and fascinating characters, played by such top performers as Henry Fonda, Joanne Woodward, Jason Robards, Charles Bickford, Kevin McCarthy, Paul Ford and Burgess Meredith; and director Fielder Cook has taken full advantage of this fact by playing much of his story off their trained, sensitive faces. Something that seems almost forgotten in this era of wide-screen spectaculars is that a close-up of an expert actor can be every bit as dramatic as a long shot of a whole tribe of Indians chasing a stagecoach across the salt flats—or, for that matter, that a sly look can often be funnier than two pages of dialogue. Television, with its relatively limited resources, has almost been forced to live with this basic

principle; and since both the story and director of 'A Big Hand' derive from that medium the picture inevitably betrays its origins. The irony is that today it takes television to remind the filmmakers of what is essentially their own art. Although his cast is largely confined to a single, smoke-filled room, Cook manages to avoid all sense of claustrophobia by adroit changes of angle and by focusing upon the most exciting stage of all—the human face in its many moods. What emerges is such deft entertainment that the film's surprise ending seems both out of key and pointless, reducing the warm humor of the central situation to the level of a clever joke."

Arthur Knight, *Saturday Review*

Jason Robards, Joanne Woodward, Henry Fonda, and Charles Bickford

Any Wednesday

Warner Bros. 1966. Directed by Robert Ellis Miller. Produced and screen play by Julius J. Epstein, based on the play by Muriel Resnick.

JANE FONDA played *Ellen Gordon* in a cast that also included: Jason Robards, Dean Jones, Rosemary Murphy, Ann Prentiss, Jack Fletcher, Kelly Jean Peters, King Moody, Monty Margetts.

THE PICTURE: *Any Wednesday* opened on Broadway without any advance interest and enthusiasm but turned out to be one of the surprise bright spots of the theatre season. That meant, of course, that there was quite a bit of anticipation about the movie version.

But Hollywood added very little of value to the dish served up by Broadway—a lot of running into streets and such, but nothing to make it really cinematic. So it was quite a pleasant movie in the way that good movie versions of such plays are pleasant, but it didn't mean much more than any similar made-for-Hollywood comedy of the Doris Day type.

Even so, Jane Fonda was crisp and attractive as the mistress turning thirty, Jason Robards good enough in a role that hardly strained his considerable talents and Rosemary Murphy, who stole all of her brief moments on stage, repeated her role of the wife and was quite as charming.

THE CRITICS

"*Any Wednesday,* which was a bright bauble of hit stagecraft when it came to Broadway, emerges not much the worse for wear. Muriel Resnick's bedroom comedy is as explicit as ever; the entendres are single rather than coyly double. Julius J. Epstein has brought over the humorous essentials faithfully enough. To fill out what were dull interludes in the theatre, he has taken the comedy out of its one set and splashed it in color, exhibited the fashionable East Side, thrown in a New York power blackout and given the whole affair an introduction to show how a nice kid could get into such a situation. It all doesn't help much. By the time everything is straightened out and love has paid its way, there is a feeling that it might have been better if it had been shorter. The funny lines, and there are a good number, would have been sharper. Jane Fonda's eyes widen appropriately, she gets hysterical, she pouts and she goes through these exquisite changes of mood like a barometer in an area of rapidly changing pressures. It's called for in the action and she delivers it with enthusiasm. Jason Robards is something else as a corporation smoothie, a philanderer whose wickedly roving eye makes him lust even for his own wife. It's not much of a challenge and his performance is no more than adequate. Rosemary Murphy, as his wife, is an magnificently effervescent as she was when she created the role

Jason Robards, Rosemary Murphy, Jane Fonda, and Dean Jones

on Broadway. . . . To take *Any Wednesday* on its own terms, it is a pleasant enough, somewhat overdrawn film that will dispose of a few hours painlessly."

Richard F. Shepard, *The New York Times*

"*Any Wednesday* is a kind of sexual string quartet arranged for four players, each assigned a key in the same flat. The flat is on Manhattan's upper East Side, and the wicked rejoinders wafting through the premises kept Broadway playgoers bounding happily into the high-priced upholstery for a couple of years. Alert to the undertones of Muriel Resnick's comedy, even a prude could relax and enjoy it, secure in the knowledge that every vibrant innuendo was just a homily in disguise. . . . 'Wednesday's' girl of the hour is Jane Fonda. Looking tempting and wholesome, she cries a lot but wears her teardrops like costume jewelry. Produced on cue, the drops are merely decorative, unrelated to any real passions or real truths. . . . The foursome manages to get through the piece roughly as written—with a few soppy sequences thrown in to justify everyone's moral lapses. The more sparkling passages, alas, lie smothered under Hollywood's big-screen Technicolor treatment. The tone is too strident, the color too bright, the running around from rooftop to picturesque playgrounds too aimless. The corporate energy expended to produce each tiny bit of titillation raises questions not of taste but of waste. Sex ought to seem less work, more fun."

Time

Jason Robards and Jane Fonda

Henry Fonda

The Dirty Game

American International-Landau-Unger. 1956. Directed by Terence Young, Christian-Jaque, Carlo Lizzani. Produced by Richard Hellman (co-production of Franco-London Films, Echberg Films, Fair Films.) Screen play by Jo Eisinger, based on a screen play by Jacques Remy, Christian-Jaque, Ennio de Concini, Philippe Bouvard. (French title—*Guerre Secret*).

HENRY FONDA played *Kourlov* in a cast that also included: Robert Ryan, Vittorio Gassman, Annie Girardot, Bourvil, Robert Hossein, Peter Van Eyck, Maria Grazia Buccela.

THE PICTURE: Henry Fonda thought it seemed like a good idea—one of those omnibus pictures with several different stories in the framework. It was the era of *The Spy Who Came in From the Cold* and the dirty side of spying was becoming as stylish as James Bond. Fonda was in Europe anyway (for *Battle of the Bulge*) and the picture would mean only a short location filming in Berlin. Director of his segment was Terence Young, of the Bond movies, and equally notable names were to direct other segments. And other cast members

would include such notable names as Robert Ryan, Vittorio Gassman, Annie Girardot and several others of note. (At least one of the promised directors and a few promised stars of distinction were out before the picture was finally made.) Fonda's role was to be that of a middle-European undercover agent but since the

Henry Fonda

Henry Fonda and Peter Van Eyck   Henry Fonda and bit player

role was virtually without dialogue—for the greater part, he played a man alone in a room, awaiting death—his Nebraska twang would not be a barrier.

And his sequence did have some good moments—closeups of his face in panic as his assassination becomes inevitable. But the other sequences were routine and even the good actors had little chance to score. The production seemed thrown together and the American distributing company threw it into the grind market, where it had a few unpublicized theatre dates before being sold off in a television package.

THE CRITICS

"St. Vitus is the guilty patron saint of *The Dirty Game,* the latest film study of that favorite contemporary sport, international espionage. How it jumps around, from one vague encounter to another, from logic to illogic. The first law of Iron Curtain spy work is to patch your cracks. Here, the seams show all too clearly, despite the heroics of a number of foreign and American screen notables and the presence of three directors. Perhaps, one of the latter would have been enough. The movie consists of three incidents which, despite American-International's contentions to the contrary, have nothing to do with each other. . . . Henry Fonda busts out of East Germany in the third. General Robert Ryan keeps arriving late at the scene of each crime, lending a certain, undeniable sense of unity to the proceedings. . . . Ryan and Fonda deliver their own lines, but the voices of the others have been dubbed—with

something less than eloquent results. . . . It's got action here and there, and its fireworks are modern enough. Other than that, dirty shame, 'Dirty Game.' "

William Peper, *New York World Journal Tribune*

"Serviceable sketch film although somewhat too pat in a high-gear, gimmicky James Bond sphere or as a more serious and probing look at the spy world. . . . Henry Fonda is miscast as a Russian type but acquits himself well."

Mosk, *Variety*

Robert Ryan and Henry Fonda

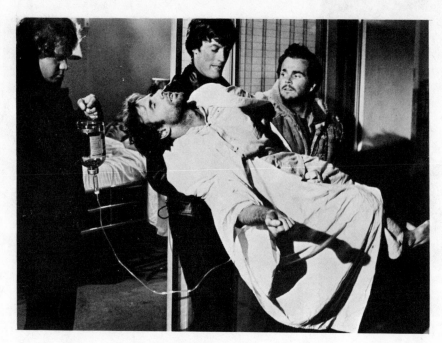

Michael J. Pollard, Peter Fonda,
Bruce Dern, and Buck Taylor

The Wild Angels

American International. 1966. Produced and directed by Roger Corman. Screen play by Charles B. Griffith.

PETER FONDA played *Heavenly Blues* in a cast that also included: Nancy Sinatra, Bruce Dern, Lou Procopio, Coby Denton, Marc Cavell, Buck Taylor, Norm Alden, Michael J. Pollard, Diane Ladd, Joan Shawlee, Gayle Hunnicutt, Art Baker, Frank Maxwell, Frank Gerstle, Kim Hamilton.

THE PICTURE: The critics sat down particularly hard on *The Wild Angels*. Most of them were outraged by its excess of violence and sex. One, for instance, was so indignant about it all that, at a press preview, he vehemently blasted Shirlee (Mrs. Henry) Fonda on the grounds that she had a connection with Peter Fonda, the star, and "Peter should have been ashamed of himself for having anything to do with this disgraceful movie."

The controversy continued to the Venice Film Festival at which *The Wild Angels* was the invited American entry. Producer-director Roger Corman defended the Festival invitation, arguing that it only proved that, in our democracy, we were free to show the less attractive side of American life.

Certainly *The Wild Angels* could not have much more luridly presented the activities of the California motorcycle gangs. Gang rapes, orgies, sadism and flaunting of conventions and the law were the stuff of which this movie was made—it went much further than had Marlon Brando's similar *The Wild Ones,* also strongly criticized when it came out some dozen years earlier. American censors snipped a few moments from an orgy scene (the picture was shown uncut in the rest of the world) but it was still much too much for most critics and censors.

Many European critics, particularly those to whom Corman is something of a cult figure, gave the picture high marks. And it did extremely well at the box office with the young and vocal taking it up as their own.

It was also extremely important to the career of Peter Fonda—finally achieving an identification and a screen personality as representative of angry, alienated youth. From *The Wild Angels* on, young Fonda, hitherto just one of many sensitive types among young leading men, became probably the leading film representative of the new generation, the first "hippy star." Posters of Peter on his "Wild Angels" motorcycle outsold those of Brando, Newman, Beatty and McQueen in many areas. (Oddly enough, a poster put out some months later of the young Henry Fonda, as Tom Joad, became a bigger seller in many college towns than the "Wild Angels" poster of Peter.)

THE CRITICS

"That notorious Roger Corman film, entitled *The Wild Angels,* opened here yesterday. This is the brutal little picture that was shown at the Venice Festival as an

Peter Fonda and the church orgy

Peter Fonda and Michael J. Pollard

American entry (by invitation) and caused a few diplomats to mop their brows. It is an embarrassment all right—a vicious account of the boozing, fighting, pot-smoking, vandalizing and raping done by a gang of sickle riders who are obviously drawn to represent the swastika-wearing Hell's Angels, one of several disreputable gangs on the West Coast. . . . Mr. Corman has shot the whole thing in color and in a *cinema verité* style that makes it resemble a documentary."

Bosley Crowther, *The New York Times*

"Realistic leather jacket delinquency yarn with plenty of shock value. . . . While not new in tone, the treatment is sufficiently compelling. The screenplay carried shock impact of the sort that occasionally stuns. As such, it is suitable mainly for those who relish their action raw and violent. . . . Peter Fonda lends credence to his character, voicing the creed of the Angels in 'wanting to do what we want to do' without interference, and is well cast."

Whit, *Variety*

Peter Fonda, as Heavenly Blues, leads the "Angels'" funeral procession with Nancy Sinatra and weeping Diane Ladd at its head

The Game Is Over

Royal-Marceau. 1966. Directed and produced by Roger Vadim. Screen play by Jean Cau, Vadim and Bernard Frechtman, based on the novel, *La Curée,* by Emile Zola. Original title: *La Curée.*

JANE FONDA played *Renee Saccard* in a cast that also included: Peter McEnery, Michel Piccoli, Tina Marquand, Jacques Monod, Simone Valere, Ham Chau Luong, Howard Vernon, Douglas Read, Germaine Montero.

THE PICTURE: *The Game Is Over* generated considerable attention when Jane Fonda sued *Playboy* magazine for using what she insisted were "unauthorized" pictures of her in the buff. The *Playboy* layout created more excitement in America than the movie itself but, in spite of some notices which found it rather old hat, there were American critics who echoed the opinion of European writers and audiences. To the latter, it was one of the biggest box-office draws and one of the most adult dramas of its year. Jane Fonda fiercely defends it against certain American critical snipes, pointing out that it did more to establish her as a serious actress abroad than any other film she has made.

THE CRITICS

"Roger Vadim's films are visual memoirs of his amours.

He has made love with a camera to former wives Brigitte Bardot and Annette Stroyberg, who glowed on the screen in response. But he has never made it so well as with Jane Fonda, the current Mme. Vadim, who is not only as gorgeous as her predecessors but also a gifted actress. Consequently, *The Game Is Over* is his best film since *Les Liaisons Dangereuses* and the finest of Miss Fonda's career. Never has she looked so beautiful—photographed in ravishing color by Claude Renoir, no less—or has been given such a good part, that of a woman who falls in love with her stepson, who is about her own age. Having trusted in Vadim completely, she creates a comprehensive portrait of a woman in love—her joys and sorrows, hopes and fears. . . .

Kevin Thomas, *Los Angeles Times*

Mr. Vadim's camera is a notorious celebrant of women and in *The Game Is Over* it scrutinizes at length with fascination the fresh face and slender, lightly clad body of Jane Fonda, who has never given a better performance."

Brendan Gill, *The New Yorker*

"Could movie director Roger Vadim do it? Could he do for his actress-wife Jane Fonda what he did for sex goddess Brigitte Bardot and for Catherine Deneuve? The answer is Yes . . . he can and he has. *The Game Is Over* is one of the most beautiful movies I've ever seen, photographed with a wealth of imagination and taste, as well as a fabulous attention to fascinating details of current Parisian life. . . . The movie is enthralling. Once you've seen the opulence of these interiors and exteriors (filmed in glorious color with sensual filters) in a mature but not sneaky look at nudity, sex and romance, you'll know how the rich live . . . and love. The acting is first rate. Vadim really knows how to pull it out of people. Jane has never been so appealing."

Liz Smith, *Cosmopolitan*

Miss Fonda appears as often as possible in her natural exterior. She has never looked so beautiful nor acted so well—and in undubbed French, at that . . . Vadim holds nothing back. He seems to have dedicated this film—the best of his career—to his wife, to amour and to the cinema itself."

Gene Youngblood, *Los Angeles Herald-Examiner*

"Roger Vadim's sardonic and sensual *The Game Is Over* is one of the best films of its genre ever to come from France. Bold, adult fare, with scenes of passion at times unnecessarily prolonged, 'Game' is, nevertheless, a film of uncompromising artistry and originality . . . 'Game' is Vadim's best picture to date and is unquestionably Miss Fonda's finest screen portrayal. The actress has of late demonstrated her agility as a light comedienne in Hollywood films. *The Game Is Over* is the first opportunity she has had in some time to display her intense dramatic ability with such a probing, in-depth characterization as that of Renée, the pampered and selfish young wife of a middle-aged businessman."

Dale Monroe, *Hollywood Citizen-News*

"In this luscious Technicolor updating of Emile Zola's *La Curée,* Roger Vadim firmly establishes himself as Ross Hunter of the nouvelle vague and Jane Fonda as Miss Screen Nude of '67 while equally firmly setting the intellectual cause of cinema back some 40 years. Seldom has such lavish and lush scenery, decor, flesh and photography been used to encompass such vapidity and slush—and used with such beguiling slickness and style that the film goes right to the top of our list of Perfectly Marvelous Awful Movies to Eat Chocolates and Play Russ Columbo Records By."

Judith Crist, *New York World Journal Tribune*

"The performance by Jane Fonda is one of her very best. She has the same capacity for acting growth so long, quietly and brilliantly demonstrated by her father."

Archer Winsten, *New York Post*

Peter McEnery and Jane Fonda

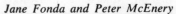

Jane Fonda and Peter McEnery

— 233 —

Hurry Sundown

Paramount. 1967. Produced and directed by Otto Preminger. Screenplay by Thomas C. Ryan and Horton Foote, based on the novel by K. B. Gilden.

JANE FONDA played *Julie Ann Warren* in a cast that also included: Michael Caine, John Philip Law, Diahann Carroll, Robert Hooks, Faye Dunaway, Burgess Meredith, Jim Backus, Robert Reed, Beah Richards, Rex Ingram, Madeleine Sherwood, Doro Merande, George Kennedy, Frank Converse, Loring Smith, Donna Danton, John Mark, Luke Askew, Peter Goff, William Elder, Steve Sanders, Dawn Barcelona, David Sanders, Michael Henry Roth, Gladys Newman, Joan Parks, Robert C. Bloodwell, Charles Keel, Kelly Ross, Ada Hall Covington, Gene Rutherford, Bill Hart, Dean Smith.

THE PICTURE: Poor Jane Fonda, so often getting into the "big ones" which turn out to be "bad ones." Otto Preminger had everything going for him in *Hurry Sundown*—a best-selling novel, a strong cast, an expensive production. Everything but taste. Almost the chief victim in the most tasteless scene of all—something to do with a saxophone luridly used as a sex symbol—was Miss Fonda, misused again.

THE CRITICS
"Slickness, soap and slobbery.... Lawsy, chillun, dey

Otto Preminger and his cast: from left, Donna Danton, Robert Hooks, Jim Backus, Faye Dunaway, John Philip Law, Diahann Carroll, Madeleine Sherwood, Jane Fonda, Michael Caine, Luke Askew, Rex Ingram, Steve Sanders, George Kennedy, Robert Reed, and Doro Merande.

Jane Fonda

The notorious saxophone scene: Michael Caine and Jane Fonda

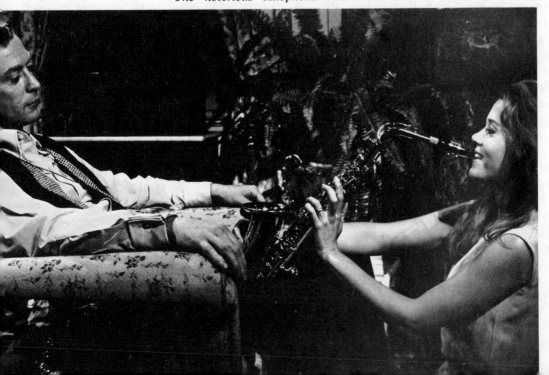

Otto Preminger with Michael Caine, Faye Dunaway, Robert Hooks, Jane Fonda and children

ain't been so perspicacious a study of Southern problems since ex-Governor Wallace's last speech on civil rights. . . . The road to this disaster is, we hasten to note, paved with good intentions (after all, being pro-civil rights is safe box-office these days) as well as with tasteless sensationalism and plain and fancy foolishness. Otto Preminger has provided us not only with soap opera plotting that gives *Peyton Place* Dostoievskian stature but also with cartoon character and patronage of Negroes that are incredible in 1967. The whole melange would be offensive were it not simply ludicrous. . . . For villainy, there's Michael Caine, speaking a dialect that out-Remuses the old Uncle himself. Jane Fonda, Caine's wife, is a good kid, fond of her mammy and really pro-Negro and devoted to her retarded son. But she's hung up on Caine, a real love captive melting at his touch, getting all boozed up and stuff—you know how these decadent high-class Southern gals are. It's a new Jane, who doesn't even melt when Caine grabs her by the breast. . . . To say that *Hurry Sundown* is the worst film of the still young year is to belittle it. It stands with the worst films of any number of years."

Judith Crist, *New York World Journal Tribune*

"Otto Preminger's *Hurry Sundown* has received much harsher reviews than it deserves. Charges of Uncle-Tomism are particularly unfair from critics who accepted and even applauded the Negro preacher and his psalm-singing daughter in *Nothing But a Man.* Still Preminger has failed to integrate his personal dramas with the massive racial theme they are supposed to illuminate. . . . Preminger's sentimental affirmation in *Hurry Sundown* is still somewhat premature and grossly oversimplified, but I still feel this is a subject with which you are damned if you do and damned if you don't. . . . On the one hand, critics applaud *Ulysses* for its audacity in allowing Joyce's four-letter words to be recited on the soundtrack, and on the other hand, they denounce Preminger for a genuinely witty stroke of visual suggestiveness with Jane Fonda and a sex-ridden saxophone. Talk dirty but don't show dirty seems to be the McLuhanistic maxim of many of the reviewers. Yet the saxophone scene in *Hurry Sundown* is infinitely more daring and cinematic and, yes, truthful a breakthrough than the culture-mongering rehash of *Ulysses.*"

Andrew Sarris, *The Village Voice*

Janice Rule and Henry Fonda

Welcome to Hard Times

Metro-Goldwyn-Mayer. 1967. Directed and written by Burt Kennedy. Produced by Max E. Youngstein and David Karr. Based on the novel by E. L. Doctorow.

HENRY FONDA played *Will Blue* in a cast that also included Janice Rule, Aldo Ray, Keenan Wynn, Janis Paige, John Anderson, Warren Oates, Fay Spain, Edgar Buchanan, Denver Pyle, Michael Shea, Arlene Golonka, Lon Chaney, Royal Dano, Alan Baxter, John Birch, Dan Ferrone, Elisha Cook, Kalin Liu, Ann McCrea, Bob Terhune, Ron Burke.

THE PICTURE: When it comes to Westerns, Henry Fonda likes to take chances with off-beat dramas, not at all the tried-and-true surefire fare. *Welcome to Hard Times* was a book he admired and he welcomed the opportunity to work again with Burt Kennedy, with whom he had done *The Rounders*. But *Welcome to Hard Times* was just too far away from the norm, with its characters seeming to be symbolic figures in some sort of parable rather than having any semblance of real life. The picture had its admirers—a small group in this country led by Andrew Sarris, and more in Europe—

but it was a box-office failure and largely a critical disaster. Within a year after its theatrical release, it was playing on television—and didn't the exhibitors raise hell about that!

THE CRITICS

"Welcome to Hard Times is a movie composed entirely of other movies. Every character has been pre-tested in scores of scenarios: the evil gunslinger; the aging lawman, poor but honest; the frightened townspeople; prostitutes with guaranteed 24-carat hearts. . . . Fortunately for the film, even the small roles are in the hands of some of the oldest pros in the business—among them Edgar Buchanan as a Government man and Lon Chaney as a bartender. Handling the clichés with the care of a cowpoke tending a tired palomino, they make 'Hard Times' seem better than it is because they have been there before—many times. So has the audience."

Time

"Writer-director Burt Kennedy forces us to come to grips with a central figure, subtly played by Henry Fonda, who is as close to being an antihero as you are

Henry Fonda, Fay Spain, Arlene
Golonka, and Janis Paige

Aldo Ray and Henry Fonda

ever likely to see in serious Western garb. It is true that
the substance of the film deals with his efforts to save
Hard Times when everyone else is willing to abandon
its charred ruins, and it is also true that he becomes
somewhat more appealing as his character expands with
his task.

"But it must be understood that he undertakes the job
only because he knows there is no place lower for him
to sink than Hard Times, that if he cannot make this
rotten town live he will be unable to find any place
worse to try the luck of his flawed character. He does
not basically change in the process of nursing the place
back to a semblance of health, and far from facing up
to Ray's return in a manly fashion, he again confronts
him with a trick and a desperate prayer. He is a Westerner practicing not a code of honor but modern sur-
vival ethics.

He and his de-romanticized environment may be a
bit hard to take for those who insist on purity in the
Western form. Certainly the violence of the film, though
infrequent, is far too savage for exposure to childish or
squeamish eyes, even though one can truthfully say
that it is esthetically justified. . . .

Burt Kennedy is a courageous man, risking far more
than most directors who attempt Westerns ever do. His
work is not just a tinkering with a tradition-encrusted
form, but a serious attempt to extend the range of its
possibilities. It may be imperfect, but it is well worth
the attention of anyone who cares about such matters."
Richard Schickel, *Life*

Barefoot in the Park

Paramount. 1967. Directed by Gene Saks. Produced by Hal Wallis. Screen play by Neil Simon, based on his play.

JANE FONDA played *Corie Bratter* in a cast that also included Robert Redford, Mildred Natwick, Charles Boyer, Herbert Edelman, Mabel Albertson, Fritz Feld, James Stone, Ted Hartley.

THE PICTURE: It's impossible to go wrong with *Barefoot in the Park*—take it from one who has been forced to sit through too many non-Nichols versions of the play (a friend is always playing it somewhere). Certainly Mike Nichols gave it a pace and style and all kinds of surprises that made it *the* comedy event of its time on Broadway. But Neil Simon had written one of his liveliest scripts and even less gifted directors couldn't keep it from being entertaining.

On the screen, Gene Saks — working against the handicap that it had all been done before—managed to keep it moving merrily. And, even if there were no surprises left, it remained lots of fun. Saks cast it wisely with two of its originals from the theatre—Robert Redford and Mildred Natwick—and added a couple of ex-

cellent ringers, Charles Boyer and, most notably, an absolutely enchanting Jane Fonda, who is always at her most beguiling when she is playing such a hip, charming and slightly scatterbrained young modern.

THE CRITICS
"No mistake about it. Neil Simon is a very funny man. He has an extraordinary knack for taking the commonplace, turning it upside down, and shaking the laughs out of it. He also has an uncanny ear for the amusing turns of everyday conversation, which become funnier still when put into the mouths of people who take themselves very seriously. Simon's people, as represented in his own adaptation of his hit play, *Barefoot in the Park,* are essentially characters—which is to say that they are quite ordinary men and women operating under a strong compulsion to do ridiculous things, but who feel that their actions are the most natural and reasonable in the world. And because Simon makes them so attractive and appealing, we are more than willing to go along with them, enjoying every moment of their temporary discomfort, applauding enthusiastically their ultimate triumphs. . . . What scenarist Simon has done to improve on playwright's Simon's original

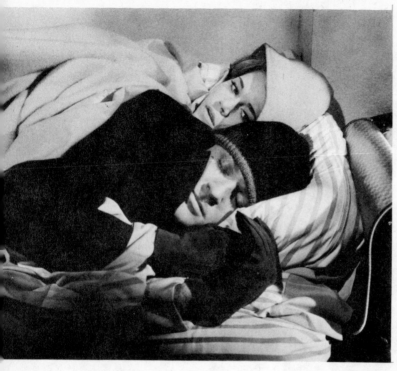

Jane Fonda and Robert Redford

Mildred Natwick and Jane Fonda

Jane Fonda says, "Not very pretty—but I love this picture"

had been to open the action well beyond the play's single setting and, except for a prolonged finale straight out of an old Harold Lloyd movie, to interlard his basic material with scenes and sequences that are so smoothly carpentered into the structure as to give no sense of superfluous padding. . . . Best of all in the film is its meticulously chosen cast and the adroit, amusing performances that director Gene Saks, here making his movie debut, has elicited from each member. Since both Robert Redford and Mildred Natwick are veterans of the New York company, their smooth expertise as the young man and his bemused mother-in-law is hardly surprising. But Charles Boyer slips just as snugly into the role of Velasco, the aging, scrounging Bohemian. And Jane Fonda, who hitherto seems to have had difficulty in determining which note to hit in her various roles, at last displays that she is in fact a charmingly fey, disturbingly sexy light comedienne, with an instinct for the timing and intonation of laugh lines that should keep her busy for many years to come."

Arthur Knight, *Saturday Review*

"Barefoot in the Park is one of the few plays to be reincarnated on-screen while playing on the Broadway stage. Happily, it loses little in transition. Essentially, Author Neil Simon has taken a plot as bland as a potato, sliced it into thin bits—and made it as hard to resist as potato chips. . . . The film is no original-cast production. Sly substitutions have been made, notably Jane Fonda for Broadway's Elizabeth Ashley. Jane's performance is the best of her career: a clever caricature of a sex kitten who can purr or scratch with equal intensity."

Time

The Trip

American International. 1967. Produced and directed by Roger Corman. Screen play by Jack Nicholson.

PETER FONDA played *Paul Groves* in a cast that also included: Susan Strasberg, Bruce Dern, Dennis Hopper, Salli Sachse, Katherine Walsh, Barboura Morris, Carin Bernsen, Dick Miller, Luana Anders, Tommy Signorelli, Mitzi Hoag, Judy Lang, Barbara Renson, Susan Walters, Frankie Smith.

THE PICTURE: Sooner or later, there had to be a movie about an LSD trip and naturally it was the kind of thing in which you'd expect Roger Corman and American International to be involved. And with Peter Fonda very much in the hippie image, he was natural casting for the occasion. Something rather startling should have come out of it.

The Trip had its moments—some imaginative camera work and some intriguing psychedelic atmosphere. It had a minor, but very vocal, band of enthusiasts.

But much of it seemed just so much phony-arty film footage, only occasionally compelling. It got very little attention, even from the turned-on generation to whom it was obviously addressed.

THE CRITICS
"The Trip is a psychedelic tour through the bent mind of Peter Fonda, which is evidently full of old movies.

Susan Strasberg and Peter Fonda

In a flurry of flesh, mattresses, flashing lights and kaleidoscopic patterns, an alert viewer will spot some fancy business from such classics as *The Seventh Seal, Lawrence of Arabia,* even *The Wizard of Oz.* Eventually, in a scene that is right out of *8½,* Fonda perches on a merry-go-round while a robed judge gravely spells

Peter Fonda

out his previous sins and inadequacies. The photographer's camera work is bright enough and full of tricks, without beginning to suggest the heightened inner awareness so frequently claimed by those who use the drug."

Time

"*The Trip* amounts to very little more than an hour-and-a-half commercial for LSD. This movie boasts Peter Fonda as a man who tries a trip in order to be wiser and it has Susan Strasberg, among other people, in the nude looking like a Venetian blind, courtesy of op and pop art painting. Neither Mr. Fonda nor Miss Strasberg is left with any place to go but 'up' after this movie. The subject matter of *The Trip* enables the director to make a totally incoherent movie with erratic, repetitious and fake-arty effects that simply nauseate, both intellectually and physically. This is one trip to skip."

Judith Crist, NBC "Today" Show

Peter Fonda

Peter Fonda and Bruce Dern

Stranger on the Run

Universal. 1967. Directed by Donald Siegel. Produced by Richard E. Lyons. Screen play by Dean Reisner from a story by Reginald Rose.

HENRY FONDA played *The Stranger* in a cast that also included: Michael Parks, Anne Baxter, Dan Duryea, Sal Mineo.

THE PICTURE: Universal, anxious to make a special splash with its feature films made especially for television, put an extremely good cast, headed by Henry Fonda, into a taut little Western drama, based on a story by Reginald Rose (*12 Angry Men*) and directed by Don Siegel, a veteran film-maker just being taken up by the upper-caste critics. The result was so good that the studio had second thoughts about its TV premiere and decided to release it first to theatres.

But NBC, for whom the picture was made, was understandably adamant about its having its initial exposure on television, as originally planned. So America saw it at home, even though it played in theatres in other parts of the world. It is still considered a model for those "made-for-TV" movies—a model which is seldom approached.

Henry Fonda

Henry Fonda

Anne Baxter and Henry Fonda

Fonda's performance as the seediest of drunken derelicts was, of course, the acting event but capable actors like Michael Parks, Anne Baxter, Dan Duryea and Sal Mineo were well cast, too.

THE CRITICS

"I think for a one-twenty [a two-hour television film] it's very good. I liked having Fonda. I like very much the fact that a man of his age is thrown off a freight car at the start of the picture. He's a bum and doesn't lick anybody. There isn't anybody in town he can lick. And then you go through a change at the end of the picture. Not that he could whip anybody, but he's a man. He faces up to responsibility. I thought the picture was surprisingly un-Hollywood—and I'm not using that term to be as contemptuous as it sounds."

Don Siegel, quoted in interview with
Peter Bogdanovich in *Movie*

"An excellent movie cast, beautifully paced melodrama, replete with social and psychological significance and outstanding performances by Henry Fonda, Dan Duryea and Michael Parks. . . . The performances make *Stranger on the Run* of particular interest beyond its being one of the few tailored-for-TV films that provide character, along with skilfully paced melodramatics. Henry Fonda and Dan Duryea are their usual perfection; Michael Parks gives his best performance to date, and Anne Baxter is so good you don't even mind her chic or her flashy teeth, hardly the hallmark of the working frontierswoman."

Judith Crist, *TV Guide*

Inger Stevens and Henry Fonda

Firecreek

Warner Bros.-7 Arts. 1968. Produced by Philip Leacock. Directed by Vincent McEveety. Screen play by Calvin Clements.

HENRY FONDA played *Larkin* in a cast that also included: James Stewart, Inger Stevens, Gary Lockwood, Dean Jagger, Ed Begley, Jay C. Flippen, Jack Elam, James Best, Barbara Luna, Jacqueline Scott, Brooke Bundy, J. Robert Porter, Morgan Woodward, John Qualen, Louise Latham, Athena Lord, Harry "Slim" Ducan, Kevin Tate, Christopher Shea.

THE PICTURE: It should have been a major movie event when old friends Henry Fonda and James Stewart got together for the first time on the screen (not counting their vignette in *On Our Merry Way*) in the kind of picture both have played so notably so many times. *Firecreek* was a Western, but a moody Western which

James Best, Gary Lockwood, Henry Fonda, Jack Elam, Barbara Luna, and James Stewart

Henry Fonda and James Stewart

had quite a little talk, much of it psychological, before the inevitable action finally began to pop. Faced with this difficult-to-classify picture ("It's too slow for Western audiences—but it is a Western,") the distributor solved the problem by dumping it unceremoniously into the neighborhood theatres and leaving it on its own. With scarcely any attention paid to it, *Firecreek* quickly expired in the theatres, to have a better run, one hopes,

on television. If you didn't see it, you are far from alone.

THE CRITICS

"Sometimes there's a sleeper, a small Western that comes along, that really has more to offer than just grist for the Western mill. For the first time in twenty years, Henry Fonda and James Stewart are on screen together and it's a joy to watch these two old pros. Fonda, mind you, is the bad guy, leader of a gang that terrorizes the town and Stewart is the aging farmer and part-time sheriff who just gets rip-roaring mad. *Firecreek* has some explosive stuff but it is, thanks to its stars and direction, a satisfyingly low-key and absorbing Western."

Judith Crist, NBC "Today" Show

"*Firecreek* is a good, sturdy and occasionally powerful little Western. James Stewart is plain wonderful and Henry Fonda almost matches him. For some strange reason these peerless veteran cowboys have never appeared on the same movie prairie before, only once together in a 1948 comedy, *On Our Merry Way*. To see what they, a fine cast and a dandy new director have accomplished on a small patch of ground has been worth the twenty-year wait.... This unpretentious little color movie, which looks as though it cost a dime, is almost exactly right every step of the way.... And, pitted against each other at the end Mr. Stewart and Mr. Fonda, as a ruthless, enigmatic loner, plays like flint on steel. Small-size *Firecreek*, sparked by two veteran aces, makes a little go a long, long way."

Howard Thompson, *The New York Times*

Stewart under Fonda's gun

Henry Fonda and Lucille Ball

Yours, Mine and Ours

United Artists. 1968. Directed by Melville Shavelson. Produced by Robert F. Blumofe for Desilu-Walden. Screen play by Shavelson and Mort Lachman, based on a story by Madelyn Davis and Bob Carroll, Jr.

HENRY FONDA played *Frank Beardsley* in a cast that also included: Lucille Ball, Van Johnson, Tom Bosley, Louise Troy, Ben Murphy, Jennifer Leak, Kevin Burchett, Kimberly Beck, Mitchell Vogel, Margot Jane, Eric Shea, Gregory Arkins, Lynnell Atkins, Timothy Matthieson, Gilbert Rogers, Nancy Roth, Gary Goetzman, Suzanne Cupito, Holly O'Brien, Michele Tobin, Maralee Foster, Tracy Nelson, Stephanie Oliver.

THE PICTURE: Some critics—like mod Renata Adler, of *The New York Times*—treated *Yours, Mine and Ours* as almost prehistoric. To be sure, it was old-style family comedy of the kind that had been popular in the forties era of *Mr. Blandings Builds His Dream House* and *Cheaper by the Dozen*. And there were moments here and there that were reminiscent of the Lucy TV shows.

But generally Miss Ball was much more restrained than usual and Henry Fonda was extremely likeable as the widower-father of ten who meets a widow-mother of eight. That their story was all based on a real-life family, the Beardsleys of California, helped give it the extra believability to put it in a category well beyond ordinary situation family comedy.

It was one of the most popular pictures of the year and, in spite of Miss Adler who supposedly speaks for youth, it was extremely well received by young audiences as well. Fonda nervously watched its premiere, held at Syracuse University's Fonda Film Festival. The auditorium, packed with collegians, was quickly rocking with delighted laughter.

THE CRITICS
"By classic Hollywood thinking, the formula should be absolutely infallible: if one kid is cute, it follows that 18 kids have to be 18 times cuter. The new math of *Yours, Mine and Ours* proves nearly the opposite. . . . Overweight and festooned with stale situations and weary wisecracks, *Yours, Mine and Ours* relies for its

Van Johnson, Henry Fonda, and Lucille Ball

Henry Fonda and "his children"

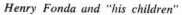

Henry Fonda and two of the "yours, mine and ours"

levity on two unassailable assets: Fonda and Ball. At 62, Fonda can still leave a line wry and dry. At 56, Ball commands a solid slapstick style that none of her younger rivals can match. . . . And they are ably backed by a surprisingly supple comedian named Van Johnson, who seems to be searching for—and finding—a new turn to his long career. Together, the old pros take the surplus corn and, like the manufacturers of all that breakfast food they buy, turn it into something with snap, crackle and popularity."

Time

"*Yours, Mine and Ours* starts from a premise that would surely have delighted Walt Disney. A widowed Navy nurse (Lucille Ball), the mother of eight, meets and marries a naval officer (Henry Fonda), a widower and the father of ten. Oddly enough, writer-director Melville Shavelson never loses sight of the fact that this is actually a real California family. The responses of both the adults and the children to this unlikely merger have a ring of truth about them, as if based on observation rather than imagination, and cuteness has been rigidly eschewed. The two stars, assisted by Van John-

son and Tom Bosley, also manage to avoid most of the pitfalls and pratfalls that their material would seem to invite. In Shavelson's hands, the film is amusing, heart-warming, contemporary, believable."

Arthur Knight, *Saturday Review*

"Now—to brighten my declining years—comes *Yours, Mine and Ours,* possibly one of the funniest farces since those golden days. This is not Nostalgia for a form of Comedy Past; it is simply joy for a thoroughly modern, free-wheeling, rollicking comedy that you can just sit back and enjoy. . . . Henry Fonda is as perfect a man as ever—remember him in *The Lady Eve?* Lucille Ball's annoying Lucy-isms have been kept in remarkable—almost superhuman—restraint by director Melville Shavelson . . . and she really proves how good a farceuse she is when she is controlled. Van Johnson shows the same old competence as Hank's navy buddy. . . . There is remarkably little more one can say about a film which gives as much entertainment as this. There is nothing to analyze, nothing to interpret, nothing to carp at. Nothing to say except Go and Enjoy!"

Peter Davis Dibble, *Woman's Wear Daily*

Raymond St. Jacques and Henry Fonda

Madigan

Universal. 1968. Directed by Don Siegel. Produced by Frank P. Rosenberg. Screen play by Henri Simoun and Abraham Polonsky, based on the novel *The Commissioner* by Richard Dougherty.

HENRY FONDA played *Commissioner Anthony X. Russell* in a cast that also included: Richard Widmark, Inger Stevens, Harry Guardino, James Whitmore, Susan Clark, Michael Dunn, Steve Ihnat, Don Stroud, Sheree North, Warren Stevens, Raymond St. Jacques, Bert Freed, Harry Bellaver, Frank Marth, Lloyd Gough, Virginia Gregg, Toian Machinga, Rita Lynn, Robert Granere, Henry Beckman, Woodrow Parfrey, Dallas Mitchell, Lloyd Haines, Ray Montgomery, Seth Allen, Philippa Bevans, Kay Turner, Diane Sayer, Conrad Bain, Ed Crowley, John McLiam, William Bramley.

THE PICTURE: Although the notices for *Madigan* were extremely good—much better, for instance, than those for the similar lurid, splashy *The Detective*—it was a film with which Henry Fonda personally was particularly unhappy. He had accepted the role in spite of his dissatisfaction with the script which had subordinated the title character of the novel, the commissioner, to the detective, Madigan. Since Richard Widmark, who was playing Madigan, had been involved in the production from the beginning, this was reasonable.

Fonda, because he likes Widmark and particularly because of his admiration for director Don Siegel, was persuaded to accept the role. An added inducement was the fact that most of the film was to be shot in New York, where Fonda prefers to live and work.

But few of the promises to revise the commissioner role to make it more worthy of the star were kept. And both Fonda and Siegel were involved in a running feud

Susan Clark, Henry Fonda

Henry Fonda and James Whitmore

that his chief inspector and best friend, Mr. Whitmore, has pulled a shady personal deal."

Howard Thompson, *The New York Times*

"*Madigan* is a good movie about some bad days at New York City's police department. . . . From the commissioner on down, everybody is up to his badge in problems. Sorting out their sex lives, remoralizing the turpitude, and tracking down a killer at the same time, makes for a tough, taut film. . . . Commendably long on documentary detail about police procedure, *Madigan* is refreshingly short on sadism. Henry Fonda is at his uptight best as the up-from-the-ranks commissioner, so righteous that as a cop on the beat he sent back the butcher's Christmas turkey. Richard Widmark is engaging as the detective who lives 'on the arm'—accepting all 'police discounts.' The skillful dramatic use of Manhattan—indoors and out—should gladden the heart of Mayor John Lindsay and further his campaign to put a movie crew on every street in Fun City."

Time

with the producer. So, although the results were impressive enough, the making of *Madigan* was far from a fondly-remembered Fonda experience.

THE CRITICS

"It's good to have Richard Widmark back on the crime beat as a detective in the title role of *Madigan*. It's also a pleasure to watch the trim, incisive underplaying of two other veterans, Henry Fonda and James Whitmore, as the hero's upper-echelon superiors on the force. If only this respectable but slack-jointed Universal offering had measured up to them as the punchy, suspense tingler it tries to be. What the picture does offer and sustain is a thoughtful police viewpoint of one particular case, and some revealing footnotes to police character and operational strategy. . . . Even more provocative is the sight of Mr. Fonda, as the police commissioner, grimly riding herd on the detective pair only to learn

"The strength of *Madigan* is the seriousness of its genre and the morally grayish tint of its characterizations. Henry Fonda's police commissioner walks around as if he has something else on his mind, and he usually has. Richard Widmark's detective on the spot lives on the edge of his nerves. Between them, Fonda and Widmark express the two aspects of life in New York, Fonda's the clouded view from the top, Widmark the desperate urgency around the next corner. New York is a city where the future is always colliding with the past and the moral arithmetic never quite adds up. The characterizations are finally wrapped up when the string runs out on a manhunt for a cop-killer and, to Siegel's credit, the ending explodes with emotional force without a wasted move or extra shot. The characterizations would not have been sufficient in themselves, nor the action sufficient in itself, but welded together by Siegel's familiar style of editing, *Madigan* turns out to be the best American movie I have seen so far in 1968."

Andrew Sarris, *The Village Voice*

Henry Fonda, Richard Widmark, Harry Guardino, and players

Jane Fonda and Anita Pallenberg

Barbarella

Paramount. 1968. Directed by Roger Vadim. Produced by Dino DeLaurentiis. Screen play by Terry Southern, Brian Degas, Claude Brule, Jean-Claude Forest, Roger Vadim, Clement Wood, Tudor Gates, Villario Bonaceil, based on the book by Jean-Claude Forest .

JANE FONDA played *Barbarella* in a cast that also included: John Philip Law, Anita Pallenberg, Milo O'Shea, David Hemmings, Marcel Marceau, Ugo Tognazzi, Claude Dauphin.

THE PICTURE: Movies derived from comic strips—and offhand you can think of such films as *Li'l Abner, Dick Tracy, Little Orphan Annie, Blondie,* all the way back to *Tillie the Toiler* and *Bringing Up Father*—are seldom as well received as their models. But, of course, one element normally missing from all such pictures is sex—outside, perhaps, of a seductive glance at Li'l Abner from Appasionata Van Climax.

European comic strips are something else again—at least, the one most familiar by reputation in this country. This is "Barbarella" and we've all heard about the saucy audacity of that strip, which combined science fiction with good old hardcore sex.

Obviously if Roger Vadim is going to make a movie version of a comic strip, you can bet it will be "Barbarella." And who would be more of an ideal Barbarella than Mme. Vadim—Jane Fonda herself?

So Vadim made *Barbarella* and Jane Fonda played it and some of the critics thought it was all too silly and trivial for words. But most of them found it high camp—with special mention devoted to the contribution, physical and otherwise, of Miss Jane Barbarella. And the public attended in droves.

John Philip Law and Jane Fonda

Jane Fonda

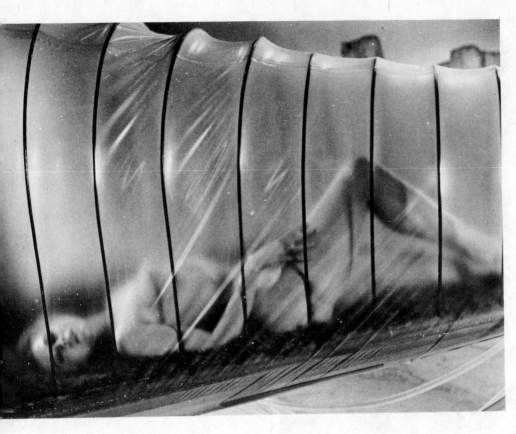

Jane Fonda as Barbarella

THE CRITICS

"*Barbarella* is not nearly the disaster it had every intention of being. Somehow its comic-strip conceits and Playboy-Bunny-in-Disneyland decor manage to sustain themselves for 100 minutes without getting too heavy or too silly. Terry Southern is listed among the multiple writing credits and I suppose he can be credited with some of the literate tone in the gags, most of which sound better than they read. But the one indispensable ingredient in this confection is Jane Fonda not only as the ideal Barbarella but also as perfect casting for Babs whenever someone gets around to filming Southern's *Flesh and Filigree*. From her opening space-suit strip-tease through every single and double entendre in the script and gadgetry, our Jane manages to exude the kind of healthy girlscoutish non-campish sexuality that should be as accessible to our children as the morbidly repressed Peter Pansy entertainments now to be imposed on them via classification.

Andrew Sarris, *The Village Voice*

"You could subtitle the film, *2002: A Space Idiocy*. Miss Fonda plays what you might call Flesh Gordon, and our first fetching view of her is as she does a strip tease floating in a state of weightlessness. We all get to appreciate the lack of gravity of the situation. (Her disrobing is technically ingenious and quite lovely, and many of the effects in the movie are equally ingenious, but never again quite so lovely.) As a film, *Barbarella* remains a thinking man's venture, although the thought required is minimal. In fact, the whole movie gives weightlessness a new definition . . . It is impossible to evaluate performances in the traditional sense. Miss Fonda plays it straight, preserving the joke by taking things seriously though not earnestly. The real credit goes to Vadim and the artists who constructed this camp visit to outré space. It is a special taste, and not for your junior birdmen, but a foolish little something for the big birds."

Charles Champlin, *Los Angeles Times*

"What would Henry James have made of Jane Fonda, an actress so much like his heroines—an American heiress-of-the-ages abroad, and married to a superb example of the Jamesian villain, a sophisticated European (a Frenchman of Russian origins) who is redolent of shallow morals, who is the screen's foremost celebrant of erotic trash, and who has the scandalous habit of turning each wife into a facsimile of the first and spreading her out for the camera. Yet Roger Vadim's evil is reassuringly "wicked"—it's so obvious that he tries to shock only to please. And Jane Fonda having sex on the wilted feathers and rough, scroungy furs of

"Barbarella" Fonda and the Blind Angel (Law)

Barbarella is more charming and fresh and bouncy than ever—the American girl triumphing by her innocence over a lewd comic-strip world of the future. She's the only comedienne I can think of who is sexiest when she is funniest. (Shirley MacLaine is a sweet and sexy funny girl, but she has never quite combined her gifts as Jane Fonda does.) Jane Fonda is accomplished at a distinctive kind of double take: she registers comic disbelief that such naughty things can be happening to her, and then her disbelief changes into an even more comic

delight. Her American-good-girl innocence makes her a marvellously apt heroine for pornographic comedy. She has the skittish innocence of a teen-age voluptuary; when she takes off her clothes, she is playfully and deliciously aware of the naughtiness of what she's doing, and that innocent's sense of naughtiness of being a tarnished lady keeps her from being just another naked actress. According to Vadim, in *Barbarella* she is supposed to be 'a kind of sexual Alice in Wonderland of the future,' but she's more like a saucy Dorothy in an Oz gone bad. The sex parodies are amusing, but *Barbarella* is disappointing after the expectations that one had (I assume I am one of many) of a film that would be good trashy, corrupt entertainment for a change. *Barbarella* isn't good trash, but it's corrupt, all right, and that's something. . . . The blind angel played by John Phillip Law is a little sickly and slightly embarrassing—not a satisfactory substitute for the Cowardly Lion—but Barbarella's other, better helpers include Ugo Tognazzi, as a hairy huntsman, and David Hemmings, who shows unexpected comic talent, as an absentminded revolutionary. Hemmings and Jane Fonda share honors in the wittiest sequence—a futuristic copulation that, appropriately, is in the genteel-but-full-of-tics style of English comedies of the forties and fifties.

Pauline Kael, *The New Yorker*

Sex "Barbarella"-style: Jane Fonda and David Hemmings

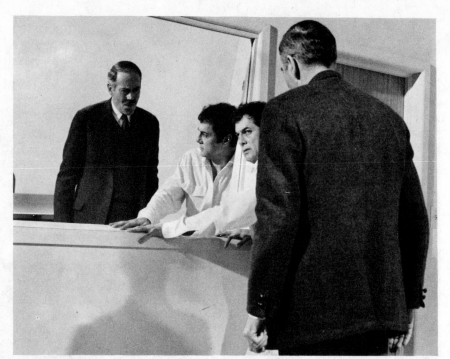

The Boston Strangler

20th Century-Fox. 1968. Directed by Richard Fleischer. Produced by Robert Fryer. Screen play by Edward Anhalt from book by Gerold Frank.

HENRY FONDA played *John S. Bottomley* in a cast that also included: Tony Curtis, George Kennedy, Mike Kellin, Hurd Hatfield, Murray Hamilton, Jeff Corey, Sally Kellerman, William Marshall, George Voscovec, Leora Dana, Carolyn Conwell, Jeanne Cooper, Austin Willis, Lara Lindsay, George Furth, Carole Shelley, William Hickey, Richard X. Slattery, Eve Collyer, Gwyda Donhowe, Alex Dreier, John Cameron Swayze, Shelley Burton, Elizabeth Baur, James Brolin, George Tyne, Dana Elcar.

THE PICTURE: Director Richard Fleischer, Producer Robert Fryer and Writer Edward Anhalt had a tough job to turn Gerold Frank's *The Boston Strangler* into a film. They would damned on the one hand for eliminating material that made fascinating reading; on the other could be accused of sensationalism and violence. That they couldn't please everybody was to be expected, and the finished picture was attacked from both sides.

By nature, the picture was rambling and episodic but Fleischer kept it as tight as possible and made particularly effective use of the split screen, used to advance plot and action, not just as a gimmick as in certain other films of the time which were also influenced by Expo techniques.

Tony Curtis broke away from his usual stereotype as the Strangler and Henry Fonda brought stature and dignity to a rather conventional role. In spite of critical dissension about it, *The Boston Strangler* was a major box-office success.

THE CRITICS

"*The Boston Strangler* represents a necessary compromise. There was too much in Gerold Frank's book to use in a single movie of reasonable length. This shortening will deprive moviegoers of Frank's great parade of 'nuts.' One no longer attends his extraordinary feat of false clues, of suspects leading away to nothing, of a grim and awful humor in the midst of that city-wide fear. The picture has contended itself with following the actual trail of the strangler and suggesting very faintly some of the perversities he practiced. Here again the book's more explicit descriptions bring one closer to the

Henry Fonda and Tony Curtis

William Hickey and Henry Fonda

Henry Fonda and George Kennedy

Mike Kellin, George Kennedy, Henry Fonda, and Murray Hamilton

actuality.... Tony Curtis, incidentally, has a makeup that subtly changes his face, so that you hardly think of him and do think of DeSalvo unless you've read the descriptions of the other man. Henry Fonda, as the dedicated coordinator of the hunt, brings his usual air of quiet intensity to the role.

Archer Winsten, *New York Post*

"*The Boston Strangler* emerges as a triumph of taste and restraint in a film era often marked by nauseating exposition and exploitation of violence. Richard Fleischer's superior direction of Edward Anhalt's excellent screen play, as interpreted by an extremely large and competent cast, distinguished this maiden film production by former legit producer Robert Fryer. A telling, low-key, semi-documentary style, incorporating the most valid and sustained dramatic usage of multipanel images seen to date, prevails in the 20th-Fox release, which falters only slightly in final half-hour....

Handsome production values, including authentic Boston production locations, and an overall muted DeLuxe color toning which is most appropriate to the mood, are the foundation on which Fleischer has built this excellent pic.... For exactly 60 of the film's 116 minutes, plot action proceeds with emphasis on fruitless attempts by Fonda, a special rep of the Massachusetts Attorney-General, and Kennedy, a Boston detective, to resolve the murders. Then Curtis makes his first appearance. Latter, trying to shake the light comedy image, is quite convincing, both in makeup and voice ... Fonda's performance is excellent, from his initial dislike of the task assigned through a quiet, dogged determination to break down Curtis' mental barriers.... After 85 minutes, the well-paced film slows down markedly as Fonda's series of interrogations of Curtis begin. What this leads up to is an excellent final scene, highlighted by a very long take in which Curtis alone on camera, gradually undergoes a mental deterioration."

Murf, *Variety*

Henry Fonda and Charles Bronson

Once Upon a Time in the West

Paramount. 1969. Directed by Sergio Leone. Produced by Fulvio Morsella. Script by Sergio Leone and Sergio Donati from a story by Dario Argento, Bernardo Bertolucci, Sergio Leone.

HENRY FONDA played *Frank* in a cast that also included: Claudia Cardinale, Jason Robards, Charles Bronson, Frank Wolff, Gabriele Ferzetti, Keenan Wynn, Paolo Stoppa, Marco Zuanelli, Lionel Stander, Jack Elam, John Frederick, Woody Strode, Enzio Santianello, Michael Harvey.

THE PICTURE: Sergio Leone grew up in Italy loving American Western movies. After he hit paydirt with his Clint Eastwood-"Dollars" trilogy, he set about to turn out his big definitive Western. In close to three hours of running time, he crammed in every last bit of plot that he had stored away in years of moviegoing. Here was a bit of *High Noon,* there a touch of *Shane,* now a nod to Hawks or Wellman, then a low bow to Ford. To head his cast, he selected his own favorite Western star—and then perversely cast Henry Fonda, one of the

most heroic of them all, as the most vicious villain to ever ride the range. (Actually, Fonda was given his choice of roles—both he and Leone relished the joke of his unexpected appearance as the Super-Bad Man.)

It would be good to say that the result of all this was a great, epic Western to end all Westerns. It didn't work that way. Much of it was fun, but sometimes the fun verged on camp. And Leone was inclined to lay on everything—the violence, the action, the plot—with a heavy hand.

Still it was something like having a whole course in the history of Western movies all wrapped up in one big movie. Although most of it was filmed in Spain, there was a trip to Ford Country—Monument Valley—for some special and spectacular footage. Claudia Cardinale was a fetching leading lady in the tradition of Maureen O'Hara and Yvonne DeCarlo. Jason Robards and Charles Bronson played their standard roles with style, and people like Jack Elam, Woody Strode, Keenan Wynn and Lionel Stander showed up in bits. Fonda, ice-eyed and deceptively drawling, started out by ordering the slaughter of an entire family, himself gunning down a nine-year-old boy, and his nefarious activities progressed from there.

THE CRITICS

"I like the kind of pure movie exchange that takes place when Henry Fonda confronts one of his men for having betrayed a confidence. 'You can trust me,' says the man. Replies Fonda: 'How can I trust a man who wears both a belt and suspenders? He don't even trust his own pants.'"

Vincent Canby, *The New York Times*

"Fonda is a cobra. It's a performance of chilling malevolence."

Sam Lesner, *Chicago Daily News*

"In *Once Upon a Time in the West,* Henry Fonda plays a villain. A double-dyed villain at that, a hired killer given to sadistically torturing his victims and shooting down innocent women and children without a qualm. It is quite a turn-up for the books, since if there is one actor inescapably associated on the screen with honesty, decency and all that is best in the American way of life, it is Henry Fonda. If, as people started wildly predicting after the success of Ronald Reagan in California, American politics were to be turned over to show business personalities, one can hardly think of better casting for President than Henry Fonda.

"When he played a liberal candidate for the Presidency in *The Best Man,* and followed it up by playing the President in *Fail Safe* it seemed like some natural law asserting itself.

Henry Fonda and Charles Bronson

"Partly this is a sign that the old Hollywood star system has been doing its work well, and partly it is the result of the actor's own reality-definition. Fonda is a curious case in this respect, since he is a better actor than almost anyone you like to name in Hollywood, yet when you come down to it he has not played anything like a wide variety of roles in his seventy or so films. His quality has been demonstrated rather by the intelligence and authority with which he has explored various aspects of one basic attribute: decency. There is no

John Frederick, Henry Fonda, and Michael Harvey

reason at all why he should not play a far from decent human being, as *Once Upon a Time in the West* reminds us: we feel no sense of shock or unreality in encountering him as a cold-blooded murderer, nor are we meant to—Sergio Leone is not the director for Hitchcockian subtleties of casting, playing deliberately on the expectations any real star will put into our minds ('But she's Janet Leigh, so she's certainly not going to be killed in the fourth reel; but he's Cary Grant, so he couldn't possibly be a wife murderer') in order to flout them.

"And yet, ability or no, the fact remains that as a star Henry Fonda has nearly always played variations on the Honest Joe, right through from his debut in *The Farmer Takes a Wife* (1935) till today. He was an ideal young Mr. Lincoln, the perfect embodiment of Steinbeck's long-suffering hero in *The Grapes of Wrath,* the upright member of New Orleans society who can take only so much from Bette Davis in *Jezebel,* and even when he was a criminal on the run in *You Only Live Once,* he was fundamentally a good man, a victim of society we could sympathize with a hundred per cent. Fundamental decency did not prevent him playing for laughs in *The Lady Eve,* where he was the innocent object of Barbara Stanwyck's machinations, and in general his gift for cool, understated comedy has been underused.

Henry Fonda

"After the war, with added maturity, his image has defined itself even more clearly as that of the thinking man, the liberal who acts on his convictions instead of merely worrying. Apart from the political roles, one thinks of *12 Angry Men* and *War and Peace* as the films which most clearly established this: his Pierre, all questions of Russian-ness apart, was a perfect meeting of actor and role, much happier than Bondarchuk's with the same character in his own mammoth Russian version of the book. But most of all, perhaps, there is the part Fonda has played in Hollywood's myth of the West. In a succession of Ford Westerns he embodied the opposite ideal to John Wayne's expansive, unthinking man-of-action hero, the quiet, calculating man, slow to anger, preferring whenever possible to work things out without bloodshed. Both heroes are an essential part of the cinema's West, and each actor has developed the ideal star persona to match. In that great hypothetical film-star battle for the Presidency Wayne would be the Republican candidate, Fonda the Democrat; and who would win is anybody's guess.

"It is altogether possible that during his long and successful career as a star Fonda the actor has had a slightly raw deal. The penalty, perhaps, of being a star. An actor is paid to do; a star is paid to be. Anthony Quinn, for example, may maintain that he so longs to escape the Zorba-the-Greek image that he would pay to be for once a Harvard man in a grey flannel suit on screen, but meanwhile he goes on playing Zorba-the-Italian, Zorba-the-Spaniard, Zorba-the-Rumanian and what have you—presumably because these are the parts which come his way automatically and because this is how the public reliably wants to see him. No doubt it came as an immense relief to Henry Fonda (as an actor, if not as a man) to shoot down that eight-year-old in cold blood in *Once Upon a Time in the West,* if only because it is the last thing he, of all people, would be expected to do in a film. At 64 one might think it a little late for a change of image. But then, who would think Henry Fonda was 64 anyway? He is a little more weathered, certainly, a little thinner on top, but as slim, as lithe, as active as he was in *The Farmer Takes a Wife* 34 years ago. He probably has many surprises in store for us yet."

John Russell Taylor, *The Times* (London)

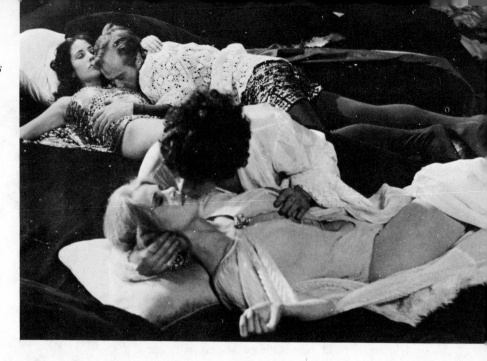

Jane Fonda and participants in orgy

Spirits of the Dead

American International. 1969. Directed by Federico Fellini, Louis Malle, Roger Vadim. Screen plays by Fellini, Malle, Vadim, Bernardino Zapponi, Daniel Boulanger from stories by Edgar Allan Poe. Produced by La Films Marceau-Cocinor. (Original title, "Histoires Extraordinaires")

JANE FONDA played *Frederique,* PETER FONDA played *Wilhelm* in the "Metzengerstein" sequence, cast of which also included Carla Marlier, Francoise Prevost, James Robertson Justice. Brigitte Bardot, Alain Delon, Terence Stamp starred in other sequences.

THE PICTURE: Although the Fellini-directed episode of *Spirits of the Dead* was generally hailed, critics were much more cool to the other two short films which combined to make up a three-part Edgar Allen Poe film anthology. The story directed by Louis Malle, starring Delon and Bardot, was particularly chastised but there was small enthusiasm from most critics for the third, as well. This was quite a family affair with Vadim directing his wife and brother-in-law. Jane and Peter Fonda played cousins in this, their personal relationship adding a titillating note, according to some reviewers. (Miss Fonda objected strenuously to such innuendoes— "It was not our intention to 'titillate' this way and in Europe, at least, no one took it like that. Not that I am against incest, but our style is more direct. When the time comes for incest we will do it head on and leave

Jane Fonda joins unbilled friends

Andreas Voutsinas and Jane Fonda

Jane and Peter Fonda

the titillating for others. Give us credit, at least, for honesty.")

THE CRITICS

"Vadim exhibits his wife, Jane Fonda, in various preposterous poses as a medieval woman who carries on a sort of love-hate relationship with a horse. This isn't as bad as it sounds because the horse is really her dead lover, who, when seen briefly, is none other than Peter Fonda. This, of course, adds another peculiar dimension to the film, which, like the absurd dialogue is quite intentionally funny. The episode is beautifully photographed by Claude Renoir and Jacques Fonteray designed Miss Fonda's clothes as if he were packaging a life-size Barbarella doll. . . . It is as overdecorated and shrill as a drag ball, but still quite fun."

Vincent Canby, *The New York Times*

"Each director contributes an individual segment, and consequently, his own individual stamp. Vadim seems to have tailored his portion strictly for his wife, Jane Fonda. The time period seems to be that of the Renaissance, but Miss Fonda's array of clothes is way-out ultra-ultra haute-monde, running to thigh-high boots, see-through panelings, chic fur ensembles, all giving extremely generous views of the Fonda anatomy. . . . It's a mood piece, nothing sensational but visually interesting with fleeting suggestions of perverted leanings, running through the thing, lesbianism, for instance, and, well, the feelings Miss Fonda has for her horse are a bit much. But as they say nowadays, whatever turns you on. The camera work, incidentally, is excellent. Good fluid shots of the bleak castle, the misty heath, and the sea foaming under lead-colored skies."

Bob Salmaggi, *New York Column*

Easy Rider

Columbia. 1969. Directed by Dennis Hopper. Produced by Peter Fonda. Screen play by Fonda, Hopper, Terry Southern.

PETER FONDA played *Wyatt* (*"Captain America"*) in a cast that also included Dennis Hopper, Luana Anders, Luke Askew, Toni Basil, Karen Black, Warren Finnerty, Sabrina Scharf, Robert Walker, Jack Nicholson.

THE PICTURE: Now Peter Fonda came into his own on the screen—and not just as an actor. For the most part, films had given him a series of nondescript parts. *The Wild Angels* and *The Trip* had enhanced his off-screen image of spokesman for outspoken youth—an image he worked hard to foster with a series of interviews and statements in which he blasted the Establishment, starting with that most convenient target, his own father. Posters of Peter Fonda on his motorcycle became best-sellers but still he was not being taken too seriously as an acting Fonda. Few took any notice of reports that he and another Hollywood rebel, Dennis Hopper, were making their own picture. (For that matter, nobody paid much attention to Warren Beatty's producing debut either—until *Bonnie and Clyde* came out.)

Easy Rider took off like a rocket. First came word from the Cannes Film Festival that it had shaken up the audiences and won an award. Full-page ads in *The New York Times* were loaded with quotes from critical raves. And the lines waiting to get into the theatre stretched around the block. A comparative unknown, Jack Nicholson, was hailed for a subtle, engaging characterization and is, at this writing, the far-out favorite for a supporting Oscar. But the enormous contributions of Peter Fonda and Dennis Hopper were not overshadowed. They had made this picture themselves and it paid off heavily for them. (And Fonda's own performance was sensitive and effective.)

The movie moguls ride with success, so, with *Easy Rider,* Peter Fonda and his associates became very fair-haired boys indeed.

THE CRITICS

"I have found that screening room audiences are often a sharp indication of what the general reaction to a film will be. Although most often on the tough side, these special audiences can put aside their scalpels to really like something. The current screening room hit is *Easy Rider,* produced by Peter Fonda, directed by Dennis Hopper, and starring both of them. Fonda, Hopper and

Jack Nicholson and Peter Fonda

Terry Southern wrote the script which will do for Fonda what none of his other roles did. That is, make him an enormous hero-star. He comes off like a combination of Clint Eastwood and James Dean. Hopper, until now most famous for his frantic pop life-style, somehow got his head together enough to pull off one of the most powerful movies I have ever seen. The less you know about the plot before you go, the better. Its bare outline is about two hip guys, their motorcycle odyssey across the country, and their hate-love relationship with America which is returned in kind. It is filled with beautifully controlled little surprises that are usually on the anxious edge of going out of control. The impact of the movie is terrifying if taken literally. Its effect on screening room audiences seems to be catatonic catharsis. Most people come out saying, 'I've got to see that again.' The other prevalent comment is 'That's one of the very few movies that doesn't cop out.' "

Howard Smith, *The Village Voice*

"The scenes are great, and the western roads and landscapes, and the little towns and restaurants. What is especially great is Peter Fonda's infinitely patient silence, and Jack Nicholson's flawless, drunken, lawyer-trained flow of pertinent oratory. That's not all that's good. Everything is good, a great deal of it very colorful, and almost everything set against music, music, music which gets performed by ten bands or people ranging from Steppenwolf, to Holy Model Rounders, the Electric Prunes, to Fraternity of Man, and on the Byrds, The Band, Little Eva, Roger McGuinn, The Jimi Hendrix Experience, and the Electric Flag. Individual scenes are so well and truly made that they remain in the mind like your own experience. . . . It's happening. It's not a movie at all. . . . Winning a prize as a 'best first' at Cannes was well deserved. It could win a prize against sterner competition."

Archer Winsten, *New York Post*

"Ultimately *Easy Rider* is the world's first real Peter Fonda movie. Nothing heroic, like John Wayne at the Alamo. You can't detect any of that charisma-of-the-silver-screen in Peter Fonda's performance. He's not even trying to resurrect the love-me-I'm-sensitive syndrome of the fifties. He's just, you know, gettin' his thing together. The cool of acting natchrully, that's why you don't get embarrassed watching him turn on. But notice how you notice Peter Fonda despite all that panamericana. Despite Dennis Hopper, who directs the film with a heavy but steady hand, and whose performance as Billy is the most vivid evocation of California hip-uptight you'll ever see on the screen. Despite even Terry Southern, who gets screen credit for the screen play along with Hopper and Fonda, and who must be responsible for the delicate rage this film projects. Despite all this—it's Peter Fonda's ride. His gangly grace (which must be considered freaky by Vistavision standards) was only a prop in those Roger Corman shlockers. But now that he has the parallel cools of actor-writer-producer going for him, it's finally been

Peter Fonda and Dennis Hopper

realized. That wouldn't matter much except that Fonda's Captain America also embodies an entire culture—its heroes and its myths. That's what's most real about this film. It dreams well. Like a real revolution or a real Spiro Agnew speech. And that alone is why it's worth a suspension of disbelief.

Richard Goldstein, *The New York Times*

"Never, it seems, have so many young Americans been so critical of their country. The creeping dissatisfaction with the Establishment way of telling it like it isn't has erupted in the streets, the classrooms and the courts. It seemed inevitable that this dissatisfaction would eventually be expressed in a new film produced by Peter Fonda. Occasionally, his sounds like the only voice in the crowd that knows why it's protesting. . . . An excruciating look at where this country is today, about as strong an indictment of America as I've ever seen in any medium. The real power of the film lies in the way it turns over the rocks of apple-pie America and reveals the slime. . . . Peter Fonda and Dennis Hopper can be proud of a movie which looks not so much photographed as actually lived! And a wonderful actor named Jack Nicholson is magnificent! A bold courageous statement of life seldom matched in motion pictures! I couldn't shake what I'd seen, even after I left the theatre."

Rex Reed

Peter Fonda

The moment before the grim ending

"These three clever chaps (Fonda, Hopper, Southern) get down to a piece of filmmaking so professional, so superbly laconic, and so savagely peaceful as to lift the picture as a whole into the category of the tragic, and to make it one of the most effective and memorable films that has so far been produced in the United States. Peter Fonda's austerely convincing and strangely beautiful performance in the leading role has a lot to do with this. While apparently fooling around in the opening sequences, he takes a leasehold of one's sympathies astounding in its extent. Then there is the deceptively simple but overwhelmingly brilliant technique with which the film's final assault on one's senses is accomplished. But at the end of the day, credit has to be given where it is due. What makes the film in the last analysis is the marvelous job done by the director, Dennis Hopper, in translating a complex idea into the language of the cinema."

Anthony West, *Vogue*

"From its deceptively amusing beginnings to its swift and terrible end, *Easy Rider* is an astonishing work of art and an overpowering motion picture experience. It is also a social document which is poignant, potent, disturbing and important . . . Peter Fonda, Dennis Hopper and their new-found co-rider, Jack Nicholson, are nonconforming but also unassertive men of peace adrift in a society they find conformist in its violent fear-hatred of their easy, shaggy unorthodoxy . . . The talk is spare throughout, and a terse sentence of Fonda's near the end of their adventure, 'We blew it,' is heavy with implications of his own dawning apprehensions that opting-out is an inadequate response . . . Jack Nicholson's performance, creating a man who reeks of bourbon and failure but who is also richly funny and endlessly sympathetic, is one of the consummate pieces of screen acting. He has engendered an individual who will haunt all of us . . . Fonda and Hopper, it should by this time go without saying, give immense performances: Hopper as the more traditional 'Hey, man' Rider impatient, self-indulgent, fearful of anything that looks like commitment; Fonda as something more of a bridge figure, sensitive and perceptive, hung up on his awareness that neither road nor establishment have all the answers or all the problems. He is at least unambiguously tragic, discovering and experiencing the truth that the freedom of the road may well only be another kind of evasion and captivity."

Charles Champlin, *Los Angeles Times*

Michael Sarrazin and Jane Fonda

They Shoot Horses, Don't They?

Cinerama, 1969. Directed by Sydney Pollack. Produced by Irwin Winkler and Robert Chartoff. Screen play by Robert E. Thompson based on the novel by Horace McCoy.

JANE FONDA played *Gloria* in a cast that also included: Michael Sarrazin, Susannah York, Gig Young, Red Buttons, Bonnie Bedelia, Michael Conrad, Bruce Dern, Al Lewis, Robert Fields, Severn Darden, Allyn Ann McLerie, Felice Orlandi, Madge Kennedy.

THE PICTURE: *They Shoot Horses, Don't They?* came along at the end of the year, just in time to qualify for the Academy Awards—and Jane Fonda won a nomination as best actress for her performance in it. Miss Fonda herself feels that her role as the marathon dancer gave her dramatic opportunities never touched in her earlier films.

The picture, based on Horace McCoy's 1935 novel, deals with the personal stories of desperate young people, against the panorama of the Depression years. More specifically, it is played against the background of a phenomenon of that era—the marathon dance craze.

McCoy's novel, well reviewed but quickly forgotten at the time of its publication, survived because of its reputation in France where intellectuals (Malraux, Gide, Sartre, de Beauvoir) hailed it as the first existential novel to come out of America. As a result of such appreciation, it won new respect in its own country and has been a strong seller in several paperback editions.

Critical reports on the picture varied widely. There were those who found it unbearably depressing, others who quibbled with other elements. But most of the more perceptive critics hailed it as one of the best pictures of the year. And all of them praised the acting of Susannah York, Gig Young, Red Buttons and others, down to such unbilled but welcome players as Felice Orlandi and Madge Kennedy. *Variety* reported that Jane Fonda "gives a dramatic performance that turns her own previous career as a sex bonbon upside down and gives the film a personal focus and an emotionally gripping power." Other critics praised her in equally glowing terms. At the end of 1969, Jane Fonda won the New York Film Critics' Award as "best actress" for *They Shoot Horses, Don't They?*, and an Academy Award nomination as well.

Susannah York and Jane Fonda

THE CRITICS

"Miss Fonda is the embittered Gloria who knows that life was rigged before she got there, longs for death and is yet incapable of executing the sentence she has cast. While all other lines bespeak her longing for death, her weary and angry regard for life, so much of the film is conveyed through an unspoken subsurface, the unspoken responses that reveal the soul of the tormented creatures in the arena. And it is on this level that Miss Fonda reveals the longing, the vulnerability, the momentary hopes and the capacity for further injury which enrich the role and the film."

John Mahoney, *Hollywood Reporter*

(Pauline Kael had faults to find with the adaptation of McCoy's novel and she despised the flash-forward device in which the audience sees things happening to the hero at a future time but without any way of knowing that these are not conventional flashbacks. Even so, she found the picture highly impressive.) "Though it staggers under this heavy load, *They Shoot Horses, Don't They?* is a very striking movie, with vestiges of the hard sarcasm of thirties lower-depth humor—those acrid sick jokes that make one wince and laugh simultaneously. Sydney Pollack is not an imaginative director, or inventive, but he stages a big, macabre, elimination-race scene so terrifyingly well, and he keeps the grisly central

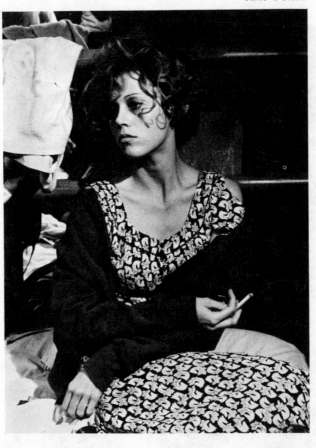

situation going with that special energy and drive that often make American movies more exciting and more fun to watch than even the best European movies. . . . Fortunately, Gloria, who is the raw nerve of the movie, is played by Jane Fonda, who has been a charming, witty nudie cutie in recent years and now gets a chance at an archetypal character. Sharp-tongued Gloria, the hard, defiantly masochistic girl who expects nothing and gets it, the girl who thinks the worst of everybody and makes everybody act it out, the girl who can't ask for anything except death, is the strongest role an American actress has had on the screen this year. Jane Fonda goes all the way with it, as screen actresses rarely do once they become stars. She doesn't try to save some ladylike part of herself, the way even a good actress like Audrey Hepburn does, peeping at us from behind 'vulgar' roles to assure us she's not really like that. Jane Fonda gives herself totally to the embodiment of this isolated, morbid girl who is determined to be on her own, who can't let go and trust anybody, who is so afraid of being gullible that she can't live. Gloria is not just without false hope, but without hope; she's not an easy girl to like when she goads the pregnant woman to get rid of her baby or when she rebuffs all gestures of comfort or sympathy. Jane Fonda makes one understand the self-destructive courage of a certain kind of

Susannah York and Jane Fonda

Michael Sarrazin and Jane Fonda

loner, and because she has the true star's gift of drawing one to her emotionally even when the character she plays is repellent, her Gloria, like Bogart's Fred C. Dobbs, is one of those complex creations who live on as part of our shared experience. Jane Fonda stands a good chance of personifying American tensions and dominating our movies in the seventies as Bette Davis did in the thirties; if so, Gloria will be but one in a gallery of briliant American characters."

Pauline Kael, *The New Yorker*

"Jane Fonda gives an admirable, bold performance as an embittered girl who fled America's heartland when she had to make love with a Syrian who chewed tobacco and came to California to be warm while she starved. Miss Fonda has her voice against her when she's playing a Texas-born wanderer, but her Gloria is still a great asset to the movie, a wounded soul swathed in scar tissue."

Joseph Morgenstern, *Newsweek*

Fonda Films
Completed but Unreleased and Unreviewed at Press Time

Fonda Films

Completed but Unreleased and Unreviewed at Press Time

As THIS book goes to press, the critical and box-office fate of these pictures is unknown. Three Henry Fonda pictures are completed but none of them is scheduled for release until mid-1970.

Henry Fonda, always cautious about predictions, will only say that he liked the scripts of all three. And, never a man to toss undeserved laurels, he feels that the directors—Aldrich, Mankiewicz and Kelly—are among the finest with whom he has worked. He can be extremely unhappy when he is making a picture in which any element seems wrong but, in each case, he feels that making these pictures were rewarding experiences.

His role in *Too Late the Hero* was a cameo. He played opposite Cliff Robertson and the plan is that their vignette will precede the titles as a kind of prologue to the military drama.

Both of the other films are Westerns but very different ones. The Mankiewicz film, *There Was a Crooked Man,* is the first script written by Robert Benton and David Newman since their triumph with *Bonnie and Clyde*. The writers claim that they wrote the script with Fonda, whom they consider the best actor in films, in mind. Mankiewicz concurred and, although the studio suggested other actors to co-star with Kirk Douglas, the writers and director stood their ground and insisted on Fonda.

He plays the role of a fast-gun lawman who is crippled in a gun battle and then becomes the warden of a Western prison in the post-Civil War era. Because he was committed to this film, he had to turn down another strongly tempting role—the star part in William Wyler's *Liberation of Lord Byron Jones*.

"That was a great role," he has said; "and, immodestly, I think I could have played the hell out of it. I really would have suffered if I had lost it because I was tied up in some pictures I have done. But I feel that *Crooked Man* is strong enough that it makes up for my losing out on *Lord Byron Jones*."

While *Crooked Man* is pretty grim fare, the other Fonda western, *Cheyenne Social Club* is wild and rollicking with Fonda playing a role vaguely reminiscent of his rowdy cowpoke in *The Rounders*. Here he and James Stewart, offscreen best friends since before either of them ever saw a movie camera, make one of their rare screen appearances together. Fonda is considerably more optimistic about the picture than he was about *Firecreek,* the last Western which teamed him with Stewart.

Gene Kelly directed the James Lee Barrett screenplay which revolves about an itinerant cowboy (Stewart) who learns he is the sole heir to a business, the Cheyenne Social Club, left by his late brother. He and his buddy (Fonda) ride to Cheyenne to take over the business to learn that he has become the proprietor of the town's bawdy house. Like *Crooked Man,* the period is the post-Civil War era.

At this writing, Jane Fonda—winner of the New York Film Critics Award and Academy Award nominee for "Horses"—is preparing to start her next picture, a suspense-drama, *Klute,* to be directed by Alan Pakula. Peter Fonda has completed a "guest star" role in *The Last Movie,* directed by his *Easy Rider* associate, Dennis Hopper, and is preparing a film which he himself will direct as well as produce. Henry is currently by-passing film offers to concentrate on his one-man show and his television series.

So this book cannot be definitive. There is a lot of future in the Fonda careers with Jane entering a new phase as one of the screen's foremost dramatic actresses, Peter scoring strongly at last, and the ever-reliable Henry remaining in greater demand than almost any of his contemporaries.

They are certainly America's first family of the entertainment world—these fabulous Fondas of the films and theatre.

Too Late the Hero

Cinerama. 1970. Produced and directed by Robert Aldrich. Screen play by Robert Aldrich and Lukas Heller. From an original story by Aldrich and Robert Sherman.

HENRY FONDA played *Captain John G. Nolan* in a cast that also included: Michael Caine, Cliff Robertson, Ian Bannen, Harry Andrews, Denholm Elliott, Ronald Fraser, Lance Percival, Percy Herbert, Michael J. Parsons, Harvey Jason, William Beckley, Don Knight, Sean Macduff, Martin Horsey, Roger Newman, Sam Kydd, Patrick Jordan.

Cliff Robertson and Henry Fonda

Henry Fonda and director Joseph
L. Mankiewicz

There Was a Crooked Man

Warners. 1970. Directed and produced by Joseph L. Mankiewicz. Original screen play by David Newman, Robert Benton.

HENRY FONDA played *Sheriff Woodward Lopeman* in

a cast that also included: Kirk Douglas, Hume Cronyn, Lee Grant, Michael Blodgett, Arthur O'Connell, Warren Oates, Burgess Meredith, Bert Freed, John Randolph, Pamela Hensley, Barbara Rhoades, C. K. Yang.

Kirk Douglas and Henry Fonda

Henry Fonda

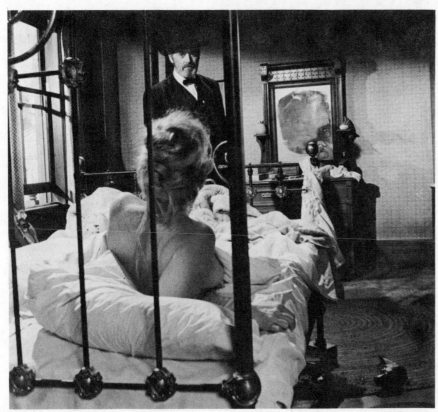

Henry Fonda and Jeanne Cooper

Director Gene Kelly, Henry Fonda
and James Stewart

Cheyenne Social Club

National General. 1970. Produced and directed by Gene Kelly. Original screen play by James Lee Barrett.

HENRY FONDA played *Harley Sullivan* in a cast that also included James Stewart, Shirley Jones, Jackie Joseph, Sue Ann Langdon, Sharon De Bord, Elaine Devry, Jackie Russell, Dabbs Greer, Richard Collier.

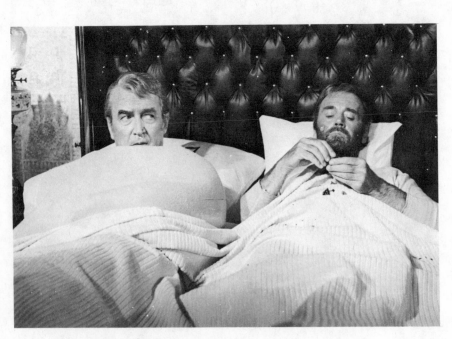

James Stewart and Henry Fonda

Henry Fonda and James Stewart

James Stewart and Henry Fonda

Henry Fonda